PRAISE FOR *SOUL CULTURE*

"This book is miraculous! Remica Bingham-Risher dives deep into not only Black poetry and philosophy, but also the lived lives of Black poets and the insights that are found there. From these troves, Bingham-Risher weaves together a book of knowledge, illumination, and song unlike any I have known, but that I might have dreamed."

—ELIZABETH ALEXANDER

"This is not an objective endorsement of *Soul Culture*, so please don't expect that—instead, this is a praise song for Remica Bingham-Risher. This is a gratitude moment for her devotion to Black poetry and Black poets. This is an embrace for a 'sweet, loving baby' who has assembled here a beautiful community, who names our souls in wonder and so much grace. How I love this woman, her genius, her immense spirit! How grateful I am to be part of this remarkable gathering!"

—HONORÉE FANONNE JEFFERS

"*Soul Culture* is the nourishment, the love, the light, the dark, the beauty. With a genius all her own, and in the blackest ink, Remica Bingham-Risher has woven us a gorgeous, intergenerational, and polyvocal history of kinship, perseverance, Black poetry, and love. I laugh, I cry, I am swung open by her radical, radiant attention. This book is a devotion. I want to share it with everyone I love."

—ARACELIS GIRMAY

"In *Soul Culture*, Remica Bingham-Risher has produced a chronicle of some of her important influences in the form of these interviews conducted with several of them, and in expressing her concrete gratitude with this book she has also produced another important documentation of how African American poets have become a realized force in American literature. Each interview is a doorway to understanding the remarkable achievements of

Black poets, beginning with the postHarlem Renaissance generation, many of whom are part of the Black Arts Movement. The opening interview with E. Ethelbert Miller gives us the sensibility of a poet whose writing, mentoring, and archival contributions have been a central nervous system for Black literature, thus clearly establishing the richness of this collection. In her own work and life, Ms. Bingham-Risher is an ambassador for Cave Canem, the organization that received the National Book Critics Circle's first Toni Morrison Award. For those looking to explore some of the tapestry of the emergence on Black poetry from the mid-twentieth century into the twenty-first, this book will be invaluable. In the faces of these faces you will see the Black and unknown bards as well as those who were first to have achieved careers: Phillis Wheatley, Jupiter Hammond, and the whole stream of us, known and unknown, but all so brave and full of hope in the collective genius of African American poetry."

—AFAA M. WEAVER

"Remica Bingham-Risher's reverence for Black poetry and Black poets shines through in this collection of essays. 'What do we save for our children?' Remica asks. 'What home do we carry? Which ghosts do we let sleep?' While this collection keeps a beautiful record of the giants who came before us in Black poetry, it also accepts that the poets of today will one day be homes for the poets of the future. She asks us to consider what kind of homes we will be. 'In Black poetry, the elders have made a place for us,' Remica says. 'So now, in their wake, what are we trying to build?' She builds a bridge between the past and the future, gently nudging today's poets to consider their place. This deliciously written collection will have you wanting to exchange emails with Aracelis Girmay, share drinks with Remica and her cousins, and, of course, attend the family's *The Color Purple* breakfast. Remica invites you in."

—ALINE MELLO

"*Soul Culture* is a necessary guide to transcendence in the twenty-first century, a nexus of ancestors, elders, and the wise among us."

—TRACY K. SMITH

"Remica Bingham-Risher's *Soul Culture* is more map than book. Reading you ask, as an early Roots album once did, Do you want more?!—and a reader can't help but to want more of this exploration of self and Black poetry. A spectacular and compelling way of turning the vehicle of poetry as a tool to remember the past and examine it."

—REGINALD DWAYNE BETTS

"Remica Bingham-Risher's beautiful book *Soul Culture*—part writer's memoir, part literary and cultural history, part conversation, part writers' guide—is at root a love song for the writers who have made Bingham-Risher's work and life possible (who happen also to be the writers who have made a lot of our writing lives possible). We do not arrive, *Soul Culture* reminds us, without the labor and love of who comes before us. We do not arrive without who dreamt us into being. *Soul Culture* honors that labor and love and dreaming. *Soul Culture* sings it. How necessary, how gorgeous, how true."

—ROSS GAY

"Love made this book: love for Black people, for poetry, and for anyone ready to embrace both. Remica Bingham's *Soul Culture* reinvents the literary interview, the artist's memoir, and the craft essay, by bringing all three together into a delicious, illuminating, deeply moving whole. Bingham invites you into her life as a Black woman in the US—shows you the things that have wrecked her and the things that have saved her—and opens up, in the process, new definitions of faith, Blackness, and the word. *Soul Culture* is testimony and trailblazing; it is book, chapter, and verse on the ways one might make a writing life—or let a writer's lifework (re)make you."

—EVIE SHOCKLEY

SOUL
CULTURE

SOUL CULTURE

● ● ○ ●○●○● ● ○ ●○●○● ● ● ●○●○ ○ ○ ●○●○● ○ ●○

Black Poets, Books, and Questions That Grew Me Up

● ● ○ ●○●○● ● ○ ●○●○● ● ● ●○●○ ○ ○ ●○●○● ○ ●○

REMICA BINGHAM-RISHER

BEACON PRESS
BOSTON

BEACON PRESS
Boston, Massachusetts
www.beacon.org

Beacon Press books
are published under the auspices of
the Unitarian Universalist Association of Congregations.

25 24 23 22   8 7 6 5 4 3 2 1

This book is printed on acid-free paper that meets the uncoated paper
ANSI/NISO specifications for permanence as revised in 1992.

Text design and composition by Kim Arney

*Library of Congress Cataloging in
Publication Data is available for this title.*
LCCN: 2022017380
Hardcover ISBN: 978-0-8070-1592-6
Ebook ISBN: 978-0-8070-1594-0

CONTENTS

Introduction · vii

Imagining Home · 1

On Faith · 25

Intimate Tending · 45

Courting Paradise · 61

blk/wooomen revolution · 81

Girls Loving Beyoncé and Their Names · 97

Who Raised You? · 115

The Terror of Being Destroyed · 137

Standing in the Shadows of Love · 155

Revision as Labyrinth · 173

Come Through · 189

Acknowledgments · 199

Sources · 203

Credits · 213

Index · 219

INTRODUCTION

F inding room for myself in any space as a child was a necessary, defiant
tending. To care for myself, to prove to myself that I wasn't invisi-
ble, despite what the world told me. Being a little Black girl in America
meant being barely evident in most spaces—incidental, inconsequential.
But in my household, in my intimate communities, in the Black family at
large—a cultural institution cobbled together by years of shared experi-
ence—I learned early on through reading that invisibility and fear were
"just another arm of God to pass through."

As I was growing up, most of my questions about identity and sur-
vival were turned over and over again in good books, and especially in
poems by those whose work I loved. In my old copy of the *AFRO-BETS
Book of Black Heroes From A to Z*, I found above the entry on *Wheatley,
Phillis*, scribbled in my third-grade handwriting, questions like "Were
books by Black people allowed, looked down upon, banned? If it was
illegal for us to read or write, how did we prove what we knew?" As a
lifelong reader, as someone devoted to and wholly invested in the power
of the word, examining the lives and work of writers always made it
easier to examine my own.

I grew up in Phoenix, Arizona, mostly a long distance from branches
of extended family up and down the East Coast. To show their love
and sacrifice and to ease the distance, relatives put together boxes of
desired things—school clothes, shoes with bows or fresh labels, but-
ter crunch cookies from the corner store, gold nameplate necklaces,
grown-up perfume, and more. Once, when asked what I wanted folks

to send me, I said, "Books about Black people," because I found so few at the library. That seemed to please them more than any other request (I guess when Solomon asked for wisdom, Jehovah was so relieved he hadn't asked to fatten his pockets like some other cousins did that God gave an abundance). From then on, books by Virginia Hamilton, Walter Dean Myers, and others arrived with each box. But even after I won a district poetry contest in the fifth grade, it took many years and books sent cross-country, stumbled upon in libraries and thrift stores, or put into my hands by teachers who saw some yearning in me before I understood that Black poets weren't an anomaly. They were plentiful; they had singular voices and lineages, and their journeys were as varied as America itself.

"Soul culture" is a phrase meant to evoke the nuanced living of Black Americans and, particularly, contemporary Black American poets. It is Black devotion; Black reclamation and reframing of the past; Black bantering and signifying; Black family structures and supports; Black joy, liberation, and a radical love ethic despite Black trauma, fear, and rootlessness. If there's anything Black people know, it's that we can be erased from history. This project was meant to be part oral history, part coming-of-age on the shoulders of giants. My goal was to ask Black writers whose work changed me, *How do you make a life as a poet?* Then, ask and answer for myself, *What questions and crafting might help you make a life as a poet in their wake?*

Black books and Black writers showed me there was a way for me to exist in the world of words and, hence, a way for me to exist in the world. My interest in this project was centering Black voices and exploring the interiority of the creative lives of poets. I wanted to provide a fuller picture for those engaging in scholarship about the Black literary tradition (not only of those interviewed here, but also of the many listed therein as part of the poets' trajectories), to record and decode cultural information shared in these narratives.

So, over more than a decade, I interviewed ten poets whose work I loved: Sonia Sanchez, Lucille Clifton, E. Ethelbert Miller, Tim Seibles, Patricia Smith, Erica Hunt, Forrest Hamer, Natasha Trethewey, Honorée Fanonne Jeffers, and A. Van Jordan.

My approach to each interview was much the same, though I came to the subjects at different times and in various ways. I conducted the interviews at each author's convenience and traveled to locations most comfortable for them. Each began with a query wherein I explained the interview as an in-depth look at the breadth of the author's work, focusing on craft, process, and the writing life as well as biographical information and major influences. The general crux of my questions followed as such: *How did your homelife and reading life shape you? Who were your influences and comrades, your cultivated community? How do you craft what you bring into the world? How do you make a life as a poet?*

I was interviewing poets who'd made their way between waves of Black art histories. The Harlem Renaissance saw a confluence of artists in the 1920s and '30s, then the Black Arts Movement saw another concentrated burst of brilliance from the 1960s until around 1975. I am certain now (as hindsight is 20/20) that Cave Canem began the next communal movement in Black poetry in 1996. Cave Canem, founded by poets Toi Derricotte and Cornelius Eady, was a Black poets' writing retreat and organization designed to help "remedy the under-representation and isolation of African American poets in MFA programs and writing workshops. Cave Canem is a home for the many voices of African American poetry." As most poets brought up in their interviews, before this time, they worked without mass community, often in solitude or as the "only" in almost every room they managed to enter. But Cave Canem, like those other art movements, began to shift that reality.

⬩⬤⬤⬤ ⬤ ⬤ ⬤⬤⬤ ⬤ ⬤ ⬤⬤⬤ ⬤ ⬤ ⬤⬤⬤⬩

Without two important entities—E. Ethelbert Miller and Cave Canem—this book would never have come to be. My reason for starting the project was simple: I had endless questions for the writers I loved, and I drove Miller, the first teacher with whom I studied in graduate school, up a wall asking about them. He wrote me a letter, said I had to get over "this awe syndrome" I had about other writers, and suggested I start conducting interviews to get some of those questions answered definitively, to assure myself that other Black writers weren't so different from me. Long before #BlackGirlMagic was trending, "magical" was a term I once used to describe a writer I loved, and Miller implied that this outlook could be dangerous too. *Who can become magical? How can one chart a path to magical?* he asked.

Though I generally recount Langston Hughes as the impetus for my love of poetry, the insatiable kernel, the spark, came just after finding Hughes, when I stumbled upon a whole book of poems—*Honey, I Love* by Eloise Greenfield—at my favorite library. There was a dark brown girl on the cover of the book, with hair in a haloed Afro like mine after wash day and before the hot comb press, and it opened up another part of me. Until then, my notebooks had been filled with short stories and diary entries, but now, I looked for poems everywhere and scribbled my own musings.

I remember being entranced by a poem that was an ars poetica of sorts, a blues that ended on an uncharacteristically hopeful refrain. Greenfield's poem "Things" was about what we can save and what goes. The little girl in the poem speaks first of what's transient, then of what she can hold onto: a poem. A made thing, a memory transcribed and beautified, a gift. The last lines of the poem make the reader snap to attention by shifting the cadence and tone, but beyond this, they posit that one could create something more valuable and lasting than the things you could find in any store. That valuable thing—the poem—could offer me something I'd been looking for: it could tell my story, which channeled the stories of the people I knew, who seemed extraordinary in their ingenuity and survival; it could be a marker of sorts, a root I'd plant no matter when I landed, something I could keep and carry.

In a fortuitous turn, while I was visiting Miller in his office at Howard University before our interview, Eloise Greenfield herself stopped by and I was introduced to the woman who had introduced me to myself all those years before. Miller told me to write about Greenfield because, as he always reminded me, we should be writing creative and critical work, striving to shine a light on the artistry that houses and feeds us. This has been the continuing path of his mentorship, and I am perpetually grateful for his guidance.

The launch of Cave Canem was the beginning of a third Black literary renaissance in American letters. Not since the Harlem Renaissance or

the Black Arts Movement has there been such a concentration of compli-
cated, compelling work shifting the literary landscape. While it's true that
Cave Canem is one force among many forces—it is not (and whatever
could be?) the definitive space or lens for Black contemporary poetry—it
is nevertheless an undeniable impetus in the permeation of significant
literary work done in the past thirty years. The ten poets included here,
beginning with Sonia Sanchez, who published her first book in 1969, are
meant to represent the changing scene from the Black Arts Movement
leading into the Cave Canem era.

I became a Cave Canem fellow in 2004 and began conducting in-
terviews just a few months before. When I went to Cave Canem, I was
entrenched in the beginnings of a writing life. I was enrolled in a master
of fine arts program and had just finished a fellowship at the Callaloo
Creative Writing Workshop. But it wasn't until I'd completed my first
weeklong retreat at Cave Canem—seven days filled with exhuming my
past, forging friendships, and studying with poets whose works I'd pored
over in solitude for years—that I understood my path as a writer.

After my first Cave Canem summer retreat, a woman in the airport
struck up a conversation by asking me what I did for a living. I answered,
"I'm a poet," quick as a flash, though it was something I'd never said or
really believed before—then excused myself, found the nearest restroom,
and wept until I heard the boarding announcement for my gate. This isn't
a book about Cave Canem, but it is certainly a book in its wake.

⁂

The writers included here represent various frameworks and ideologies:
Black studies, women's studies, mixed race studies, LGBTQIA+ studies,
and avant-garde studies, though these labels seem to narrow rather than
account for them. The poets share their childhood memories, failures,
successes, and details about their most intimate selves; many discussed
topics never broached with other interviewers. Each essay begins with an
epigraph from the poet's interview, includes words of wisdom through-
out, and ends with an exchange from the interview as well. I hope that
by giving each poet extended space and time this text will help crystallize
the fluidity of the Black aesthetic and how it is influenced by the personal,

social, and historical context of each poet. Black poets aren't easily lumped into any single box for scholars, students, writers, or readers.

It's no wonder that two prose writers, James Baldwin and Toni Morrison, the Grand Father and Grand Mother of the Black literary landscape, continued to appear in the conversations with these ten poets and are sprinkled throughout the meditations here, even as I purport to be a poet focusing solely on poets. Though not in all of the essays, both were cited frequently in my interviews as influences. Baldwin and Morrison transcend genre and sight; they are the still point for many—if not most, if not all—Black American writers, as their root work and life's work continue to explicate our place in the world, binding and driving us as we move toward our own understanding.

In the South, the term "grew me up" is an endearment tied to love and discipline. The body of Black poets continues growing me up in their intimacy and radical love. We're such a small group, often shaped by perilous times and circumstances, that we must be faithful—to each other and to the art in particular. Of course, in resilience and building, there's always joy: we jone on each other, talk smack, laugh loud and rowdy when we are blessed to be crowded in a room of us. We've often come from isolation and spaces that trivialized or misunderstood us, so we grow each other up and into being when there is proximity, when we are allowed camaraderie and freedom, when there are places where race can become an afterthought or a crown, where craft—how well you tend a poem, your work and technique—is paramount. Throughout my life, poets I met first through their poems and books, then in classrooms, at retreats, or at conferences helped grow me up by writing their own stories, answering my questions, and coming back to me as guiding voices on and off the page.

Many are missing from this collection. *Soul Culture* is not meant to be a comprehensive look at the writers who have made their mark on the literary scene since the Black Arts Movement, nor are these necessarily the most seminal writers from that period. These are writers I loved personally and was given the opportunity to sit with. If given my druthers, I would have also included others (like Nikki Giovanni, Marilyn Nelson, Sharan Strange, Afaa Michael Weaver, Kwame Dawes, Patricia Spears

Jones, Rita Dove, and the list goes on) who continue to change the way I understand literature, Blackness, community.

Much of this work is woman-heavy because my life and aesthetic is woman-heavy; there are several overarching themes found in my work, but I am most intrigued by the way we (as humans and especially women but, even more especially, women of color) are asked to maneuver in such narrowly carved spaces. In editing this book, I realize that my maternal grandmother—Mary Knight, born in Scotland Neck, North Carolina, in 1922—appears on the periphery of many of the pieces. I was often consumed by her closeness and care before she died, just as I was planning the *hows* and *whys* of this project in my head. My grandmother had the same wiliness as so many of the ancestors remembered in this collection, and she still colors every part of my life. In many ways, this book, like all of my books, is for and because of women like her.

Around the same time that I started thinking about converting the interviews into a full-scale project, I began teaching in community workshops and at universities. Consequently, many of the essays and questions turn to teaching, as I translated my trek as a writer for students. Some essays began as presentations; others were just a way to address my own trajectory and understanding, my own place in the soul culture as well.

The enduring question I ask daily—when writing, when watching the news, when praying—about Black folks is: *How is it possible we've survived?* Soul culture is rooted in deep pain, longing, and incessant innovation, so this book is about singular experiences illumined by memory, mortar made possible by genius, grit, mother-wit, and sleight of hand. My overarching question for the interviews was, *What do these poets know, and what have they lived that is of value to us?* Emerging as a poet in my own right, I've been forced to think about acceptance, desire, and profound Black love amid perpetual fear. When asked during an interview about the implications of history, culture, and how I think of success, I explained, "I am asking myself and my poems each day, what do we have to live up to?" This book is about all those things.

SOUL
CULTURE

E. Ethelbert Miller

IMAGING HOME

If you look at me as an outgrowth of the Black Arts Movement, then that is a period in which Black people were talking about loving oneself, loving one's Blackness and loving one's people. I was sort of baptized by that.

—E. ETHELBERT MILLER

My first encounter with poetry was probably hearing my mother read the Psalms, but the jolt that still thrills and guts me is hearing Diana Ross's "Missing You." Not just the words but the anguish in her delivery, the gravity in the tone. How could I *not* miss whatever was gone?

Somewhere, there is a reel-to-reel recording of me as a three-year-old singing "Missing You" as a roomful of family watched. My parents and I had driven eight hours from our house in Augusta, Georgia, where the army had stationed my father after we'd left Germany. We were visiting my mother's hometown of Norfolk, Virginia. Both of my mother's parents were still alive, and a host of cousins, aunts, and uncles crowded a living room. The whole lot of them whooped and hollered as I sang. My mother had already dazzled them a year before with another of my party tricks—at two, I could "read" a whole book with inflection and drama and did so until my tough-edged granddaddy declared, "That baby is something else!" and asked me to do it again each night I was there. (My mother read to me while I was in the womb and nightly thereafter, until I'd memorized several pages of *My Book of Bible Stories*, a Little Golden Book about Winnie-the-Pooh and the Heffalumps, and a few others she'd carry with us wherever we went.) I'd begun memorizing songs and singing them with such vigor that my mother had me send up whatever missive I was most enamored with when we found a listening ear. That summer, we had twenty or so—what with my mother being one of seven siblings and all and sundry of us, the children and children's children, descending on the place my mother and her siblings thought of as home.

My grandparents moved to Norfolk in 1939 soon after they were married. They'd grown up in a town you'd be hard pressed to find on most maps: Scotland Neck, North Carolina. After sixth grade, the Black folks there left school to work in the fields. They longed for somewhere they could have bigger dreams. But which did they call home? The city that raised them, or the city where they'd raised a house full of children? And which helped them figure out their place in the world, their calling, where they fit?

I wondered always about this for the lot of us—we'd venture out, we'd witness, but what would steady and bind us? What loves would make a place? Is home a door opening? After time and distance, I wrote about this:

MISSING YOU
Everybody sings it. It can be
hollow, juked or spare. I grew up there,
in the middlearth of music.

All along they'd used it, and I was unaware
until the reel-to-reel resurfaced and my voice—
squeaking, grainy, blare—mimicking Diana, rooted

out the heart of the heart, *Tell me why the road turns?*
No one had the answer. We were a convoy
of melancholy or joy. Little unsaids,

before or after the final mix; this is where
the art lives, the open of the full mouth kiss.
My parents did this. Fled here and there. Loved each other.

Burdened me. Their history now—its brass and clang—
something like a crier's flame, this burning knot I cannot name.

I didn't know then that when Diana Ross sang "Missing You" she was mourning Marvin Gaye after he'd been killed by his father. I read all I could about his life and found that Gaye stewed in his own misery, his own mystified and missing identity. His father shaped him and they hated each other for it; they argued frequently whenever Gaye left the whirlwind road and came home. I only knew that the assonance and lilt of the song's declaration built out of love and longing reminded me of something dazzling and grave, something the people around me knew intimately, something I'd trek across the country and learn myself.

When home had changed hands for me many times, I started trying to carve out my place in the world. My first book, *Conversion*, came to light just as I got a job teaching creative writing at a university. I found out I'd won the Naomi Long Madgett Poetry Award and that my book would be published by Lotus Press. Lotus was legendary—it had ushered in many of the books I'd packed on my shelves and one in particular I'd been coming back to, E. Ethelbert Miller's *Season of Hunger/Cry of Rain*.

Miller's poems paint him as a world watcher, light chaser, purveyor of quips and sharp one-liners, deep lover of love. I chose to study with Miller my first semester as a grad student at Bennington College in the hopes that he would offset some of the complete misreads I knew there would be of my work and life by my classmates and maybe other faculty. He was a known "connector"—all around DC and beyond, he'd been putting poets of color in touch with each other, and I welcomed this community building as part of his praxis. He led the charge for Dolores Kendrick to become the city's second poet laureate after Sterling Brown. He'd been director of Howard University's African American Resource Center for nearly half a century. He hosted reading series, radio and television shows; collected artifacts; and coordinated efforts to link writers, scholars, and students, whether they'd just been bitten by the poetry bug or, like him, had already spent a lifetime championing the power of the word. Literary politics—memory, place, legacy—played a part in everything, he'd teach me.

Teaching June Jordan's "Poem about My Rights," I think of Miller, as they were dearest friends and unequivocal supporters (maybe lovers—I could never quite figure which and didn't have the gumption as his student to ask). Jordan wrote the introduction to *Season of Hunger/Cry of Rain*, relating that Miller was an invaluable resource for poets and a staunch advocate for Black poetry.

How much Miller and Jordan loved each other is in the poems they wrote back and forth in their books for years, how much of his life he spent missing her is in their letters. Before our interview, Miller was working on getting the two-hundred-plus letters he exchanged with Jordan into the hands of someone who would see this bond and honor it. He said: "I have a letter from June in which she told me that she gave all my letters to [Harvard's] Schlesinger Library years ago. So, my letters are there, but her letters to me are in my house. My letters belong to the estate . . . I wouldn't release any letters that may be harmful to people living, but I would release the ones that could help people understand her career."

He continued: "There's one letter in which June writes about only having a few dollars. I have another letter where she's going to debate William Buckley and she lists everything she's reading to prepare for the debate. Those things are important. Before she died, June was honored in Philadelphia for lifetime achievement. In the beginning of her speech, she cites her mother, her father, and me as the biggest influences on her life. If you're a biographer, you're going to take notice of a remark like that." In her introduction to *Season of Hunger/Cry of Rain*, Jordan says Miller's poems reflect on the ordinary, how our daily living adds up to the shadows of our devotion. In his poem "October 31," dedicated to June, he dreams of being the silver streaks in her hair.

My students read Jordan's "Poem about My Rights," a multipage manifesto for freedom despite the body one might be born into or where that body might land. Afterward, I ask: What does poetry—in its repetition, language, and specificity—teach us about love and history? Why is it better at this than most research papers or newspaper articles? Every semester they come up with a variation of the same response. "The poem punches me in the gut," one student says. "She's angry at all the limitations people put on her, and you can feel it," says another.

While I am alone preparing for class, reading the poem again, I get to the repeated phrase "I do not consent" and raise my hand involuntarily. The gesture is mid-shout, mid-hallelujah, mid-I-see-you-and-you-see-me. I leave it there until I get to what I remember is coming: "Wrong is not my name." Because my name means what Jordan's means, what Miller works so hard to leave everyone some knowledge of: she is full of wonders. We are full of wonders; I am full. I am complex and worthy. I will make a place for myself, despite where I'm coming from, what I've come through.

⚓ ● ⚓ ● ⚓ ● ⚓ ● ⚓ ● ⚓

The truth is I hated growing up in Phoenix for all the wrong reasons. Mostly the problem was how my mother and I ended up there. A few years after that reel-to-reel was made at my grandparents' house, my parents split when my father began using cocaine. We lost our own house near the army base in Augusta, his military career, most of my mother's assurance, and much of what I thought I knew for sure. The army afforded us a final move; my mother's sister Shirley, her husband, Bobby, and my four cousins were all the family we had in Phoenix, Arizona, but they were happy to have us, so that's where my mother and I landed after the fall.

I didn't know the phrase *culture shock* as a seven-year-old, but I felt it. Moving out West was a lot like landing on a distant planet. The landscape was wild, foreign. I was used to kudzu covering the highways, forests of live oak and red cedar, four seasons, oceans near enough to call to us, and Black folks everywhere—they were my teachers, babysitters, and neighbors, laughing across the aisles at the Piggly Wiggly grocery store.

In Phoenix, nothing was the same. I was the only Black child in each class, we were the only Black family in our Bible study group, the only Black mother and child walking the aisles of the discount clothing store. Phoenix was less than 5 percent Black when we arrived in 1988, though the city was the most heavily populated in the state. In the decade or so

we were there, it wasn't strange to see a KKK or skinhead rally material-
ize in Cortez Park past the old Indian School (opened in 1891 as part of
the federal assimilation policy for Native Americans and closed in 1990).
There was no Martin Luther King Jr. holiday, well after the nation recog-
nized it, as Phoenix wasn't a place that recognized us.

I'm not sure when I discovered Isaac Hayes's cover of "By the Time I
Get to Phoenix," but from the start I thought he was singing about me:
"By the time I get to Phoenix, she'll be rising . . . she'll find a note I left
hanging on her door." Now that I'm older and have heard the whole
nineteen-minute missive, I realize it's a vamp about a woman breaking a
man's heart and him running as far and furied as he could. I kept hearing
only what I wanted to as a child: that there was a young girl and she was
rising. Was it a metaphor—was she the city, was she the sun? Or just one
searching for who she'd become? The church organ's verse-long notes
under Hayes's baritone gave it a mournful, eerie tone. Even if you were
barely listening, you knew the music was leading to something lost, some
heart breaking and someone getting left behind.

Three years after we moved to Phoenix, on the first day of fifth grade,
I was shocked to enter the class and find Darlene Myers, a yellowbone
Black woman, Creole and young enough to surprise us now and again
with the latest slang or dance moves. She was thick like my aunties, stern
but so funny, and the only Black teacher I'd have during all my schooling
in Arizona. I was so grateful for her, as was my mother, and we were all
drawn to each other, as she was the "only" in school board meetings, on
cafeteria duty, and at district performances too.
    One day Ms. Myers read Langston Hughes's poem "Mother to Son"
aloud to the class, then asked what it meant. While everyone else seemed
uninterested or confused (I don't recall us being read poetry or intro-
duced to it in any other class in grade school), I was awestruck by the
mother persona Hughes had chosen. She sounded just like my grand-
mothers. She told her son that no matter what he faced, he would have

to keep pushing, like my grandmothers said at family reunions or when I complained about being far away on the phone.

I was a voracious reader but hadn't yet found poetry outside of song. I was bowled over, in love. This poem was Blackness, insight, tenderness, and beauty all in a neat package, like an heirloom jewel that had been waiting for me.

Years later, I'd tell Miller about my love of "Mother to Son," and he'd stop me in my revelry. *And why do you think your teacher knew Hughes?* he'd ask, raising his eyebrows at me. While I was taken with Hughes's voice, Miller was concerned with place and the politics of the Black poet's trajectory. He traced Hughes's legacy from where we stood a few years into this new millennium back to the Black Arts Movement, then the Harlem Renaissance.

In our interview, he said, "When I started learning about the Harlem Renaissance, one of the first questions that popped into my head was, *You mean to tell me that there were only three or four people writing in the 1920s?*" He smirked and shook his head. "I saw that the reason we read those writers today was that they had access to two of the key journals, *Crisis* and *Opportunity*. Back then, just by studying and being a close reader—I didn't have to wait for a biography to come out or anybody's letters to be published—I could tell that Georgia Douglas Johnson was having an affair with Du Bois. I figured that out because here's young Langston Hughes sending poems like 'The Negro Speaks of Rivers' to the *Crisis*. Georgia Douglas Johnson says, 'Oh, that would be nice if you dedicated it to Du Bois.' That's how he got in and that's why I have it with the dedication in [the anthology I edited] *In Search of Color Everywhere*. Dedications are very, very important. Everything is important when you study literary politics."

It's then that I realized Miller wasn't just a poet, he was an archivist—"a literary activist" is what he called himself. Looking around his office at the African American Resource Center at Howard or his home, his life's work came into focus. Artifacts graced every corner. On the third floor of his house, there was a small shrine to his father and brother. A copy of his memoir, *Fathering Words,* was the centerpiece on his living room table and he explained: "Poetry is good, but it has its limitations. For me to deal with the loss of my father and brother, I had to write prose."

Priority Mail envelopes addressed to students and filled to capacity adorned tables and chairs in another room.* There was an entire bookcase full of his writing, another that held only autographed books. There was Walter Mosley's artwork, even a rare copy of *Time* magazine with James Baldwin gracing the cover—this, too, was signed.

In his sunroom, pictures crowded the desk. One was a framed flyer from the 1997 Ascension Poetry Reading Series featuring Reetika Vazirani and Zoë Anglesey—good friends of Miller's who died within months of each other. He said of this: "Becoming an elder, I have to start putting things in order and taking care of stuff. I'm trying to make sure I set the records straight. That's also how I'm responding to Zoë's and Reetika's deaths. Here are two people I loved and I'm trying to keep their memory alive."

He felt as though his most important accomplishment was the effect he'd had on the lives of others. I asked about people coming to him, almost on a daily basis, looking for feedback on their work or direction, some help to find their place. He conceded that some were just in search of a hustle, but we should try to be nurturers, to open doors for each other: "At any given time, I am promoting at least two or three writers. For example, somebody may contact me and ask me to give a talk. If it doesn't fit into my schedule, I tell them, 'I can't make it, but call so-and-so' . . . If you believe in someone's talent, you find the doors and

---

*I still have many of the envelopes Miller addressed to me while I was his student. Each month, he'd not only send detailed feedback about poems I'd written and books I read, but he'd also scour his personal collection and put together what he called an "E-packet" for each student. These packets consisted of any given number of things: articles, book posters, special edition Langston Hughes and Zora Neale Hurston postage stamp lapel pins, a signed Sweet Honey in the Rock CD, or a VHS tape of an A. Van Jordan and Shara McCallum reading from the Folger Shakespeare Library. I learned quickly that sharing his vestiges with us was a particular kind of nurturing. I asked him about why he did this and he said, "I started looking around and saw that my colleagues were teaching from their strengths. I wasn't operating from my strength. My strength is African American culture. Now, I'm making sure that people get a good dose."

push them through until they reach that point of takeoff. That's what literary politics is all about."

In that fifth-grade class, after reading Hughes, we wrote poems about heritage, where we came from, and who we wanted to be. I wrote one called "Africa" that began: "I'm a Nubian princess with a voice like a song / . . . I am a village woman with nothing to hide. / I am Africa, filled with Black pride." I thought nothing of writing a poem that broached race, a theme I'd be circling forever.

Another poet I've learned much from, Forrest Hamer, told me about a similar convergence that brought him to poetry during our interview: "When I was in the fourth grade in 1966, specifically during Negro History Week, we learned about slavery and 'the Progress of the Negro since Emancipation'. . . I think I developed a kind of double-consciousness I had not had, and the struggle to understand who we were not only in our own minds but in the minds of the whites around us—my world at that time was strictly segregated—lodged in me as a problem. I wrote my first poem as an effort to 'solve' that problem."

Like Hamer, I'd been asked to see myself in a poem. To tangle heritage, I'd have to wrestle "the race problem" and make a claim to my place, where I hoped that heritage would lead me. I was writing me and finding me at once.

A quick word of caution: if your first impulse is to write poems that contend with race, then you probably won't be satisfied writing about pet cats, the whip-poor-will, or Cezanne. Honorée Fanonne Jeffers has a fabulous poem called "Blues Aubade (or, Revision of the Lean Post-Modernist Pastorale)" where she signifies about this kind of name-dropping and navel-gazing, whatever artsy folks might do or expect you to do. Your impulse will be to write about things others will label *political*—personal poems that you will recognize as your own aunt's suffering, your grandmother's penance, your child's undoing, your faithful reckoning with your own Black life.

Ms. Myers liked my poem so much that she entered it into the district poetry contest, and it won. A few days later, she seemed unsettled when she told me the principal was on the way to the class to congratulate me. The principal, a white woman with an endless array of Ann Taylor power suits, kept her honey-brown hair in a wavy bob and could be heard clicking her high heels up and down the concrete outside our classes most days. She peeked into the classroom and asked me to step outside for a moment as Ms. Myers cut her eyes and went back to teaching.

We stood on the long sidewalk that connected the buildings for each grade. "It really is a compliment," the principal kept saying. "They want to be sure you wrote it, which means it's really very good." Then again, "It's a compliment, a backwards kind of compliment, don't you think?" She wanted me to agree with her; she shook her head the way you do when you try to get a baby to mimic your nodding. Then, a bit reluctantly, she said she needed to ask if the poem was mine because the judges had to be sure.

I'd never been called to her office. I didn't misbehave. I sang solos at every choir concert, and as one of the few little Black girls in the entire school, I was hard to miss at any event. I was the consummate overachiever; in fact, when I got a B a few years later, I grounded myself for two weeks, much to the chagrin of my family and wily friends. For two years running, I'd won every academic award there was to win. The principal was always in the group of administrators on stage, waiting to shake each student's hand at the awards ceremony, yet here she was asking if I'd done the work. I hadn't understood why Ms. Myers cut her eyes at her, but now I knew. Surely the principal had told her they needed to "verify the authenticity" of my writing, and surely Ms. Myers had jumped to my aid. But here we were.

A few weeks later, they gave me a trophy that is still the only one on my mantle (they don't give many trophies to people who mostly just excel at reading), and my mother sent the poem to my family scattered about. My paternal grandparents, at the time living in Korea where my grandfather was stationed, had the poem handwritten on silk and framed, then sent it to us as a gift. It is still on my parents' wall near my college diplomas, and we cherish the poem more than the credentials. It was a start for me, an entryway into all my layered dreaming. Now, I had a voice to tackle what I saw on the news or in my own house, a voice to carry what harbored me, to bridge the distances, to question everything.

Of course, Ms. Myers was my best and favorite teacher. She understood me, praised me, and, when I confided in her, even talked to my chorus instructor about why I missed a concert, then offered to come and get me for any other after-school activities (my father would intermittently return but began disappearing for days, taking the car and our little money with him). We trusted Ms. Myers so much that when she surprised me and another student with a trip to Disneyland a whole state away for two days during spring break—something my mother *never* would have agreed to with any previous teacher—I was allowed to go.

In class and at parent-teacher conferences, Ms. Myers liked to mention the more than ten foster children she'd raised over the years. At Disneyland, a young Black boy around our age with a flattop and braces, plus the coolest bomber jacket I'd ever seen, accompanied us: her newest son. He vied for her attention almost as much as Brandi and I did. Brandi was my best friend from our class. She lived a few blocks from our apartment in a run-down ranch style on a tough block. Brandi was smart and kind; we matched our tights and sweaters, even hairstyles when we could. Her blond hair, crinkled with mousse, and my large puffs, when straightened, both could be anchored into sleek high ponytails. We shared lunch and BOOK IT! challenge books because she was also a star student.

At the end of the year, I left Ms. Myers reluctantly. On the last day of school, we both sobbed, then pulled ourselves together until my mother arrived and started us to crying all over again. I went to a middle school in another part of the city, and soon we lost touch.

Imagine my surprise when, one evening, my mother came to the dinner table with the newspaper, looking grave. The headline was "School Learns a Tough Lesson in Deceit" and it was about Ms. Myers, who'd gone on to become a principal at St. Mary's Elementary. The article said: "When the Catholic Diocese of Phoenix hired Darlene Myers as principal of St. Mary's Elementary School last August, it had no idea it was getting a thief and imposter with a lengthy list of felony convictions and aliases." She'd been arrested and jailed for embezzlement, stealing thousands of dollars ("tuition funds and even money that schoolchildren had raised by selling candy") in the last few years. The article went on: "Police say Myers, 41, has prior felony arrests in New York, Illinois, and Connecticut, has served prison time, and has used at least 10 aliases in her crime career."

I was dumbfounded and confused. How long had this ruse been going on? Had she used that money to live lavishly? Was she something like a modern-day Robin Hood, using it to house children and spoil the less fortunate in her classes with trips and rides and books when their parents were poor or absent, like she did for me? Did the principal who wondered about my poem really have questions about Ms. Myers's authenticity? Didn't Ms. Myers know all the Black folks were lumped together by most who saw us? How could she embarrass us—herself, her children, my mother, and me? My mother already had to explain each time my father went missing, and now she was faced with demystifying another of my heroes. "This is terrible, but she was a great teacher," she said, probably meaning, *All this bad shouldn't erase everything she was to you.*

"What a waste," I said, meaning, *Things aren't always what they seem.* Thinking back, I guess Ms. Myers was a certain type of hustler, but she still opened a door for me. She let me see what words made possible, what light they carried, and what I could hope to be.

But I also learned then that people, like spaces we called home, could be different than we'd imagined. People, like home, could be all sorts of things.

Ms. Myers's duplicity was just one of the life lessons Phoenix taught me. There was also racism and poverty. My mother was rebuilding our life from the ground up, as we'd lost the house and the cars had been repossessed. We were on welfare and lived in Section 8 apartments for a time; we often relied on the help of others. All of this led to shame. Violence, too, was rampant, spilling over from the gang sets in LA, and we felt it in different ways. The walls on each side of our apartment were tagged every few months with graffiti, there were colors we couldn't wear, and the boys in school each year picked sides—some disappeared soon after, dropping out, getting locked up, and becoming the victims of jump-ins or drive-bys. Being Black hadn't been an anomaly where we'd lived before, but here this was an added strain. We were so few that it was easy to make us feel invisible, freakish, or outnumbered.

The first time I remember being called a nigger, I was coming home from Bible study with my mother. I was around twelve years old. We had just gotten out of the car, dressed in skirts well past our knees with books in hand, cutting across the grass to the steps that led to our apartment on the second floor. A truck full of Mexican boys—two in the front and several more in the open bed—slowed as they passed us in the dark, and one said loud enough for us to hear, "It's just some fucking niggers." They didn't speed off or even speed up, just crept down the street as I stared at them and they stared back.

A few months later in what had become one of my favorite escapes, my middle school library, I searched the card catalog for "Black + poetry" out of curiosity. To my surprise, a book appeared titled *The Black Poets*, so I went to find it on the shelves. I remember looking at the birds converging on the cover, the black lettering, and wondering who Dudley Randall was (this was, perhaps, the first anthology I had encountered). I read down the table of contents and got no further than page five: "Run, Nigger, Run!" What I immediately assumed about the book—wrongly— was that it was a collection of "Black" poetry put together by white people. Most of the Black or Latin American or Native art I'd encountered in Phoenix was neatly curated as part of city enrichment programs downtown or framed in other libraries and only addressed the surface of who folks were.

I don't remember thumbing through the rest of the table of contents or reading any other piece, but I turned to that folk poem credited to no author. It was in dialect; it made us sound foolish to my untrained, unknowing eye and ear ("Dat Nigger run'd, dat Nigger flew, / Dat Nigger tore his shu't in two"). I was livid. I marched up to the librarian and raised my voice. I told her the book was inappropriate, that it used racial slurs and needed to be banned from the library. She was taken aback, immediately apologetic; she'd never seen me behave disrespectfully. I was also in tears, so this could have aided in her willingness to find some truth in my claim. She took the book out of my hand, handed me a tissue, and said she would take care of it *right away*. I thanked her and went to my favorite corner, tired but triumphant. At least I had done something about the riffraff and now I could go on with my all-important prepubescent life.

When I went back to the library the next week, the book was gone, from the catalog and the shelf. For the rest of the year, the librarian smiled sympathetically and waved each time she saw me check out or return. Together, we had done something for the greater good; she was happy to assuage her student and I was happy to have spared another the humiliation of that word splayed across the first pages of a book that should have been about our brilliance. It wasn't until college that I realized the book was indeed an example of that.

Before I went to college, my family moved back across the country to Norfolk, Virginia, to help take care of my grandmother, who'd become ill. She'd suffered from depression off and on throughout her life and, as Granddaddy had died more than a decade before, she was having a hard time living alone. All the family had moved back East, in fact—my mother, aunt, uncle, and cousins. Our whole cohort departed Phoenix my junior year of high school and I was so grateful to leave it behind.

When I decided to major in English and minor in African American studies in college, I was chasing all the things I felt I'd missed. In my very first class, I was given a list of "Texts in the Cultivation of African American Arts and Letters," and what was at the very top? Dudley Randall's *The Black Poets*, and not far below it was E. Ethelbert Miller's *In Search of Color Everywhere*. *The Black Poets* was required reading for the course (and for several others). I spent years cringing at the sight of it and my stupidity for not knowing it was indeed ours—and seminal—all those years earlier.

Dudley Randall, a writer, translator, the book's editor, and the director of Broadside Press—an indispensable home for Black poetry in Detroit, alongside Lotus Press, during the Black Arts Movement and beyond—was invested in offering the full range of Black poetry as it stood when he compiled the anthology. Hence, looking at the women poets alone, one finds slave songs and folk poems like the one I'd read, but also poems by Lucy Terry, Phillis Wheatley, Mari Evans, Gwendolyn Brooks, Lucille Clifton, Nikki Giovanni, and Sonia Sanchez, among others who, in time, helped shape me.

Sanchez especially would make me feel a little less alone in my aloofness as a girl. During our interview, she talked about stumbling into the gaping holes in her knowledge of Black literature as well. Once she left home in Alabama, even after she'd made her way through Hunter College, she met Jean Hutson, curator of Harlem's Schomburg Center for Research in Black Culture, a library and archive that is part of the New York Public Library. Sanchez related: "The first three books she gave me were *The Souls of Black Folk*, *Up from Slavery*, and *Their Eyes Were Watching God*. I started *Their Eyes Were Watching God*—that one was on top. I read about a quarter of the book and I got up and knocked on her door. At the old Schomburg, she was enshrined in this glass room. She came to the door and said, 'Yes, dear?' I said—and I had just met her—'How could I be a graduate of Hunter College, how could I call myself an educated woman, and not have read these books?' and she said, 'Yes, dear. Now go sit down and read.' And I kept coming there."

When I raged against the poetry book in my library, I was presumptuous, confused, and outraged about how my Blackness was being reflected, given that there were so few other books I could find at the time about who I wanted to be. I was probably wrong. Had I not been so fiery and quick to jump to the defense of *all* Blackness by railing against the book based on its opening pages, I might have looked through the table of contents like any sensible person and sought out the work of other poets one by one. But sometimes we are left to our own fears and intricacy.

Through the years, I have tried to remind myself that I was just a child. I was headstrong and vigilant in disarming what I thought was prejudice—but there is still no way for me to convey how much I regret what I did. I had recently been called a nigger by other folks of color, who I believed in my untested heart should have been on my side, so I was hyperaware of every perceived affront. But for me, getting a book banned—especially a collection of Black voices—and taking it out of the hands of other students for years, possibly forever for all I know, is an almost unforgivable sin. It's certainly the worst thing I can think of ever doing, though my mother will tell you that getting caught kissing a boy behind the movie theater was the worst thing I did in middle school. I eventually married him, but she still won't let it go.

As I am someone invested in doing the work of a poet and invested in Blackness and all its complexities, I've used and published the word *nigger* in my work. I've used language some might find more offensive than this. For some of this crafting (especially as it pertains to women's sexuality), my book *What We Ask of Flesh* has been banned in at least one high school. Maybe this is cosmic payback for my jumping to the wrong conclusion all those years ago.

To make some kind of amends to the poetry gods, I buy a copy of *The Black Poets* every few years and put it back into the universe—donate it to a prison, give it to a used bookstore, hand it to an eager student. I did learn from my stupidity, so I suppose all wasn't lost. Now, my hasty actions remind me that context is everything. I've learned that the best way to defend Blackness (or any marginalized thing) is to let it be just as it is, or was, or could be.

Part of Miller's life's work, like Randall's, has been to collect Black voices and curate them for others, to document their vision and experiences. "We know culture is key in terms of the exchange of values and traditions. That's how people learn. That's the beauty of being a human being," Miller said, when I asked about his approach to editing.

With *In Search of Color Everywhere*, he said he "tried to create the anthology for the everyday person . . . [this anthology] was a book I didn't have when I was growing up . . . I wanted to do 'the one' book. This desire comes from my job in the African American Resource Center.

If you ask a body of young African American students what poems they like, you're going to hear some of the same poems over and over again. I said, 'Okay, I'm doing this "one" book. You name the writer and I want their signature poem.' That's what I tried to do."

Curating voices is also a way to trace Black lives, Black living, what we've inherited from home and what we've shaped ourselves. Miller said, "[I]f I took the first section of *In Search of Color Everywhere*, which deals with freedom, you see those poems go from the creation, to Africa, to the Middle Passage, up through slavery, all the way to the last poems in that section, which deal with freedom in terms of incarceration. I could take this unit of poems and I could teach a history class using the work. The same thing goes for the section on love or the celebration of Blackness."

We're a whole world in the hands of curators like Randall and Miller; they help transmit experiences and voices, save what has been heard, ferry us across place and time.

• • • • •

When we left Phoenix and moved to Norfolk to take care of my ailing grandmother, she still had sisters in Scotland Neck, North Carolina, and had been waiting for us to "carry her there." For the first time in a long time, riding down South, I noticed what I'd never seen as a child. There were Black lawn jockeys with their lamps to guide the way of passersby, field after field of the unknown, cemeteries split on either side of the road ("One side colored, one side white," my grandmother explained), and huge, columned, stately homes next to small, rotting ones.

Despite living in Phoenix, where cotton was still harvested outside of the city, I had never seen a field of it, so I asked my grandmother what all the trash was along the road as we headed to visit her sister Doll. Much cotton had broken away from the bolls, so the roads were lined with thin white, almost like pieces of muslin. The fields were wide, and each belonged to someone, so Aunt Doll said, "Don't pick nothin' that ain't ours," when we got to the house and I asked if I could feel a bit of cotton on the stalk. She pointed me toward the edge of the family field and I picked a boll to find white fiber locks on brown burs, brown seeds inside, and a rough-skinned stalk with thorns. The cotton was lighter than a strip of gauze in my hand, but an article told me that slaves were expected to haul "200 pounds per worker per day." I couldn't understand how this was possible, or how much of the land and its markers remained unchanged.

What was I imagining? What was I hoping to find? Years later, I was tasked with writing a poem for the MLK Day program at Norfolk State University, an HBCU where I took a job out of college to help oversee writing assessment for students. In my research, I was shocked to find that Dr. King, when he was ten, sang with his church choir at his town's premiere of the film *Gone with the Wind*. I wrote in King's voice; I imagined him singing "Dixie" and still longing for the things it held, despite its complicated history. I wrote all that, then the lines:

> That's how you know what home is:
> The place you keep coming back to.

Home is what we most desire, not just a mark on a map, but the dream of the thing we hold onto. Place, on the other hand, is where we fit in, or is sometimes the cramped road that what you think of as home gives you.

Home, for me, was an ideal—a city of memory, a firm ground and shining mirage—what I thought I remembered in the way I wanted it to be. When you're a child, even when there's been upheaval and chaos, you have a way of remembering things with nostalgia and longing. In the distance, everything is pretty. What seemed unmovable was, in reality, already-shifting ground. Every city I knew, I only knew as I'd fancied it. Even now, I wonder how I could have envisioned Augusta, Georgia, which had erupted in race riots that made national news less than a decade before I was born, to be a perfect landscape for folks like me.

While I listened to family stories and devised stories of my own, I became obsessed with sussing out the past. But what most shapes our thoughts of home? Theano Terkenli said in her article "Home as a Region" that "[a]s definitions of home change, people yearn more for home and thus tend to become more intensely attached to it. In other words, they value more what they seem to be losing." Memory is unreliable and skittish. I looked back on Augusta, Phoenix, and Norfolk with a child's mind—what was bad was wholly bad in my heart's summation and what I was missing was entirely good.

None of this was accurate. Everything was gray and garbled—my experiences had taught me this, but I fought hard to ignore it in my memory. People have many sides and land (where we stand on it, what it has held before) does curious things to us all.

When compiling her anthology *Black Nature: Four Centuries of African American Nature Poetry*, Camille Dungy, much like Miller and Randall, claimed a space for Black poets, allowing them room in the conversation about ecopoetics as they examined their ties to the land and how they're estranged from it. In *Black Nature*, my poem "The Ritual of Season" tests the storms, calls fury God, challenges everything. Reading Dungy's anthology tells me what I didn't seem to know as a little girl under Southern skies or on desert dryland: Black folks are haunted everywhere. Even when we're home, we're not free of fear and unrest and longing. Even when family's nearby, we are worrisome. Even when our children are with us, we lose sleep.

Learning about Blackness from a distance was a gift—I realize this now but resented it then. I had such awe for what I thought I was missing, for folks I really did miss, for land I might have learned to hate had I stood to grow on it much longer. America is a fraught country for many of us, and we can't escape this odd juxtaposition—this pining mixed with unease—no matter where we stand.

Now, after being in the South on the East Coast for more than twenty years, home feels like the thicket of trees across from the ocean, less than a mile up the road from my little Virginia cottage but nearly impossible to make a way into without much struggle, probably pain, though it looks beautiful from afar. I've grown up here too—found and lost loves, graduated several times, buried my grandmother, bought my first house, worked under Confederate statues. I wrote books and taught students much like myself. My relationship with every space I call home is knotty, intricate. This complexity, the weight and wonder of it, is indivisible.

All the time I've been imagining home, I've also been thinking of a place for myself, a home in Black poetry. Hughes set out those first bread-crumbs for me to follow, and I've tried to widen the path of my wondering. In "The Negro Artist and the Racial Mountain," Hughes's voice comes back to me, affirming that some of the struggles I carried would help ground me. Common folks are folks too; we love each other and hold joy deeply. There might be a steep hill to climb, a maneuvering around politics to make a place, but the common living should also be praised. To succeed in this, I should cobble together a wide swath of community, of family intent on questioning. During our interview, Miller asserted that a successful living as a poet is about "the distance you've traveled inside yourself." How do we dream a larger, more expansive space for ourselves than has existed for those who came before us? How do we walk in the shadow of those who walk alongside us, who teach us, and set a table for those coming after?

No matter where I was, that "problem" of race, of longing and displacement, was my spark from the beginning. For a long time after leaving Phoenix, I prided myself on surviving the city, on finding who I was despite it. As a child, I believed questioning what was thrust upon us was a small act of resistance. But now I know it's a lifelong striving. It's revolutionary, finding beauty in what haunts me.

Once a year, two girlfriends and I load up a car and head South to eat, laugh, read, and write. We've gone to Myrtle Beach, South Carolina; Norwood, Virginia; Kitty Hawk, North Carolina; and other Southern haunts. We ventured North once, but things weren't the same. We couldn't find the right barbecue, found no cotton gins or markers about Nat Turner's revolt, no lawn jockeys to shake our heads at, no wide swaths of untilled field. We had so little to challenge, so little to balk at and return to—we weren't comforted or angered by what we saw heading North, so we go South, home away from home, for inspiration. We are three Black women writers setting out to find a space that allows for us, or one with which we are eerily acquainted. Mostly, we want soul singers blaring on the open road, food our aunties or mamas used to make, long naps and long sun. We want to follow the water. We want to be far enough from our everyday that when we encounter pieces of our familiar, they underscore what we should be saving, what lines and conceits we can let go and which reveries we must keep. What do we save for our children? What home do we carry? Which ghosts do we let sleep?

BINGHAM-RISHER: How do you feel about the popularity of poetry from open mics and the spoken word movement?

MILLER: What you see taking place in the cafés and the clubs is really good, because it's giving more support and appreciation to the field in general. I remember getting on the Metro a few years ago, there was a young brother sitting close to me and he had a poem. A few stops later, his buddy got on. They were excited and started talking about their work. I'm listening and it's some tired stuff [laughing]. But here are two Black guys who didn't know each other that well—they'd met at a reading or something—talking about poetry. They couldn't have been more than eighteen or nineteen years old, but here they were, two young Black men, not arguing or shooting at each other. They had a love for language that was bringing them together. That's priceless.

Honorée Fanonne Jeffers

ON FAITH

What leads me to the page is spirit.
—HONORÉE FANONNE JEFFERS

FAITH (fāth): **noun. 1.**) *The duty of fulfilling one's trust; allegiance owed to a superior*—I owe ancestors and elders my reverence, faith, and take seriously my charge to speak truth to power, meaning I will tell it like it is and not how others pretend it was or should be.

I am trying to find joy in destruction.

Me and my cousin Richelle, my always accomplice, were sitting just outside the kitchen, listening to the women who raised us tell all they know about who's low-down and who's gotten back up again. We were younger than ten, so I didn't know it yet, but these are "the Poets in the Kitchen" Paule Marshall wrote about, the women whose down-home speech will change the way I hear music, intersperse rhythm.

The ways Black folks speak (and speak to each other, family or not) is a love language built on wordplay, indirection, humor, and affection. We call this articulation *signifying*, which is apropos as it is often meant to be a heads-up, a sign, a portent about some coming action.* There are

---

*For a critical study on signifying, read Henry Louis Gates Jr.'s "The Signifying Monkey and the Language of Signifyin(g): Rhetorical Difference and the Orders of Meaning." Not only does it teach much about the creativity of Black language, but it also gives context for why Gates would reportedly say, "I'll speak with your mama outside!" as a cop wrongfully arrested him on his property in Cambridge a few months after Barack Obama took office.

endless variations of Black rhetoric. Signifying often depends on the re-
gion you're in or were raised in, your church home, the way your friends
joke, or how your family shares its own lore. When I read Major Jack-
son's poem "Urban Renewal—Block Party" written for The Roots from
his book *Leaving Saturn*, I was bowled over by his calling Shakespeare's
Prospero a "sucker-emcee." I loved it when Patricia Smith sounded like
every street corner barbershop comedian/philosopher in her poem "Ter-
rell's Take on Things." And just coming to the title of Lucille Clifton's
"why people be mad at me sometimes" made me want to know her se-
crets because they sounded like secrets my cousins might keep.

Signifying women raised me with an understanding that destruction
can be made into sugar, something gritty and sweet on the tongue. Worry
can be undercut and buried. Getting up every day, turning the music on,
cleaning house, cutting up in a warm room, then putting your hands
in the pot means you can go on living, despite what the world has left
you with.

•● ● ●●●● ● ●●● ● ●●●● ·

When I interviewed Honorée Fanonne Jeffers, much of our talk was about
the politics of race, the elders, and what we owe for all their generations
of bearing these burdens.* She believes the elders are, in part, why she's
a poet, why she is given gifts. She told me, "[T]he only reason I've been
given what I've been given is because the ancestors reward me for tending
their altars." This return to the ancestors defines her work and mine too.

I believe in the elders and in their being straight with me. I can lis-
ten to the "poets in the kitchen" and hear snippets of what my great-
great-grandmother sounded like, then let her descendants tell it from our

---

*At one point, Jeffers broke the "politics" part down nicely: "'[R]ace' is used as short-
hand for 'Black people.' If I write about a fish fry in my grandma's backyard, how
does someone think I am writing about 'race'? Because there are Black people there?
Because there aren't white people there? That first poem [in her book *The Glory
Gets*]—'Singing Counter'—is about race because you only have 'race' issues when
you have two or more people from different cultures in conflict. If there is no conflict,
you only have 'culture.' Race is an artificial construct too, but that's another issue."

beginning. That is why as a child and even now, I sit with the elders and listen.

•● ● ●●● ● ●●● ● ●●●

FAITH (fāth): **noun. 2.)** *Confidence based on evidence, testimony, or authority*—what others said and wrote, what they hoped would come through me. Faith is recognizing a voice, a tenor or note; a handwritten missive; something somebody's mama said, a heart-mending.

In graduate school, sitting in a large lecture hall at Bennington College with some of the most well-known literary writers in the country—Robert Bly, Donald Hall, April Bernard, David Lehman, and others—listening to a lecture on "The Great American Writers," I had a clear revelation: they don't see me, they don't even know I'm here.

A twenty-year-old Black girl with dreams of being a poet—or any Black writer, as the lecture hadn't mentioned one in the hour it labored on—was nonexistent in the sight of the writers all around me. But Black American poets had changed my life, and their voices, lives and paths, triumphs and tragedies, were worth illuminating, as they had led me here.

Rumor had it I was only the second Black woman poet the program had ever admitted and the youngest poet ever, at twenty, to enter. There was only one other writer of color, a quiet Nigerian visual artist and novelist, who would later become my dearest friend from that class. Ada and I were drawn to each other partly out of necessity and partly because opposites attract. I was boisterous; she was reserved. I fussed in the back of every lecture about what was missing; she sat with her forehead uncreased, sketching gorgeous abstracts, unfazed. We were quickly swept up into another group of second- and third-year students, some of color, some outsiders who fancied themselves kind of cool-kid misfits. We called ourselves the Bennington Bitch Club and had shirts made the next year so everyone would know it.

In addition to the Bennington Bitch Club I was gifted with the presence of Jeffers, a visiting writer who would show me another way to be a Black woman poet in the world. Her work meditated on the South, family flaws, the blues, and spirit—we were kindred in many ways.

At Bennington, at the end of every residency, most of the students gathered in The Commons—a large building in the center of campus where we'd eat, get our mail, and lounge between classes. We'd sing there in front of the fire well into the night. Peter, Paul and Mary's "Leaving on a Jet Plane" made its way into that last evening's set each time we prepared to head home and I liked chiming in, but it wasn't a song I knew well until I'd sung it with the others again and again. I'm sure plenty of students there thought it a fitting, sweet rendering of goodbye and maybe also felt like it was the story they had to tell loved ones each time they came to campus for weeks at a time to write—*I'm headed out to follow this other love of mine and not sure how far it could pull us apart, or if I'll be the same person when I return.*

I shuffled back to my room fairly early most of those evenings. The Vermont dark was like a cloak. What seemed like miles of sparkling snow lay beyond The Commons along the field called The Edge of the World where we'd set up a firelight maze in summer. I remember heading out into the eerie quiet (once you left a building, even one full of singing comrades, almost all sound was lost to the dull ambient light and biting cold). Most nights, I was enveloped there by loneliness. So little of what the crowd thought pertinent lodged anywhere near even my distant memory. When Jeffers arrived, we fell in step almost immediately and I'll never forget when we discovered we could sing. She mentioned being in a band that played jazz and blues once and I said I'd always wanted to be.

I already looked up to her, as she was invited as a visiting writer and I'd been reading her first two books about down-home Georgia and love as a many-tiered wonder of a thing. There was fatback, pot liquor, barbecue, passing cousins, wandering husbands, backtalk, and shouting. She wrote about family just as it was. She didn't see the need to clean everything up and make it pretty. Some of the living, even of folks we loved, was foolhardy, but it all taught you. She'd left me messages in both her books, reminders she might have known I'd need to return to: "Sister-girl, what a treat you are! I am so glad to have met you. Keep in touch. / Remember your own gifts as you move through this world. Peace and grace and joy."

While Jeffers was there, our last night around the fire, I mentioned how I thought Aretha Franklin's "Ain't No Way" was a perfect lament and how I loved the ethereal notes floating in half-echo, half-awakening. Jeffers had a deep alto and began singing Aretha's part low but loud, her voice full of power. I blended in Cissy Houston's soprano all along the background. Everyone in earshot—a few dozen students and faculty lounging while the sun went down—hushed themselves and turned to watch. We knew every note but bent a few to our liking, and we'd never sung together before, but she sounded like home to me.

In an essay Jeffers published in the *Virginia Quarterly Review* called "The Subjective Briar Patch: Contemporary American Poetry," she said much of what I was feeling in that lecture hall: "What does it matter if the faces of contemporary American poets are different colors if ultimately the writers of the 'best' poetry in American literature—the Modernists—are all white and overwhelmingly male? If a poet cannot make her literary god in a subjective image, how can someone who isn't white or male pray at a poetry altar of her own making? The answer is: she can't."

During our interview, I pinpointed that time, not long after we met, when I was still a student at Bennington and she'd visited the semester before. I remembered sitting in that lecture thinking, *I'm invisible to these folks,* to which she replied candidly: "You're not supposed to be seen! Ms. Lucille [Clifton] had to hip me to that. She came out here [to Oklahoma] for a reading, and at the time, I was dealing with all these little racist microaggressions. And I was so dramatic, I threw myself at her feet and I said, 'Ms. Lucille, they're trying to destroy Black women this week!' And she said, 'They are always trying to destroy Black women. They have been trying to destroy Black women since we got off the ship. So you better get yourself together.' You know, Ms. Lucille was sweet as pie, but every once in a while, she'd get a little bass in her voice."

Clifton, another of our heroes, could be tough when she needed to be. The interesting thing is, Jeffers is mostly (even notoriously) tough, but soft when friends are in need. When I called her crying that night, she had faith, comforted me: "Baby, they don't know your power," she'd said, and when I reminded her of this, she immediately called up another sister poet: "No, they don't know your power. That's not actually my saying, though. Lyrae Van Clief-Stefanon used to say that to me: 'They don't know my power.'"

I do know the power that other Black poets have given me: Enlightenment. Scrutiny. Camaraderie. Words to subvert fear.

• • • • • • • • • •

FAITH (fāth): **noun.** 3.) *Belief, trust*—"The evident demonstration of things unseen," what creation teaches me about God's sense of humor and color palette, about his love of song and our voices. I have faith in relief coming, about Earth always being here, about the dead rising again sometimes at our own hands.

Death hasn't come for me much and for this I am grateful. I almost drowned once, was car number twenty-nine in a sixty-nine-car pile-up on an icy bridge in December fog, but I left the water and the bridge mostly unharmed. But when death comes for others, I'm worn and warned. I set out to do what's needed of me.

When I was headed to the last room my grandmother would ever see, it weighed on me. At the stoplight, cars were honking on all sides. The light turned green but everyone was stopped behind me. It was pouring outside and I'd put my head down on the wheel, praying.

In the hospital, I held her hand and greased her hair. My aunts were there. Everything I'd prayed for—*let me make it on time, let me know what's coming, let it be easy*—had come true. As I was running in from parking the car, wet with rain and tears, her doctor materialized and said, "I remember you. Let me tell you what's going to happen soon." As he talked of kidney failure, I asked if I should prepare for the worst. He said,

"Make no mistake: this is a terminal event," meaning he had given me something to direct my steps, a way to walk toward what I'd told God I needed, the clarity I'd put my faith in. She died in a few hours and I was at her side—her body still warm and skin smooth. And I was already thinking of how I'd immortalize her, how I'd continue to tell it, to build a steady room.

Faith doesn't fail me in death, as it does some others. In poems, as in my belief, people are resurrected. When loved ones die, I go back to familiar voices, to homage. I reread Jeffers's poems "The Gospel of Barbecue" and "What Grief Is." They elegize her Uncle Alvester and a whole generation of folks, like my grandmother, at home in the South. Those accustomed to souse, chitterlings, and scrapple. They have bodies full of trouble and houses full of folks who'd like the plates they've served up sopped clean. When they go, there are houses of worship lined with tearful, weary congregants bidding them stay. I find whole books of poems for almost every moment death arrives, which gives me faith that others have survived this and told about it, that I, too, will refuse to let the past be the past.

On the morning of my interview with Jeffers, March 20, 2015, I was driving to work listening to National Public Radio and heard the story of Otis Byrd, fifty-four. He'd been missing since March 2 and was found March 19 hanging in the woods in Jackson, Mississippi, in a possible lynching. Before our call, I went back to Jeffers's poems "Where the Song Stops," "Incident at Cross Plains (The Lynching of William Luke, 1870)," and "Giving Thanks for Water," all fearless in their take on racist history. I asked her if the job of the poet was to be a historian? A muckraker? An elegist? A keeper of difficult things? She told me: "I'm lucky as a Black poet writing at this particular time that I don't have to consider in the beginning [of writing a poem] what my role is. There are other Black poets in the past who have done that work for me. I no longer have to consider whether the people reading my work consider me a human being, like Phillis Wheatley did.

"But if you're writing about lynching or writing about race . . ." she went on, "if you are writing for the people but the people don't know what you're saying because the language is so dense and difficult, then how effective is it? I think poets should strive for clarity."

Jeffers is not about hiding the truth of the thing in a maze of language few can understand, no matter what time we're venturing into, no matter whose lifeline we strive to exhume. This is evidenced by Jeffers's *The Age of Phillis*, a biography in verse about Black poetry's foremother, Phillis Wheatley. She said of it and of the necessity for clarity: "I want regular people to get Phillis Wheatley. I don't think I'm any more important than any scholar or historian, but my role is to talk about who she is for the regular folk. To be able to go to Mt. Calvary Baptist Church and break it down."

She went on: "I'm an antiquarian, I do historical research, but I'm not an academic historian; I don't know their particular vocabulary. In the same ways, I'm a critic, but I don't do post-structuralist theory, etc. I think that it takes someone like me—my late friend James William Richardson Jr. used to say this—a plainspoken sister to explain things."

Part of being plainspoken, for Jeffers, is putting faith in transparency, despite how this might harry others. It takes a kind of fearlessness, or faith in tending, doing the work of the greater good no matter what heat it brings you. I'd read Jeffers's book *The Glory Gets* the day before our discussion. I thought of how some might take issue with the opening poem, "Singing Counter," about Mary and Hayes Turner, a married couple lynched in 1918 (along with their unborn baby). The poem eschews metaphor, insisting on plain talk about the mob, zeroing in on individuals who bring their children to watch, who claim Christ and good living. I think the poem is brilliant, but many would find it shocking. Another poem, "I End in Winter," says, "Every blade I sharpen / is sure of its intentions." I asked what were her intentions, what did she have to say to readers who might call this biased, call her racist, or note that all of this is political racket, conjuring the nation's dealings that led us to this present? She said:

"But these things go back to 1619. What bothers me now is that folks are acting like this is the first time this has happened. I'm like, 'Sweetie, that's why I have a library card and you, too, might want to get one.' People who are so surprised by this haven't been reading. Yes, I'm surprised by the audacity of these violent events, but not by killings. It's the same thing with Otis Byrd. . . . I've got a friend that says, 'I'm tired of people talking about the past.' My thing is, as Faulkner said—and I'm sure I'm butchering this—the past isn't dead, it isn't even past. These aren't issues that are just coming about. This is not a remix; it's a symphony."

This is love and devotion, this is faith: listening to the continuous maelstrom of echoes and following them wherever they might lead.

·•● ● ●●●● ● ●●●● ● ●●●● ·

FAITH (fāth): **noun. 4.)** *As a collective term. Obsolete. One of many alleged group names found in late Middle English sources e.g. A feyth of Marchantes.*—For their love of reclamation, of finding and overturning the obsolete, a community or collective of Black poets should hereby be referred to as a Faith, i.e., A Faith of poets made me.

Writing is such a reclusive exercise—even more so when you are a Black poet in America, where intellectuals are touted but not compensated for much. And even when family loves you dearly, as mine does, they rarely understand what the heck you are doing with all your time.

My family, and many Black families, still lean more toward the Booker T. Washington philosophy of vocation over observation—i.e., *Girl, what is your job?* For instance, I wrote the following for an anthology of notable quotes from Black voices, and though the project came to nothing, the accuracy didn't wane:

1. I've found that, to most, "Black intellectual" is an oxymoron; "Black poet" is little more than an absurdity. This bothered me, until I learned to embrace the absurd and use it to my advantage in my poems and otherwise.

2. Try not to act a fool when your friends and family start asking questions about the finer points of your work/life as a poet. Some of the best questions posed to me thus far have been:

> [Mama] You gone put them nasty poems in the book too?

> [Cousin] You been publishing all them poems. Don't you have enough money to get your car fixed yet?

> [Auntie] So, I hear you got your book published. . . . Is that hard?

3. My grandmother praises every word I write and will flip through any college journal that lets me in, but her bragging rights were limited because she couldn't ever find my work in a store, nevertheless tell somebody else to go out and get it. So, when *Essence* decided to publish one of my poems, as far as she was concerned, I'd hit the big time. I think my family bought out every issue from Jersey City to San Jose. It was just like poet Jarvis DeBerry once said, "With Black folks, the only thing better would be the *Jet*."

Being Black also means community dictates mostly everything. If you are a Black person, and especially a Black poet, you are part of the tapestry that is the Black family, immediate or otherwise, whether you desire this or not.

Some find this limiting, but I've found a real comfort in this Collective "I," as it has been the way of my life. There are always "cousins" and "aunts" who are close as kin but not of the same blood. Blood doesn't matter as much as shared experience, and this is made evident each day in my writing life. I mine (and steal) and create the stories that shine a light on people the way I see them. No matter how folks enter, I look for ways to keep them here.

Ed Ochester, another of my wonderful poet-teachers at Bennington, said, "Cave Canem is where you'll get your real education," despite the fact that I was paying $30,000 a year to get an education there. My teachers in grad school were supportive of my work and willing to dig deep into craft, not just my life as a Black woman. They had no problems separating the page from what might have been their own theoretical experience of my living. As they all understood the MFA program on the whole to be a majority-white space, they encouraged me to seek out other workshops that might offer me more than Bennington could. And meeting Jeffers, part of the inaugural group of Cave Canem fellows, was like finding another segment of kin that wouldn't overlook or undervalue me.

Each summer when I left the retreat, something I looked forward to were the love letters that would come as an email chain. Here are snippets of our dispatches from 2006, ten years after the retreat began:

From: Remica Bingham
Subject: RE: CC Love Note

Dear Family,

Remember the lessons we learned on our nature hike: snakes cross our paths for a reason, and some flowers have to fight for sun. Take what you can from these lessons now, and know that you are in my prayers. To all, yes, love is a funny thing. I feel like giving up on it so often during the year, but then I'm blessed with all of you. Spread your poems out in front of you tonight, look at what you've done in such a short time. Know that you are capable and that there are more stories to tell. Know that we are all waiting, listening. I hope everyone is at home, or at least where they want to be, safe and full.

Love, Love, Love,
Remica

From: Amanda Johnston
Subject: RE: CC Love Note

So, last week was crazy! CC to the 10th power! I enjoyed laughing, writing, dancing, impromptu aerobics set to Kanye's "Workout Song," droppin' it like it was hot with Rita D, Elizabeth A, Patricia S, Cyrus C, even Big Daddy Kwame D slid in on some Beenie Man! I saw y'all . . . thank you for being fabulously human!

Love to all my new and old family . . . everyone that I kicked it with, cried with, shared with, worked with, laughed with, and lived each day with. As Lucille Clifton said, this isn't a coincidence. We are in each other's skin. This love is cellular . . .

Cornelius & Toi—For your generosity, strength, and for loving us with such passion that you built us a house where there was none. Thank you for gathering all my brothers & sisters, aunts & uncles and bringing us home . . .

Love Always, All the Time,
Amanda

From: Reginald Dwayne Betts
Subject: RE: CC Love Note

Yeah, this was the realest experience I've had in a minute. Thanks for the openness, caring, understanding and talent of all of y'all. I'm blessed to have had the opportunity.

Now, I'm at the airport. My flight has been cancelled three times. I've slept in the airport, I need a massage something fierce, see how many reasons come up to miss CC. Anyway, y'all be cool. First time I've literally fell in love with 60-plus people in a week.

dwayne

From: Aracelis Girmay
Subject: RE: CC Love Note

Family.

So good to be around the love & wise of you. To have spent time with my several hearts—& to have met new loves—& to have laughed & cried & danced on like that. To have learned new songs & opened my eyes wide to the poems you carry. You are brilliant: machete, ax, cane & balm, salt & sweet, straight-backed & lightning, smooth & bird, low-voiced & high-voiced, filled up & wise, keen, keen, keen . . .

I love you, I love you, I love you (you see, three times—not two, cause that's what Ms. Lucille said).

Yes, I love you, peacocks of my heart, wine in my glass—so glad to spend this life knowing you & doing this work in the world—so glad we get to go back to our homes & carry the shine & the questions & the deep work & the joy & all of it, really. So glad the net of our knowing each other is a wider thing now.

So glad that I will know you & know you.

until tomorrow, pa'lante, pa'lante,
Aracelis

From: Christian Campbell
Subject: RE: CC Love Note

Cave Canem Massive,

I have been back here in Nassau now for what seems like months. It is hurricane season, heavy heat and rain. I don't know why it took me so long to gather my words to you all but here I am. I went to Cave Canem so exhausted— to be honest, part of me didn't want to go because I was (and still am) feeling so behind and paralysed with my dissertation work. But I went, for the last time. And here I am, still cradling my small joy about the reminder of what a marvellous thing it is to be an artist, what a life.

I give thanks for this space. I give thanks for Erica Doyle who, as I was remembering sometimes feeling displaced at Cave Canem, reminded me (in a restaurant, in New York, in April) that Cave Canem is ours, what we make. Which I take to mean that it grows and shifts and shrinks and curves, does not stay still, is HERE. That it is ME + you + you + you . . . The making and re-making of us. We MADE this!! I felt that fully at my last retreat.

From Cave Canem, here I am learning even more about what it means to be at once fierce and generous of spirit, what it means to be loving (and, for me, to be clear and fearless about that love), to surrender to possibility. People you give me courage.

The bigness of us, the smallness, the beauty of us all and all and more. I left my last retreat worn and glad to be here (the here where we all are), with the silent pact we made to each other, trodding in the light of my purpose.

Love,
Christian

Every year it was like this; the lovefest went on and on for weeks. We needed each other in the void of all the others who never saw us. We carried this light we recognized in ourselves. This community, this radical Black love ethic, gave me faith that I would be able to go on questioning and creating despite what might try to hinder me. In that space, we were the wide world. We gathered each other and made a home of us.

⋅ ⋅● ● ●●● ● ●●● ● ●●● ⋅

FAITH (fāth): **noun.** 5.) *Sincerity of intentions*—Black folks advise you to step out on faith, take yourself seriously, carve out a place.

I have been given many monikers in my life. If you are family, you probably call me Meekie, except my Daddy, who calls me Little Face, and a few cousins like brothers who yell Chocolate Chip or Muffins whenever I walk into the room. If you are my grandbaby, you call me Mimi. If you are my friend Eugene, you call me Midget. If you were my friend Rumain, you called me Little One or Shorty. If you are my husband, when we were children you called me Small Fry, and now, Lucky Charms.

I believe if someone loves you enough to give you a new name, you have become something special in their heart, a possession and sparkle, an inheritance, a gift.

Sometimes you are given a new name, a term of endearment, because you are nearly drowning and someone sees it. Jeffers called me Loving Baby for a long while (she watched me get jobs, write books, get married, so I guess I'm a bit grown for it now). Miller calls me Rem Rem. He left me a note in my mailbox at Bennington once, probably not long after that invisible feeling I called Jeffers about, but never mentioned to anyone else. On the outside, in his tiny handwriting, I found:

Rem Rem

Freedom Papers

(A Love Pass Too)

And inside, a poem:

DARK NIGHT IN BENNINGTON

(For Remica)

Did they catch you?

I'm still free—

Canada is close.

Keep running Rem—

Write when you can.

—E. Ethelbert Miller

January 13, 2004

Bennington, VT

Maybe he saw me struggling, even if I never said it. Maybe he knew I needed humor, rapport, and the ancestors too. I kept that note, just a piece of lined college-ruled paper in a trifold, all these years as assurance that faith is someone taking you into account, someone seeing you.

So many fed me, fed my spirit, shored me up with their quips and gifts and urging. Jeffers became a sounding board and mentor. Each time I reached out for some new opportunity—a job, a grant, a fellowship—I took her advice with me. After years of frantic emails and phone calls lasting long into the night, we couldn't help but become friends. We talked most about faith, spirit, godliness as we passed poems back and forth. We missed and scrutinized Georgia, our shared home. For her, the land was sacred and piercing. The red clay of backcountry roads held as much providence for some as the lines on an open palm. The ritual of heading where it may lead, returning and shedding fat, inexplicable tears while leaving, became an act of devotion to dirt paths, yellow jasmine, porch swings, and unmarked graves.

We lamented parents and their imperfections. We ran to and from family, then had stories to tell. I assured her it was alright to be leery of folks who'd purposely hurt us in the past, and she reminded me often about my power. A few years after the first inscriptions she left for me, she wrote in my copy of her book *Red Clay Suite*: "Sweet, Loving Baby, Fierce Poet—all Capital letters! If it weren't for you, where would this book be?—Languishing on the red dirt! :-) Thank you for being." I could have written the same about her in every book I wrote, as without her, so little of my work and hopes might have come to light. A sister to me, she grew me up by teaching me to remember those who came before. Also, to lend a hand, and eye and ear, to those coming after, so they'll bear fruit and carry on the tending.

To shore each other up, Jeffers and I share Scriptures back and forth. We've done this for many years, for inspiration through joys and miseries. She's written about Hagar and Magdalene; I've written about

Peter's wife and mother-in-law, about Jemimah and other unnamed women who seem to escape the spotty memory of some touting Scripture. We examine and rewrite it, deliver it to each other like love notes. It makes me feel good to know I can give a word of comfort, sometimes without knowing what's needed, just send things that speak to me. In an email exchange, I wrote: "Here's your scriptural thought of the day: Proverbs 25:11—'As apples of gold in silver carvings is a word spoken at the right time for it.' A kind word from a good friend is better than riches. In fact, fine words from anyone—talented poets and fiction writers, perhaps?—can do the heart good, so words are more valuable than material things. Keep this in mind when your deadline is looming and it seems too much. As one of these poems or stories drifts out into the world, it might save someone's life. God knows, on many a day, good words have saved ours."

In our interview, I asked how she negotiated being the daughter of well-known Black Arts Movement poet Lance Jeffers and trying to make her own impression without the expectation readers may have had for her work because of her lineage. She explained how her faith set her and her father apart: "I do feel like I am in his tradition, as much as I have tried to fight it. But, at the same time, I feel like I am able to access ancestral and spiritual powers that he could not access because he was an Atheist. I don't think there's anything wrong with being an Atheist; I feel like we can have different realities. There can be a reality where there truly is no God, but in my reality, there is."

•••••••••••••

I was drawn to poems because of their radiating spirit—they are mostly a snapshot of one moment, one arc, but upon inspection, they circle the lives of one person, one street, in a particular town, in a particular country or culture. They suggest that we are all one body, leaning into the lives of other similar bodies in the great universal. After years of ruminating on faith, on the "Poets in the Kitchen," on the ancestors and learning my power, in a book of love poems, I wrote:

YOUNG, SMALL AND GROWING, OFTEN VIOLENTLY
Music can't save you but it marks a place
 and the knife can be a fierce negotiator.

I learn this reckoning from the women raising me:
 my mother's four sisters, my father's three,

grandmothers, play cousins, surrogate aunties.
 They crowd the table, throwing cards and customs,

warbling. I take a shining to everything
 they allow me to hear—*The Wiz!*

and Kingdom Melodies, Motown, Handel,
 every haunt and opening.

They tell me singing is my gift, use it
 for rapture *not* apology,

and to cut any boy who messes with me.
 At funerals, weddings, school assemblies—

my voice is their tender yield.
 Boys brave enough to try me

always learn what I'm learning to be:
 a straight blade, a canticle, bigger

than their scattering, curve and contour
 of mothers' hands, echo,

aurora, an orchestra,
 a galaxy.

Words help me navigate the strange space that is often our living and
help me place myself in the context of an ever-changing, ever-strange,
and difficult world. My faith gives me perspective, a grounding, some

freedom from the unrelenting worry. Just as I come to each poem differently—with my own associations, experiences, and understandings different from the reader next to me—I don't interpret and apply my faith in God in the exact same way as another reverent person next to me, and this frees me. So what I think is important for any artist, any human, is to find spirit wherever it finds you.

The knowledge that we're all built with a longing for connection to something larger and greater than our possibilities sends me back to the page again and again, walking in faith, questioning.

BINGHAM-RISHER: You've said you sometimes feel like a racial ambassador interacting on social media. There's nothing controversial that seems to be off-limits in your work. This is a really personal question: when—as a poet and in your life—do you let go and let God?

JEFFERS: When you read something by me, a story or a poem, understand, this is my backing down. I am more hardcore than you can ever imagine [laughing]. This is politesse that you see in those books. And as a person, letting go of hurt is still a very big hurdle for me. I think that comes from the fact that I'm holding on to the ancestors; I am a tender.

Lucille Clifton

INTIMATE TENDING

*I think if I do anything like the "unsayable," one of the
things that people tell me I do and I think that it's true, is
speak for those who are not yet able to speak for themselves
and also to say, "You are not alone."*

—LUCILLE CLIFTON

M y father was mortified when I started asking about body parts be-
fore age two. I was an only child, accustomed to following my
parents everywhere in our small apartment, into the tiny kitchen, into
the bathroom, jumping in the shower with either or both whenever I
wanted to. I was promptly put out one day, before even being soaped up,
after I fixated on an appendage only my father had and yelled, "What is
that hanging down there?" From then on, I wanted to know everything.
Where do babies come from? How are we born?

I was a talkative child, so much so that my Pop-Pop, my father's
father, gave me the handle Chatterbox when I wanted to talk on his CB
radio. My mother would sing Run-DMC's "You Talk Too Much" almost
as a lullaby to get me to close my eyes at night and leave her be. So she
should have known better than to let me venture along with her mother
to get the clothes when we visited her that summer.

Grandma dropped the basket of hand-laundered, sunswept sheets
into the dirt when I said matter-of-factly, certainly without her asking, "I
used to live in my daddy's penis." She stared at me, wide-eyed, and shook
her head no, which I took to mean continue: "Grandma, Grandma, do
you know where else I used to live? I was a little tiny seed. I used to be
in my mom's stomach then my parents . . ." to which she finally shushed

me and led me back to my mother upstairs. "What are you teaching this child?" she asked, and my mother just laughed.

⸪ ⸫ ⸪ ⸫ ⸪

When I began elementary school, the practicality of poems, for me, was that they were written as small verses, much like Scripture, which I was already familiar with. Sometimes the lines broke in the middle of sentences or verses; sometimes the beauty held it together and I missed the meaning but got the tone.

Those Scriptures and poems with language beyond me I could look up line by line and write definitions of words therein in the margins. The dictionary was also a favorite book of mine. (I toted a pocket-sized one a woman gave me at a yard sale when I asked how much it was and she said, "A kid who wants the dictionary? For you, it's free!") The Bible and dictionary each helped me find new words and thus gave me new gifts. As I grew, my thirst for words grew with me.

Words were a comfort, and the body held the secret to so many things. What did Black women writers teach me that others couldn't? They led me to a particular kind of intimacy, others who saw me. Looking at the Black women on the covers of books I've held onto since childhood—like *The Friends* by Rosa Guy, about two teenage girls finding solace in each other, or *Let the Circle Be Unbroken* by Mildred D. Taylor, a family saga helmed by their high-spirited daughter Cassie—gives me pause. I suspect this is because I never guessed how many layers there were to Black women's living, or how far this love of reading them would move me.

This intimacy from Black women writers was a many-tendrilled thing. For me it was: double consciousness of race or the relentless possibility of erasure turned over in the mind; uncommon familiarity; peeking into the front room window of an upstanding house; family business out loud; friendship as the bearing of secrets; sex (learning one's self or another); powerlessness and agency; unfed desire; love transcending; a door to an inner ear and heart.

Intimacy as a young reader also meant I searched for writers who made sure I knew they were writing for *me*, those who intoned the value of Black girls and hence were writing on behalf of them and for their own complicated sensibilities. Devotion—an offshoot of the tree of intimacy—was, then, a commitment to the truth of Black girlhood. Whether it was a nod to inward conflict (beauty dysmorphia, historical hierarchy), fragility (bred by circumstance or generational trauma), or other grown-up hardships that threatened to sweep Black children from one side to the other of the dangerous, imbalanced world, I looked for books that shined a light on this elaborateness.

For a long time, I only knew novelists who were doing this kind of tending, but once I discovered whole books of poems by Black women writers, I found intimacy doubled in their hand—tripled in its heightened imagery when I found queer Black women writers like Cheryl Clarke, Audre Lorde, and Nikky Finney. I wanted these double-tongued libraries living in me.

I was long past childhood when I happened upon a copy of Lucille Clifton's *Quilting*. The poems were small, unadorned (few periods and commas, no capitalized proper nouns, not even the personal "I," and titles seemed optional), resembling the squat verses in my miniature Bible and my little dictionary worn thin. Clifton turned me topsy-turvy. I had never seen someone do so much with the little she'd written. Honorée Fanonne Jeffers and I would joke that it took other writers (ourselves included) two pages to do what Clifton could in four lines with no punctuation and no title. She was a master of minimalism but never sacrificed humanity, complexity, or her wry sense of humor.

Sitting with her, I asked if when she sat down to write she knew in advance what a poem would look like and how it would (or more likely wouldn't) be adorned. She said: "What I do know is I try to use every word, I try to use the right word, the most precise, the most responsible word. So, every word stands for the definition, the size, the history, the possibility, all of that. So I don't need a lot of words."

Lucille Clifton was well into her life—finished with an abbreviated time at Howard, married with six children—when she published her first poem.* She'd seen Robert Hayden in *Negro Digest* and thought, "*Whoa, a black guy. This is cool, I'm going to send him some poems.*" Her bravery led to her winning the National Endowment for the Arts–sponsored Discovery Award, a reading in New York City, and an editor asking to see the manuscript she'd read from. Clifton said: "I was always very particular with my work. So my manuscript was in the order I would have had it in and all of that. . . . I gave it to her and Random House bought the manuscript. It was so nontypical."

Since then Clifton has written numerous books of poetry, poetry collections, a memoir edited by Toni Morrison, and more than a dozen children's books, including the numerous adventures of Everett Anderson, a character she designed for her children. Clifton is the only poet ever to have two books—*Next* and *Good Woman*—selected as finalists for the Pulitzer Prize in the same year.

"Can you keep a secret?" she asked during a follow-up conversation we had about our interview. "I've won the Ruth Lilly Prize. They'll announce it next month in *Time* magazine." She was genuinely happy and honored, giddy even, at the thought of the accolade. What pleased her the most, it seemed, was that the award was for her entire body of work and that a group of her peers saw fit to acknowledge what she'd done over the past forty years. When I asked her how she was going to celebrate winning the prize, not to mention the $100,000 purse it carried, she

---

*When I asked Clifton about being among many of the elite Black artists who attended Howard University in the 1950s, she said: "I wouldn't call it elite. I was on full scholarship at Howard. I was never expected to go to college. I never knew what it all meant. My father told me when I got the letter, because I took a Howard scholarship test. They had eight scholarships in the country and in the diaspora and they paid for everything, and I won one of them." She was only sixteen, so I offered that she must have clearly been brilliant and she said: "Oh, well, I thought I was. You know how you are when you're sixteen." But riding high was short-lived, she explained: "I loved writing, but I was wild and young, and I didn't see why I had to know about chemicals. I did very badly in chemistry, so I lost my scholarship. It was very disappointing; my parents were very disappointed. My father said, 'God has done this to show me that my idol has feet of clay.'" I told her if that didn't make a child cry, I didn't know what would, but she was practical, resilient. She said: "Yes, I cried for a while, and then I got another job."

said, "It's not about the money; it's about the honor . . . but maybe I'll buy a new dress for the ceremony. I think I can swing that."

• ◦ ● ◦ ●●◦ ◦ ● ◦ ●●◦ ◦ ● ◦ ●●◦ •

Clifton makes plain in her poem "surely i am able to write poems," about what's lurking beneath the trees and ocean of Black longing, that there is a "two-ness," a layering, as our living is political whether we want it to be or not. This, it seems, is really what Countee Cullen was railing against—the forced politicizing of the Black writer voice—in his row with Hughes that shows up in Hughes's essay "The Negro Artist and the Racial Mountain." But this is also what I've come to understand as density in the poems of Black writers and is now what I seek out and am often disappointed not to find in the writing of those without the birth-burden of double consciousness as part of their living and, hence, breath, breadth, and work.

When I read *Quilting*, even more than her precision, I was taken with what Clifton chose to write about—the intimate body, Black existence, women's realities, godliness, the past and our legacies, people she pulled from obscurity. One of the most pertinent observations that came from our interview was an aphorism someone else, an avid reader, had used to describe her process. She said, "Someone once told me, 'You find the myth in the human and the human in the myth.'" Clifton made many question how flesh was linked to spirit, how the body was an extension of the Divine, and why so many of us were extraordinary but left wanting.

• ◦ ● ◦ ●●◦ ◦ ● ◦ ●●◦ ◦ ● ◦ ●●◦ •

As I waded into the world of poetry, I realized Clifton herself had become rather mythic—most poets idolized her as much as I did. In the way that Toni Morrison is the mother of Black fiction, Lucille Clifton is in many ways the mother of Black contemporary poetry. To illustrate: one summer, I was walking with a group on the campus of the University of Pittsburgh at Greensburg, where the Cave Canem retreat has been held, and Clifton appeared. She was sprung on us as a surprise by co-founder Toi Derricotte, who was just now exiting a car and reaching out a hand to Clifton, who moved slowly about fifty feet away from us. The whole group stopped on the bridge just to watch her make her way into a building we were headed to. We were awestruck—any Hollywood starlet wouldn't have commanded as much breathlessness from a group of young Black hoping-to-be-poets. She wrote of the miraculous with such clarity that we thought *she* was miraculous. "Lord, she's just walking like she's a normal human being—she ain't even floating or nothing," I said, as she made her way down the same path we were to cross, and the group exhaled into a loud hollering stint of laughter.

Clifton sat in on a workshop I was in that week. I'd written a poem called "Genesis" that would make its way into my first book. I was writing midrash—Biblical retellings—ever since I'd read Clifton's work and was given permission to reevaluate what I knew of creation, of privilege, of God. She weighed in on the poem—I'd rethought how different Lucifer might have been if he'd been born instead of made, and though she liked the work (and said so!), I'd also made the massive misstep of using the wrong adjective. "Never use the words *black* or *dark* in a negative light in poems. Other folks do that enough," she said. Every poet in the room began marking out whatever dreary musings we'd linked to Blackness because others had said nothing of this in the past, but when Clifton said it, it seemed obvious and concrete: don't denigrate yourself. Don't emulate those who would deny your fullness.

·ᴥ•◦ ♦ ◦ᴥ•◦ ♦ ◦ᴥ•◦ ♦ ◦ᴥ•·

Clifton specializes in transformation. One of her major themes, the work of women—their bodies, their sensuality—had her pegged as a leading feminist (or womanist) poet of her generation as well, though it's not a term she embraced. She didn't consider herself a political poet, just an observant one. Not religious, just intensely spiritual. She told me, "I don't label myself at all. Other people label me . . . As far as being a womanist poet is concerned, I really truly think that you have to be a woman, and everything that means. I've said a lot of times, when my first book came out, my children were seven, five, four, three, two, and one. Back then, I just decided what mattered. Having the most spic-and-span house wasn't that high on the list." Being a womanist to her meant setting priorities that included making room for yourself—your full-bodied self, your mothering self, your sensual self, your selfish stealing-time-from-chores-to-do-what-you-love self, your daughter and granddaughter self, the whole of yourself.*

I was taken with all the taboos Clifton wrote about openly—things whispered about elsewhere that I got shushed for as a child. Throughout *Quilting*, it seemed Clifton got progressively more brash and subversive, defending a woman's tongue, uterus, hips, even the blood that came and went against her will. In "fat fat water rat," she turned a woman rendered invisible by a childhood taunt into a thick-hipped goddess rising in her sexual prowess.

What light she shed for me, more than any high school course on sex ed, on the import of the vastness of the woman's body.

I asked about any pushback she got from work like "poem in praise of menstruation," "poem to my uterus," and "wishes for sons" and she told me: "I once was asked by a male poet, why did I write about so many female body parts? This was my sassy answer, okay? My sassy answer was, 'If I only had one interesting body part, I wouldn't write about it either.' We've got a lot of interesting parts, you know?"

Since she was being sassy, I took it a step further and brought up an early poem she was brave enough to put in her first book that opens with the speaker naked in her window for the world to see and poems like "homage to my hips" that had become her signature pieces. I had to know: was being so comfortable with her sensuality empowering, especially now

---

*I asked about the role of the feminist, especially early on in her career, during and just beyond the Black Arts, civil rights, and women's lib movements. Clifton also gave a sidelong comment about economic and social class issues that let some women head up the movement and others do the hard daily work of living, though most leave this out of the story. She said, "I'm acquainted with some of the women who were part of the women's lib movement, like Rita [Mae Brown] and Minnie [Bruce Pratt] and all of them. I always thought they were interesting because some are friends. For all they did for the movement, I think they're amazing. But I thought, now, some woman talks about raising three children and all that, but often somebody else raises her children, a lady comes into town to help her. Nobody helped me raise my six children; they wouldn't even babysit. I had four in diapers at once. So, there's a little edge of, *come on.*"

at seventy? She said: "I'm going to write some more poems about it, about being sensual at this age, and what's the matter with men? . . . I love those poems; I loved when male poets did it. I do a lot of Bible poems and I find sensuality in them all the time. I am a grown-up, sensual woman, even at this age and size. People would think you wouldn't be. I'm open to the whole of human experience." I told her, paraphrasing the end of the poem, "You've got everybody trying to figure out how to 'spin somebody like a top,'" and like the young poets watching her cross our path, or like my mother raising an artful wandering girl-child, she laughed wildly.

• ◆◐ ◐ ◐ ◆◐◐ ◐ ◐ ◆◐◐ ◐ ◐ ◆◐ •

Besides reclaiming the body, many of the poems in *Quilting* turned what I knew of Scripture on its head. Clifton gives voice to figures that are usually silenced in religious tradition, antiquity, and patriarchy. One such poem is "eve's version." Diametrically opposed to the slow-witted and easily coerced Eve portrayed in most Biblical accounts, Clifton's Eve is so in tune with her own sensuality that she's enticed by it. In the Scriptures, any movement toward "being fruitful and becoming many" would have ultimately been Adam's. Debunking the myth of Eve's traditional asexuality, submissiveness, and naïveté, the poem ends with Eve hungering for her "own lush self" and pegging Lucifer as a sweet talker.

Clifton sought out the human in characters most resigned to fairytales, science fiction, or speculative fantasy. Part of her aesthetic was to use those voices as an outworking of her own. She, too, was a daughter with strange gifts; "the ones" called to her, she was given messages, foxes found her front door. Her once-twelve fingers reached out into the wide world through her daughter and back to her mother, clairvoyant and whispering to them both. Whatever undertaking, mortal or immortal, Clifton chose, the work spoke to all of us. She gave voice to ordinary people who have extraordinary things happen in their lives. "What if Mary was just an ordinary girl who got pregnant?" Clifton asked in our interview. "What would become of her then?"

I heard Clifton's questions echoing in my head all while I wrote my first (and every subsequent) book. I wondered what part desire had in man's long descent into sin and how being the creation of God's desire—the only

extravagant light brought to life—would add to the power of women. So I
wrote "Adam's Conversion":

It must put danger
in your relationship
if you're the last
creature on the planet
to get a mate.

When that day came
you'd gladly mask
the ache in your side
and vow allegiance
to her creator.

After the snake appeared
walking upright and speaking
in the tongue of God, her eagerness—
newly formed breasts
rising, nipples peaked
and plummed—got you
carried away. You sensed the warm
pooling between her thighs and thought
of nothing else.

She said *Taste this*
and love like God slithering tongue
over taut skin, severing flesh
with her teeth, and you could only
obey—fall down
on your knees, bow your head
and taste it.

I read Clifton's *Quilting,* then *Blessing the Boats, The Book of Light,*
and on and on until I read every poem in every book and her memoir,

Good Woman, about her father's people, Dahomey men and women. She beckoned to almost-gods and made the ordinary (barren but not broken women, mothers with poems and fire in their hands, even one worn breast calling and comforting the other) unrivaled, sharp-tongued. Clifton's economy and precision made clear that every body is a useful body and every poem can speak in a plain-faced voice; no poem or suffering has to labor on.

⚬● ● ●●● ● ●●●● ● ●●● ●

When I went to work for Cave Canem behind the scenes, Clifton had returned to teach again. A few days into the retreat, word spread that one of the poets there had suffered a terrible loss. Their mother had died and the poet would have to find a place to stay and withdraw from school to save what little money they had. I was typing up itineraries on a computer in the workroom where the faculty gathered as they discussed this sad turn of events.

"All the money you're paying me to be here," Clifton said, pointing at Derricotte and Cornelius Eady, the other cofounding poet who taught each summer, "put it in a check for that child." I tried so hard to do what people caution young ones to do—stay out of grown folks' business—but my head snapped up from the task at hand. I could tell I wasn't hiding my surprise by the way Clifton looked. "Not a word of this," she said to me, "the child has to go to school, and not everybody has to know everything." She taught me that day not only about illuminating the lives of the ordinary in poems, but also much about taking care of your community. Sometimes the practical, immediate thing is the most important thing. You should help someone get what they need, but you don't have to run and tell it all through the streets. Care for the suffering of others— live the way your poems sing.

⚬● ● ●●● ● ●●● ● ●●● ●

When I sat down to interview and share a meal with Clifton at the Dodge Poetry Festival in Stanhope, New Jersey, she couldn't get a moment's peace. It seemed as if every person in the small room wanted to be near her. Well after her table was full, people made their way over to try to commandeer seats. She was gracious and patient, though exhausted. As the seventh or eighth unknown approached her and reluctantly left, I asked her, "How do you deal with all of this?" While she acknowledged it was challenging to find any quiet space at Dodge—the largest poetry festival in North America, which usually hailed over one hundred thousand attendees—she said, "It's not always like this, and they all mean well. That poetry can do this still amazes me." More miraculous than the hordes of people who sloshed through the mud and cold to sit in a tent and hear Clifton read poems was the fact that, despite many obstacles (recurring health problems, breast cancer, losing babies and her beloved husband Fred in death), she was still here reading poems with such hope, such joy. She taught me that if you've created what moves people beyond their understanding, you are a light to them, so they may be drawn to you. If they are and you can stand it, share pieces of yourself in the flesh; let them hold your hand, let them come to you.

·◖ ● ◖●◗◖ ◗ ◖●◗◖ ◗ ◖●◗◖ ·

Reading Clifton opened up the world of the body for me. But when I happened upon Toi Derricotte's *Tender*, all the extensions of intimacy collided, many of which I thought of as anathema, even those that return time and again in all my questioning.

The book has seven sections in which it seemed the poet tackled all of the most difficult dirt (the transatlantic slave trade, colorism, mental illness, suicidal ideation, abusive parents, self-loathing). It also breached the most sensitive harborings (self-pleasure, orgasms, decentering the ego, homage, and awakening). *Tender* revolves around intimacy; it vacillates between all the definitions of tender or tenderness (a form of payment, something soft-hearted, a genuine kindness, a caring attendant, an easily coaxed animal readied for the killing, supple meat). There's much personal indictment—the Black woman poet's perception is a part of the complex set of values and distortions that rule over all who harbor the Black skin we're in.

In *Tender*, Derricotte's poems are brash, interior, vast, and varied. There are prose poems bordering on lyric essays; six-page poems cordoned off into sections with shifting points of view; almost-found five-line commentaries and one-hundred-line confessionals. If anything is off-limits, I haven't found it yet. Poring over *Tender* gave me permission to disclose, query, transform, and see my way through my own wandering.

It is surely because of poems like "Clitoris" in Derricotte's book, which compares the organ to a girl who must be treated tenderly, that I am able to write a section of my poem "The Body Speaks" that begins:

> Say vulva and make it clean
> say labia   say lips slip
>   not folly   not force
> or flinch   or fist

What I learned from Clifton and Derricotte is that a woman has the right to command her body be treated the way she wants it to be, despite all the world's intended misuse.

They insisted I examine the social implications that come from our bodies as Black women, even our skin. My skin is dark, and I hadn't yet thought of how, in the presence of other Black folks, this darkness might free or hinder me until I came to poems like "Brother" in *Tender*. It's about siblings with different mothers, one darker than the other, and lays out how color can be a rift in a family, for onlooking neighbors, for sisters and brothers in a mishmashed house. The poem tells of the brother marrying a girl darker than the others and bragging to any who'll listen, equating Black with godliness and ending with the brother finding solace and love in it, with the family's divisions still mounting.

In a poem like "When My Father Was Beating Me," *Tender* unflinchingly looks at an ugly, inside thing. A father beats his daughter as the mother—washing dishes in the other room—surely hears, maybe prods, maybe approves or directs the breaking. The speaker tries to make sense of this joint mangling, the silence her parents demand of her, her broken personhood and self-esteem, a pain near death, an almost unbearable humbling. Clifton taught me the body's power, then Derricotte showed how much of ourselves we could lose if the body wasn't handled lovingly.

There's much talk lately of the importance of representation—*If you see it, you can be it* was a mantra I remember teachers making us repeat—but, until these Black women poets, I only saw slivers of my-self, of creative freedom, of fearless inspiration. Writing is part of my self-care, and if I'm censored there, inside my own wondering, where else am I allowed to question freely? Writing rarely gives me answers, but it helps me articulate questions I have about the world and my own longing. It's a safe space, with many rooms, a house Black women have tended for me.

In February 2010, Honorée Jeffers called me overcome with grief. We cried, reminiscing about our "Ms. Lucille"—about her candidness, spirit, and style (*Girl, remember when she flexed on all of us last winter, pulling up to the conference hotel in a black stretch limo and full-length mink coat?!*). We shook our heads, laughed, then cried some more about her leaving this Earth. But, as most old folks will tell you, death comes in threes, or at least hard and fast enough to make us feel this way. So when the call came about Ai (Ogawa) in March, then about Carolyn Rodgers in April during a storm, the sky seemed to be swallowing up all the poets who helped shape us, who carved out places for audacious women of color in the writing world.

In September of that year, culture worker Joanne Gabbin directed a tribute for Lucille Clifton at the Furious Flower Poetry Center on the campus of James Madison University. More than seventy poets read po-ems for each of Clifton's seventy-three years, and all were aglow with her lessons that night. Two of the poet's daughters, Alexia and Gillian, attended and shared in honoring her. In a group poem-song fashioned by co-director Nikki Giovanni, all of the participants stood on stage and recited what Clifton's work and life had taught us best: "come celebrate / with me that everyday / something has tried to kill me / and has failed."

In *Tender* and *Quilting*, in Black women writers' intimate longing, the mother (or father or self, anyone, *anyone* who has a hold on you), per-fect or imperfect, could be faced. They could be examined, dismantled, unnerved, followed, or left to their own path. As in Derricotte's poem

"Invisible Dreams," all thinkers and dreamers must make a place for ourselves, within ourselves—outside the mother, outside all others.

In their disclosure and revolving doors inside and outside the body, *Quilting* and *Tender* disassembled me. I'd written poems about the things that plagued me, but only things I felt wouldn't get me into trouble (i.e., wouldn't shock anyone I loved)—someone like my grandmother, God-fearing and interested in decorum, much more subtle and tactful than me.

But the truth is, I want the body put to good use—in books, in bed, in life—and I want the poems to be uncluttered, singing. Intimacy in my writing before I found writers like Clifton and Derricotte was saddled with quietness, duty. But after reading them, like in Derricotte's poem "Family Secrets," I was unburdened, free to love any unrighteous gods out loud. Free to name everything.

BINGHAM-RISHER: You write a lot of
poems about your family, some of which
they might not consider very flattering;
"donor," "here rests," and "mercy"
are just a few that come to mind. Do
they ever get upset about the poems?

CLIFTON: I never tell anything but
the truth. My daughter knows that
I tried to get rid of her. Because she
always says, if she could have talked,
she would have said, "Give me thirty
years. You're going to need me." And
she was right. So, I always tell nothing
but the truth. What can they say?

A. Van Jordan

COURTING PARADISE

*[I]f you don't want to preach to people, you read
them poems; you present another voice and they find
that there are these elders out there who have been
articulating your experience in their work, which
they've never had access to before.*

—A. VAN JORDAN

Someone who's an "old soul" is usually a child who knows too much
about the world, or who sings all the lyrics to Billy Paul's "Me and
Mrs. Jones" right and loud when it comes on the radio, though her par-
ents haven't taught it to her and she is strapped into her portable potty
chair in the back seat when she is three years old. Or, perhaps, a child,
even younger, near two, who can be smuggled into work at the fire de-
partment because there are terrors in the neighborhood and at home, so
he has learned to play almost silently, with little coaxing or attention,
under the desk of his mother for ten-hour shifts.

We are old souls in this house, my husband and I. People said, when
we were too young to understand why, that we'd "been here before,"
meaning we were carrying our sorrow or acumen, wearing it like a cloak.

When we were thirteen, we were sneaking kisses and spending count-
less hours on the phone. After we'd been calling each other boyfriend
and girlfriend for nine months, an eternity in teenage years, every night,
without pretense and without fail, the boy with the old soul would say
to me, "We're just too young, it happened too soon. But, I swear, I'll find

my way back to you." He meant this deeply. "How do we even know what love is?" I asked him, and he was crushed at the thought of this, the thought of me not being sure of what I'd been saying and agreeing to all this time. He said, "I know I love you. I know what this is," and never wavered, despite my level-headed questioning.

But he knew we'd move on, be fleeting as children are and miss what light there might be in our hands. I thought his deep voice was smooth, that his high cheekbones made him gorgeous, and that he was a little quixotic, what with all his devotion. But I also knew he often went home to a place that was imbalanced, violent, and, over time, he had learned to wait silently, to let others flit around him, banging or yelling, busy with their own chaotic shifting. He knew, though I doubted it, that he and I would cling to some dream of this improbable love between us for the rest of our lives, even in the distance. So when we had been out of touch for years, when I had moved across the country and become a writer, when he had fathered children and helped his mother escape a burning house, when we were living peacefully and almost thirty, he hung his hat on reckless desire and came to find me.

•• • •••• • ••••• • •••• •

I'm asked to be on a panel of Black poets fighting assumptions about what we're allowed to house in our work. My thoughts on the matter are anchored by Octavia Butler's lines from her book *Parable of the Talents*: "Paradise is one's own place, / One's own people, / One's own world, / Knowing and known, / Perhaps even / Loving and loved."

In my book of love poems, *Starlight & Error*, I asked, in as many ways as I could: Is Black love revolutionary? Are faith and forgiveness? Is desire a part of our futures; can we claim it as part of our past? I rummage the interconnected legacies of love between couples—aunts and uncles, mothers and fathers, newlyweds and hopefuls—as well as what's left for children and their children's children, retold through the lens of imagined memory.

But when I was knee-deep in love, the Charleston church massacre upended the world again. So the larger question for me as a Black artist became the question being asked of the whole of us: Are Black poets allowed to write love in the middle of crisis—not just personal but communal trauma? Are we allowed happiness, in our art and otherwise, when the whole of us is mourning?

I think of Butler's definition of paradise, then a tenet that theologian Monica A. Coleman laid out, namely that Black women artists *counter* "the oppressive aspects of society that prevent Black women from having the quality of life and wholeness that God desires for them, and for all of creation." Black artists have long known God does not desire for us one lane, though there is no mistaking what at least America loves and expects of us. Black art centered on Black oppression, Black pain, has long been considered triumph in America.

But in the midst of terrible national tragedy, my desire was to craft what had been and would be coming to me, what would sustain us. I wanted to tell the stories that made my aunts say, "Alright now!" and point at each other when we sat around the den recounting what good a lover could do. Stories like those old pictures we printed on T-shirts for the family reunion—the first of us all hugged up and young again, top branches of the tree that housed all our surnames. I wanted to write those glimmers we wanted to fill our children's heads with, not the riders coming for them despite their innocence, but first house party slow dances, love letters with photos, the bodies worn and ringing, singing to each other in a quiet house after dark. All the wonders of paradise, the wonder of being human beings.

· ···· · ···· · ···· ·

The year Rosa Parks died, I drove to North Carolina to interview A. Van Jordan, just a few weeks before Hurricane Katrina would barrel in. We met at his favorite coffee shop, the Green Bean in downtown Greensboro, two blocks away from the site of the only thing I knew the city for—the historic Woolworth sit-ins of the civil rights movement in the 1960s.

He noticed I was wearing a small ring on my left hand that had LOVE written in script, and as we settled into our booth, he said, "All you need is one that says HATE on your other hand!" but the reference was lost on me. Jordan was conjuring a character from Spike Lee's *Do the Right Thing*, Radio Raheem, who wore rings that spanned both fists with LOVE and HATE etched into each. Raheem would appear in Jordan's book *The Cineaste* years later.

The import of being so near the old Woolworth I understood, but I missed the film's homage as I was a few years younger than Jordan and still tracing my way back from my mother's careful tending. I was allowed certain glimpses of ugliness, but was not allowed to watch violent films (even Black ones, ones of cultural significance, ones my teachers could have made an argument for but didn't) until I was grown and thus had missed most of Spike Lee's oeuvre. When Jordan alluded to it, I laughed politely, vaguely remembering a scene where Raheem's fists come at you on screen that I must have seen in a trailer. I watched the film—mourned Raheem and lost summers—after our interview. In fact, I watched several films Jordan mentioned once the tape recording stopped and we entertained each other with memories, most of which seemed like a mosaic of history and reality to him.

His love of film came early, but Jordan came to writing accidentally. He told me he'd studied English literature at Wittenberg University because he'd gone to a vocational public school and was unprepared for college when he arrived: "I was failing everything I touched my first semester and, consequently, landed on academic probation. It was a liberal arts school, and everything I did there was based on essay tests. We had the largest class of Blacks that had ever entered the school and we were dropping like flies."

He went on: "I met this upper classman, a brilliant brother named Jeffery who was an English major, who told me, 'Listen, man, if you can learn how to write, you can get through this.' I was sent to a place called the Writing Center. I had to sit down with a white kid who was about my age and go through these drills, which was really humiliating to me. Finally, I ended up getting some grammar books and spending time locked in my room, going through the stuff by myself." By the time he had to pick a major, Jordan had taken so many extra English classes that it made sense to stick with it. His plan was to become a journalist, which he pursued until poetry got the better of him. I asked if his folks were worried about how he'd survive when he headed down this path and, like most of us, he had to make the case for love. He said, "I come from a working-class, blue-collar family and community. I'm the only person in my family who has a college degree, so it took some selling."

We talked about how I'd begun to go back to his first book, *Rise*, religiously. It's a book of devotion and fervor, cadence and sound. A thread of music runs throughout it from the opening poem "Notes from a Southpaw" to the last section, which bears the book's title. It's chock-full enough to be some blues legend's box set. It reads, in many ways, like an album with constant references to funk, jazz, and all the customs Black folks created in between. I asked how music served as a catalyst for his writing and he said: "The music was a common thread. I used it in the way that historians use wars or the presidents to chart American history. The music served to tell a bit of my history and the history of the culture from which I come."

I am curating a playlist for a class called African American Literature and Its Cultural Traditions. I explain to my students that the evolution of a people can rarely be separated from their music. This is especially true for Black American artists, who created the only original music forms that come out of the United States and that are the faith songs, in one way or another, of the marginalized. My class begins in 1619, so we start with spirituals, then folk songs, the blues, make our way to soul, funk, hip-hop, and how art and pain are clues for the type of burden people try to overcome in any given moment.

Why was there singing in the fields? Why did folks juba on Sundays? How has soul music, and soul culture on the whole, become, as cultural critic Emily Lordi calls it, a promotion and outworking of Black thriving? Between World Wars and Red Summer, Jim Crow to COINTELPRO came the crossroads, Motown, Wattstax. Through Vietnam, after Reagan, we glittered until they hated it, we beatboxed, bent bodies, made another way to truth, flipped ourselves and the world on its spinning head. I make my students playlists and call them mixtapes, so they'll know what eras I'm harboring, what faith I'm ferrying, where I'm coming from.

I caution them: Just listen, let the people who've made their way through hard times give you a leg up. Learn what those folks had to set to heart, set to paper, beat out on the piano, the bass, the drums. Then, like Jordan, you'll be able to sing your own stories, and all the while be singing the past too.

＊❧ ❦ ❧❧❧ ❧ ❧❧❧ ❧ ❧❧❧ ＊

When I asked how he discovered poetry, Jordan said: "My understanding of myself as a poet came through, unfortunately, writing bad love poems to girlfriends." He started writing verse the way so many did—trying to woo somebody—and it showed. I'd been returning to *Rise* because, despite the difficult odyssey funneled by the music therein, Jordan also scattered in love poems that make you fan yourself or purse your lips, shaking your head by the time you get to the last line. Mostly I read his work all through graduate school while I was diligent (filling the bed with books each night to pore over) and happy (teaching workshops to second graders and teens, getting my own bearings about which poets I wanted to mirror) but "relentlessly single," as one girlfriend put it. I loved dreaming about love but was decidedly alone.

In Jordan's poem "Tamara's Dance," the speaker ends up prostrate, at the feet of a woman, his allegiance bound to her unfathomable percussion and alchemy. Her dancing is a siren call, a welcome spell. The speaker in "What Does It Mean When a Man Dreams of Lingerie?" roams Victoria's Secret and finds nothing but the shadow of the love he's lost. Richard Pryor enters to philosophize about the pendulum swing of Black love. (Jordan said of Pryor, who shows up in other poems in other books as well: "Not only was he talking about the issue of the color line honestly, but he also was talking about male vulnerability honestly.") Mingus floats out of a store's speakers to play what no one wants to hear but everyone needs to: *if you'd have treated her right, she wouldn't be gone.*

In all of Jordan's books, male speakers are vulnerable to women; women, in turn, are powerful, almost beyond mortal beings, and this intrigued me. MacNolia Cox, the subject of his second book, seems supernatural at times. She was a young Black girl who advanced all the way to the National Spelling Bee in the 1930s. Then she was thrust back into Jim Crow living and anonymity but still found love with her husband, John.

This recurring juxtaposition of the power shift between men and women in his work is especially evident in poems like "On Stage," "Sunshine," and "How Does a Man Write a Poem." I asked why and he told me: "There might be two reasons: First, I don't think I need to show conflict to show strength. I wanted to go against the cliché of Black women being these sassy-strong figures that, I think, is counter to the real greatness of Black women." He continued, saying that in some works in the past there's been "a distortion of the Black male/female relationship. Black love isn't always dysfunctional. Of course, relationships have problems in all cultures, but that's only part of it. These poems were an attempt to deal with that issue in verse in what, I felt, was a more realistic rendering."

I am consistently impressed with Jordan's ability to build nuance and gentleness into Black women's love and life stories in their own voices. He went on to explain: "Secondly, I think I'm also conscious of the perils of the male gaze when representing women. I don't always transcend it, but I'm aware. I don't care whether I'm dealing with issues of race, class, or sexual orientation and gender, I always have to write against the hegemonic gaze that beams down on that group. When you grow up Black in America, you have a keen sense of what that's all about."

We're taught in so many ways—in music, in films, in the Valentine's Day marketing machine churning summarily after each New Year's resolution about making the most of our lives—that poetry is a tool reserved mostly for edifying the romantic heart. I started writing "for my people" like (I hoped) Margaret Walker and to tussle with heritage and discrimination, because these were realities for me long before love. But by high school, I was as sappy as the rest and poems became my witness. Love poems— good, effective ones, not overly maudlin or embarrassingly explicit— were difficult to write, so I read plenty but mostly avoided writing them until Michael returned and eros would no longer loosen its hold on me.

Michael left a message on my answering machine. A group of girlfriends and I had just returned from a weekend in Philly where we danced and slept piled on pallets in the studio apartment of other carefree women we knew. I came home smiling and full. I played the message and was startled by how excited I was to hear from him unexpectedly. Later, he would tell me the backstory.

He was visiting family at a reunion in Detroit. His cousin Talib asked, "Whatever happened to that girl you were so in love with?" And Michael said my name. But Talib, always the loudest, silliest, most truthful, ran the thing together in his excitement: "Yeah! Remicabingham, Remicabingham"—one nimble word in his approximation—"where'd she go?" Michael told him my family moved to Virginia when I was sixteen. We'd lost touch.

It had been twelve years. Michael had two children, a whole life, but still thought of me. Talib was incredulous and enlisted the family. "Have you googled her? We gotta find Remicabingham!" He told his mother, then other cousins, who started a slow chant that spelled out my name letter by letter. Things were taking a turn for Michael and he couldn't be sure anybody would be quiet again. He was reluctant as the family crowded around a computer.

I'd begun writing. I'd published a book. I'd paid a girlfriend to make a website for me. I was a writer-in-the-schools, a program for those who want K–12 students in their area to learn poetry. I'd been asking them for months to remove the phone number they published on their contact page, but nothing was happening. They'd send me to high schools nearby and the kids would open up a bit, write their dreams and lives for me, so I forgot about the number, the programmers' excuses. I was just happy the word about Black poets was getting to some earlier than it got to me.

It was just a few weeks after Michael Jackson died, so my Michael had just lost another lifetime love, and maybe this was why he agreed to search for me on his great-aunt's computer while everyone looked over his shoulder. They found a few sites with my name, but pictures took forever to load. Talib was impatient, said: "We ain't never gonna find your Remicabingham, cause this famous Remicabingham is all over the place." They discovered the phone number; my picture materialized slowly. "That's her!" Michael said. "She's a writer!" The chant grew louder as Talib prodded him to call me. They went back and forth. Michael had all the right excuses (*What if her husband answers? What if she's asleep? How do you know she'll remember me?*) But Talib was relentless, daring, hopeful until Michael gave in. Before he dialed, he told Talib, "If she calls me back, you're gonna be the best man at my wedding." And nine months later, he was.

·•● ● ●●●● ● ●●●● ● ●●●● ·

I am from the Lucille Clifton school of poetry and understand that I am to inhabit the spirit of both/and, not either/or, so writing love poems does not mean I have the luxury of looking away.* It means, among other things, my love must encompass: poems to my husband on our wedding night, contrapuntal riffs about my parents' summertime meet-cute, missives for forgotten names, what the present best-we-can-give love is and how it has been shifted by the trauma in all our histories.

Jordan seconded this when I asked why he chose to include the stories of historical figures like Richard Pryor or Josephine Baker in his book M-A-C-N-O-L-I-A, though it is essentially the story of MacNolia and her family. He replied: "I felt like her story was a part of a larger story. It was emblematic of the story of most African Americans, but if I tried to explain it to someone who wasn't Black, they may not immediately get the significance of a kid being cheated out of a spelling bee. If we factor in this other element of racism, it's not just a lesson about how you lose, it's a lesson about *why* you lose. That's a real turning point for most Black people. We usually learn that lesson at some point and it changes our whole outlook."

So the lane I chose—my conscious craft and labor during this time— was to continue to write poems purposely and actively *centered* on

---

*In a workshop, Clifton told us, "Black women artists don't have the luxury of being from the land of either/or, we must be from the land of both/and," meaning we most often are called to juggle responsibilities, to try our hand at multiple things, even those to which we aren't accustomed. Sonia Sanchez echoed this during our interview when she told me she wrote her most famous play, *Sister Son/ji*, in one sitting. She said: "Every time I was asked for something, I agreed. Ed Bullins said, 'Do you write plays?' and even though I had just done [*The Bronx Is Next*], I said, 'Oh yeah, I write them.' So, I went home and did *Sister Son/ji*. It took me all night long to do that one."

devotion, tending and cultivating joy, intentional exchanges of Black love that might go undocumented, forgotten. Some of the poems start with song titles; in some poems the lover beside me wakes up singing.

One story I extracted while interviewing my aunt for *Starlight & Error* was how she and my uncle, a Black marine, wrote letters every single day of his deployment to Vietnam and then after. I hounded her for months to find the letters. She said she had them, but they never materialized. Because I knew the import of this delicate, ongoing fostering of daily love, I wrote the letters myself (and named them after their favorite Marvin Gaye song to boot):

DISTANT LOVER
Dear Bobby: Cambodia, Vietnam, it's all on the news.
If I watch too long, the lines run together and
I can't tell who's who.

My sisters been my company,
especially Dee. We use an old map
to show the boys where you might be.

I listen to music, passing time.
Marvin's singing sweet in this new cut, he say
When your lover leaves you, you got nobody, a lonely
    hour's come over you.

He's live on stage, somewhere far like you
and those girls screaming behind him
must know he's telling the truth.

Remember that day we left the boys with my mama
when the bank gave us that loan?
The rain came down, drops big as pennies

and we didn't care, walked all the way home.
When we got back to Dunbar Street, we were a mess:
hair slick, clothes muddy, our shoes and hopes

in your hands and we just laughed.
People couldn't understand what it meant
to have someone believe in what we started.

We danced ourselves silly, soaked as we were
through and through—the rain came down like that today.
Days like this, I sure do miss you.

While I was courting paradise, it seemed all the other Black poets were writing the body politic. Reading journals, judging prizes, reviewing drafts for friends, I found us railing against injustice, counting bodies and naming them. Every few weeks, I asked myself if it was irresponsible—callous, even—not to be doing the same. What is our lane in times of crisis? Are we mirror? Spectacle? Prodding stick? I published a few of the *Starlight & Error* poems in a journal and was grateful when good poet and friend L. Lamar Wilson called to say, "I'm so happy to read Black poets writing love poems, real love poems. When was the last time we were allowed to do that?" I understood that he meant the importance of the love poem is a different kind of political act, an important outworking of a greater faith.

My family is the praying kind, full of women who love hard and show this by taking their children to Bible study each Wednesday and Sunday, spending Saturday ministering to others, and finding God on their own every other day of the week. So the massacre at Emanuel AME Church in Charleston, South Carolina, rattled us. Then a month later when Sandra Bland died mysteriously in police custody—though they'd call it suicide—I was left reeling. These losses stand in a steady line in the Black Lives Matter movement, born from fear, exhaustion, and losing loves with no accounting on anyone's part. Just asking to *matter*, as Michael Che famously joked, is such a bare minimum kind of plea. Beneath Black Lives Matter, then, is the hope that we would be allowed an ordinary living, that our children would be allowed to grow up, find love, find joy, and give the wisdom of experience to as many others as the heart and life will hold—in other words, near paradise.

During our interview, Jordan told me when another kind of love set in: when the poems he heard shifted his understanding of himself and others. He said: "The turning point, or demarcation line for my understanding poetry as an art form and a craft, came when I heard Cornelius Eady read at the Folger Shakespeare Theater on November 15, 1994. Cornelius read his poem 'Gratitude' and in the middle of the poem I started crying. I had never had anything like that happen to me before. I'm not demonstrative in that way; I don't cry at movies or things like that. I could hear my life story being told through the poem and the way he framed it blew me away."

He'd held that date, those words, in his mind like a memento, a blossom pressed and saved. We talked about how teaching shifts your perspective and how he tried to recreate that moment when he found Eady for his own students: "[I]f I bring in the work of Tim Seibles, Yusef Komunyakaa, Ethelbert Miller, Cornelius Eady, Toi Derricotte, or Elizabeth Alexander, the students connect with it in a different way. There's such a diversity of voices, so much life in the work, that people 'get struck.' You walk into a workshop full of young sisters and bring in Lucille Clifton, who they've never heard of before, and their concept of what a poet is changes. Before being exposed to the work, at best their understanding is usually a rapper or somebody on Def Poetry Jam, which is fine, but it isn't the full spectrum."

We came back to this importance of familiarity as I pointed out that I'm sure Jordan had also encountered students like me, well-read but still left wanting. When I was taught "the classics" through high school, there were *never* Black poets in the curriculum—and I was fortunate enough to have had a brilliant Black classical poetry–loving AP English teacher, Dr. Borbie Davis. (I'd graduated from Booker T. Washington High School, the only historically Black high school in a nearly majority Black city; Dr. Davis wrote iambic pentameter for fun between sermons on the weekends.) Sure, I knew "O Captain! My Captain!" by Whitman and can still quote lines from Andrew Marvell's "To His Coy Mistress," but what of poets who looked, sounded, and loved like me? Jordan said: "[O]ne thing I find is that there is no way for a student to really access poetry before they hear their own voice in the poem. No other culture asks you to read the work of someone outside your culture *first* and then come back to your own voice." He continued: "Of course, you have to read Whitman, you need to read Keats, but if that doesn't in some way represent the direct iconography of your life, you're going to have a hard time connecting with it."

⋅•● ● ●●●● ● ●●●● ● ●●●● ⋅

Sometimes poems, in a familiar voice, showed up unexpectedly. Like when someone in our family announced that they were getting married, my mother's mother would point at the starry-eyed lover and repeat the same refrain: "Courting is a pretty thing, marriage is a blossom. If you want to get your finger bit, poke it at a possum!" Then she'd double over in a fit of laughter. Though we had no idea what it meant, and she never explained, we'd come to her to seek out the verse as a kind of incantation, a blessing. She'd been gone two years before Michael came back to me, so my mother said it instead at our engagement party.

When I asked Jordan how he'd done the double-work of crafting love written in the voice of mothers, daughters, cautioning women, he said: "A big part of it was just listening to the women in my life. I come from a family of strong women. My mother is a good example, for one. Before I got to college, I had to graduate from the Bessie Jordan school of home training. Then I had a host of aunts, cousins, and girlfriends who were good examples. I didn't really have to invent a lot of it. I just had to listen."

I'm glad to have my mother's voice and my grandmother's voice, the ritual of us unfolding, resonant and ringing. The little poem-song as a kind of hand-me-down, a kind of warning.

To start *Starlight & Error*, I researched all the love poems I could find. I think of it the way one might research the history of hair salons, planets, or marble flooring. I try to start at the beginning, with griots, Sappho, Rumi, Shakespeare, then move up through time. I stumble upon a version of Grandma's ditty in the book *Love and Marriage in Early African*

America edited by Frances Smith Foster. "Love Is Jes' a Thing o' Fancy" is the name of the anonymous folk song. Seeing it amid other declarations—warnings, doctrines, and missing dreams—reminded me love makes a way out of no way and those women cutting a path to me held onto their hope and caution. When Grandma pulled us aside to repeat it, she told all we needed to know about love: sometimes it comes in a foreign package, pretty and pressed to fade; sometimes it has a face of stone. The harder it is, the better it holds on.

Our Black joy is the house we build for the children, the house we tend for ourselves.

Michael and I keep our friends close, we keep the music and dominos and table-smacking laughter closer, joy on joy on joy. We don't take each other for granted; we see God in our likeness, in all we have and do. I sing him Michael Jackson's "Got to Be There" at our wedding. He reads me e. e. cummings's "[i carry your heart with me(i carry it in]." He lets me scatter books on the bed, then fall asleep. Some nights in my turning, I find him making bookmarks out of tissue or receipts, so he can save the place I might have lost. Fewer and fewer nights now, he has the dream of his father and brothers, whom he has to fight in his slumber. I put my arm on his shoulder to calm but not wake him and he settles into softness sleeping next to me.

Joy is tending to each other, two-stepping in the hallway, oversized children crowding our bed to watch a movie they know I will fall asleep on and that they can quote word for word. It is going to see *Fela!* and *The Lion King* and *The Trip to Bountiful* on Broadway, escaping to the lights together, discovering some shining, binding, boundless new thing. Sure, there's too much laundry and most nights the world is burning, but we forgive the world for this, as there are also brownie sundaes, poems scribbled in most margins, and early morning ocean waves with the sun making paintings of the sky as we throw the football around. We pray so much we think God tires of us. We believe paradise is a real thing. We plan to make it together, despite what ails and chases us; people see it on our faces: we are a blinding, dancing light. All the while, I write.

Jordan is invested in not just snippets but rather the trajectory of whole lives fleshed out. He explained: "I'm certainly interested in the ability to tell a story with a book of poems. I think that's a part of the literary poetic tradition that isn't tackled enough. I'm fascinated with books like Marilyn Nelson's *Carver* or Rita Dove's *Thomas and Beulah*. When I see a book that does that, I think, *This is what poetry is supposed to do.*"

He undertook this in his book M-A-C-N-O-L-I-A as well as amplifying the interior lives of historical figures in his next two books, *Quantum Lyrics* and *The Cineaste*. Jordan examines the past with the aim of taking back the humanness of figures that have been idols of sorts—forefathers of science, industry, film, music, and myth. In *Quantum Lyrics*, comic book heroes Green Lantern, The Flash, and The Atom are as real and conflicted as Richard Feynman and Albert Einstein, fathers of modern science.

In a section titled the "Quantum Lyrics Montage," Jordan's fondness for history and film are combined in a series of poems that have Einstein as their axis. In the series, Einstein, his first wife, Mileva, his second wife (and cousin), Elsa, and several public figures weigh in on the burdens of ardor, genius, and the politically charged times. Rarely do any of us think of Albert Einstein as a lovesick beau, but in Jordan's examination, love influences Einstein as much as any other force. In "Thought Experiment #1: $E=MC^2$," Einstein's discoveries, mistakes, and losses are sworn into memory. Indeed, every action has an equal and opposite reaction. He knows the push and pull of pairing. And what is missing—the love of another—can make even the most rational man question everything else that binds us: gravity, light, hope.

Jordan uses times past to ask fundamental questions no scientist has been able to master: how does the inexplicable inertia of the heart affect theories that govern the details of our lives? Under Hitler's anti-Semitism, the comfortable embrace of Einstein's own homeland faded. Worse still, the United States he fled to recognized the sanctity of scientific thought, but not the inconceivable prejudice it held dear. Even Einstein couldn't understand this, as Jordan depicts him, in a letter to W. E. B. Du Bois, postulating that expunging race is as impossible as slowing the growing universe. How frightening it must have been for a genius like Einstein not to be able to control with equations and theorems all the moving parts of his own life, all the people and beliefs orbiting him, while he could figure out what caused the orbit, how it held, and why. But in Jordan's hands, under any circumstance, even with the world's inequities colliding, how buoyant and resplendent is falling in love.

The filmmaker, in most of the poems in *The Cineaste*, is part historian, part truth-seeker, and the audience is an astute voyeur of human inclination. Among others, Jordan illuminates Black films or filmmakers: *The Mack*, *The Brother from Another Planet*, and Oscar Micheaux's lost silent film *The Homesteader*, made just four years after *The Birth of a Nation*, which Jordan also frames loosely. Oscar Micheaux's work and biography make up several series of sonnets in the center, more than half of the book's text and subtext. Jordan casts the sojourn of a nation being reborn into some new hybrid of what it once was, a reluctant mix and measure of social upheaval and burgeoning industry at the beginning of the twentieth century.

There's no way to overestimate Micheaux's wisdom and gumption: he was a Pullman porter, himself a homesteader, a best-selling novelist, and the first Black feature-film creator, writing, directing, and producing more than forty of his own films, many based on his life. Jordan resurrects Micheaux as he does Einstein, along with all their haints, successes, and aspirations, none of which curdle and shift them more than love or want of it. Micheaux falls in love with the untouched prairie, the dream of a wife, and a charlatan preacher's daughter. He marries her, and they suffer, can't devise a happy end. Like most of us who find our way to understanding by creating, Micheaux turns to his art to comfort him. Were it not for love and all its struggle, there may have been little need for his prolificacy. By asking questions of our past like Micheaux, Jordan helps to open the discussion of what the future could hold if only we focused on what has already been salvaged, on a reel-to-reel or in the lives and voices of time immemorial. Jordan's is the kind of art that elucidates and fascinates us—a montage of all our echoes and intricacies.

What is paradise in the world imagined on the other side of a camera, the underbelly of the drum, the scribbling pen? Perhaps, for all of us, paradise is each angle, multiple voices, the wide berth for desire and forgiveness, illuminated in the hands of a deft storyteller. During times of crises—all throughout history—the apprehension for Black artists especially is real, but I have a deep, abiding faith that nuanced art can humanize and complicate us. Daily, we are countering the mess we see without context in textbooks and on the news. So, for me, centering Black love and community—enduring relationships, present men, laughing women, growing children—still thriving despite our fear is not just complicating but *counteracting* tropes that sully us.

To be sure, there have been Black poets and there will always be Black poets writing about love. But the inescapable Black aesthetic that trumps love, trumps all, is community (the Collective "I" in many manifestations). We are often, out of choice, obligation, circumstance, or desire, railing against injustice—not to mention the Black womanist poet, who has another complex body laboring alongside her other consciousness. But art pivots, fills in the lines and frees us. As I write this, I'm so grateful for the *Black Panther* film and the #WakandaSoLit phenomenon that followed. I felt and intensely understood the profoundly necessary communal joy spawned by it, as we are living in critical times. I took my son to previews, I took children who are like my children; I wanted them to see beauty reflected, power in their hands, love and admiration passed through calamitous days.

To court paradise, as Black poets, we must find what is outside the expected, what is hardest to do in the hardest of times, to see hope now and beyond. When *Starlight & Error* is finally finished and brought into the world, much of the hardship we all endure is there, as that, too, is part of our dailiness. But we are the subversive, wonder-working, almost unimagined. Suffering, the undercurrent riding in the midst of triumph—a challenge to our existing condition, God in the details of our resilient living.

BINGHAM-RISHER: You never shy away from the reality of race and racism in this country in your books. Why do you think it's important for us to attend to the truth, despite it not always being welcomed?

JORDAN: In intellectual circles, there is the idea that race is a construct, the philosophy of K. Anthony Appiah and others, which I can get with at times. However, I feel like racism is the real social construct and that there's nothing inherently wrong with acknowledging race. The question comes up all the time: "How do you feel about someone calling you an African American poet?" Well, I'm flattered that they recognize what I am. . . . You know, a culture developed from having people who look like me on this soil; I'm just trying to represent. So, if someone wants to take my book and say, "This is *also* what Black is," I have no problem with that. I would prefer that than for them to only have a monolithic view of who we are.

Sonia Sanchez

BLK/WOOOMEN REVOLUTION

*I think that's the point of being this poet at this particular
time. I want to have a conversation about not only surviving
and attempting to change the world, but also how to love.*

—SONIA SANCHEZ

W hen the documentary about Sonia Sanchez's life called *BaddDDD
Sonia Sanchez* aired on PBS, it was the middle of the semester, my
sixth wedding anniversary had just come or gone, my son was battling
a barrage of school tests, and most of the world was at war with itself. I
caught bits of the film between grading and cooking, cleaning and writ-
ing, before sleeping or after Bible study, as finding two free hours is a
rare luxury.

Sanchez read one of my favorites, "To Anita," a poem for her daugh-
ter and for the mass of Black women warring with themselves, colorism,
and community. As Sanchez's voice breaks on camera, I hear the pain in
real time. A few days later, I caught the film just as she was explaining
what it was like building a Black studies program at San Francisco State
in the 1960s, and I remembered I'd been asked to present a list of courses
about my "most sincere areas of interest" that might be taught at my
university. As students protested on screen, I made the list:

- The Black Interior: Contemporary African American
  Women's Poetics
- The Light That Was: Exploring the Works of Lucille Clifton
- The War Works Hard: Women's Poetry of War and Conflict

- Our Mothers' Gardens: Womanist Poetics from 1950–Present
- Writing Across the Lines: Poetry Exploring Gender, Race, Culture, and Ethnicity
- The History of Us All: Personally Political Feminist Poems
- Leaders of the New School: Intersections of Contemporary Poetry and the Hip-Hop Cultural Movement
- Gospel of the Southern Road: Examining Blues and Mythos in Women's Literature of the South

In hopes that one of the courses would be offered, I pulled Alice Walker's work of womanist prose *In Search of Our Mothers' Gardens* and Elizabeth Alexander's *The Black Interior* off the shelf while Sanchez's work is set to music in the documentary. Alice Walker calls for a revolutionary Black artist—one who centers love as the crux of the work—in an essay published the same year as Sanchez's second book, *We a BaddDDD People.* In the essay "The Unglamorous but Worthwhile Duties of the Black Revolutionary Artist, or of the Black Writer Who Simply Works and Writes," Walker lays out a framework—a list of things one must do or may be called to do—to be a Black poet subversive.

She says revolutionaries must face the Truth of each situation, even if it means plain-faced laboring for the artist. For instance, if the children in your class can't read, how will poems serve them? The Truth of the thing must be faced before anything can be made beautiful.

In addition to teaching beauty, the revolutionary poet teaches how to enter and inhabit it. The revolutionary artist can't create in a vacuum; they must embrace all avenues, be open to the future, and help us dig our way out of the present even with all our scars. During our interview, Sanchez said the same of artists all over the diaspora holding up the stories of the everywoman and everyman: "When you travel in the world and you see the emotion and movement of poets from Neruda to [Nicolás] Guillén, to poets and writers like Ngũgĩ wa Thiong'o, Chinua Achebe, when you see [Keorapetse] Willie Kgositsile, people all over the world have not only written and written well, but have engaged the society also as to what it is they must do for the populace. We not only speak out loud, my dear sister, but beautifully sometimes and harshly sometimes, but we also at the same time speak for the people who cannot speak for themselves. It is incumbent upon us to do that."

Sanchez echoes this with her own insistence on the hard labor necessary in lifting oneself, then doing the same to help others, despite what stands in the way.

I met Sanchez at the second Furious Flower Conference in 2004, where she performed with her band Full Moon of Sonia, and interviewed her a few years later. As we had just begun to get to know each other and I was a young mostly unpublished poet, I was surprised to be invited to a gathering at her house that first evening we sat together. At Sanchez's party, there was food spread from end to end on a large wooden table; people filled the house and were almost as interesting and varied as the art stationed in every room. There were pieces by Thelma Burke, Elizabeth Catlett, and Jacob Lawrence. There were many African statues and masks, along with signed prints and photographs with artists from every genre. Sanchez smiled with entertainers on one wall and Bearden's autograph graced a print on another. Ngũgĩ wa Thiong'o sat in the living room signing his latest epic novel *Wizard of the Crow* and took pictures with guests. This went on until well after midnight. Sanchez stood in the kitchen, beckoning when she saw me: "Dear sister, here's a camera. Document everything, make sure you see everyone. Bring it back to me when you're done."

Months later, when I saw Sanchez at a conference in Atlanta, she remembered we hadn't finished our interview, as we were cut short by the gathering at her home. I fumbled when she asked me why I hadn't tried to reach her, explaining that my grandmother had just passed away and that the last few months had been grim. She cut me short as I tried to beg her forgiveness and said we could finish whenever I was ready.

Before I could thank her, a group of editors came. As she was being swept away, she took my hand. "We're having a get-together tonight at a local poet's house. You should come. Here's the address, here's the time, bring poems, bring friends."

In her book *We a BaddDDD People,* I was introduced to the Sonia many fell in love with during the civil rights era. When we met more than forty years later, her poems had grown quieter and more mild-mannered in their way. Those in the Black Arts Movement subverted tradition by breaking rules of English grammar and syntax, especially poets like Carolyn Rodgers, Ntozake Shange, and Sonia Sanchez, whose work from that era utilized satiric or phonetic misspellings; slashes for word dismemberment, abbreviation, or fusion; and incorporated one of the most distinguishable features in Black English, using the verb "be" almost exclusively to mark aspect in verb phrases.

Of course, using Black vernacular wasn't new. It was a medium in the tradition of Paul Laurence Dunbar, Zora Neale Hurston, and others. But these artists of the 1960s writing in the language of the people understood how reading and hearing the language of one's heart might change the reader's response. Moreover, Black feminist poets were railing against *each* institution that bound them—racism, sexism, ageism—and were precise in their subjects and audience: they were writing Black poems for and about the common Black citizen, especially the youth they believed would be most adept at listening to and acting on their messages. Sanchez explained her revolutionary craft when I asked about the biting tongue in her earlier work: "[Y]ou must remember, all the death and dying that happened during the time that we were writing, and we had discovered how much we'd been enslaved in this country. No one had taught that in the universities, our parents had not even talked about it. So when we discovered it, we weren't going to say, 'Well, by golly, I think this is important.' We came out hitting and slapping and alerting people to what had happened."

She went on: "In [my book] *Home Coming,* you see concentrated bloodletting. We had to alert people who had not been alerted to what was going on. When I got up on the stage and said, 'I'm Black,' people booed me, because people wanted to be considered Negroes with a capital N. So, you had to use curse words, because then you engaged people. When I used curse words, I engaged the younger people and they said, 'Ooh, stop, look at that!' Then, after I got them engaged, I didn't have to curse anymore."

Among the leaders of the civil rights and Black Power movements, Black youth in the 1960s were bodacious in their stand against discrimination and maltreatment. This made them kindred spirits with the artists of the time. By speaking in the voices of those in their communities, Black poets validated those silenced for centuries. During the Black Arts Movement, numerous brave—sometimes irreverent—new voices like Sanchez's began to sing in poems, on wax, and in politics.*

A cursory glance through *We a BaddDDD People* is nothing like looking into *Morning Haiku*, a collection of Sanchez's formal verse published in 2010. There is little discernible structure for most poems in *We a BaddDDD People*—words sprawl down the page or bleed into others with forward slashes in between; the spelling is invented and divisive in its raging; expletives, derivatives, repetitions of letters or phrases, and wild capitalizations abound. This is obscenity-slinging, English-breaking, loud-mouthing, Afro wider than the photo filling the back cover, revolutionary Sonia—unapologetic and abrasive, full of fire and righteous love. The documentary proves that Sanchez has never been afraid to tell people about their mess. Mess as in James Brown's soul-fire "Papa Don't Take No Mess!" Mess as in staying down in your own dirt. In the 1960s, this is what Sanchez believes plagues the Black community she holds dear, and in *We a BaddDDD People* she wills the real, revolutionary work to begin at home. In the poem "blk/rhetoric," she asks who is going to walk the walk, not just talk the talk about revolution. She wants more than lip service for the new Black Is Beautiful movement. She wants more than simple capitalistic appeasements ("cad / ill / acs" or, if the phrase is

---

*I asked Sanchez about when, during this convergence of folks, she met Nikki Giovanni, Haki Madhubuti (who was Don L. Lee then), and Etheridge Knight, who would make up the Broadside Quartet, and she made sure to get my history straight. She said, "Well, turn it around—and I'm just saying it for accuracy—Nikki was younger than us, so she was with us. The great thing about us was, what we did is, we opened up to everybody. She certainly came along with us for Broadside. When you talk about the Black Arts Movement, the people who started that were an interesting bunch of people. You had [Amiri] Baraka, Askia [Touré], Larry Neal, Bobb Hamilton, myself, and then the musicians who came and the painters who came. All those people who came into that facility, BART/S, the Black Arts Repertory Theatre/School, to begin this thing called Black Arts."

drilled down, ill-bred, dishonorable ['cad'], sick [ill] actions [acs/*acts*]) by those pushing materialism over substance. She wants more than racial, sexual repression and street mongering, more than artificial highs from drugs and cheap hooch, more than temporary pleasures, pain, or sensationalized fascination with difference. She wants legitimate, continuous change, a real about-face for society.

For Sanchez as for Walker, revolution is both a verb and noun, an action and event. In the documentary, Sanchez fights with and for the people in great or small things. She does what Walker posits she must do as a revolutionary artist. Sometimes poets must help move students from one reading level to another, fill out government forms for assistance, help people eat. Revolutionaries must do the regular work to get folks from day to day, be in the trenches, not just pontificate about art and adornment without helping to beautify the lives on the ground. Sanchez teaches and fights for Black studies to be recognized by campus administrators; she is arrested as a grandmother against war. In our interview, I was especially tickled when Sanchez talked about bickering with a manager for fresh produce at her inner-city grocery store. She is fighting against disparities, food deserts, and neighborhood deprivation. In her community, she is in the midst of revolution.

We talked about Sanchez's fight to establish Black studies as a field and how real the work got for her before most of the knowledge had a chance to trickle into a groundswell. She said: "It's amazing how long it has taken people to catch up. Now, it's normal, it's commonplace, the things we talked about, things that people should have been doing in the early 1970s. Now, in the twenty-first century, it's normal to have a Du Bois House, but when I talked about Du Bois and taught Du Bois's *The Souls of Black Folk* at San Francisco State, the FBI came to my house. They knocked on my door and told my landlord he should put me out, because I was one of *those*—they didn't call us radicals, they called us militants. He said because I was teaching Du Bois—but he pronounced it wrong—Hughes, and Robeson. Well, you can't very well do the first semester of African American Lit without including them."

She continued: "I must admit that I was naïve about the process of teaching them, as I told Ms. Jean Hutson, who was the curator of the

Schomburg. When I finally called her after the FBI had left, I said, 'You know, I've just been visited by the FBI!' I had tears in my eyes, and she said, 'Dear, dear Sonia. I thought you understood that if you taught some of *those* people, you might have a little difficulty,' which was the understatement of the year [laughing]." But being a revolutionary often means troubling the water for good.

In his introduction to *We a BaddDDD People*, published by his own Broadside Press, Dudley Randall opens with a delineation of the true revolutionary spirit: "Some people think of revolutionaries as troublesome, but I have found the ones I know to be kind, gentle, generous . . . Those who are revolutionaries, however, want to make this a better world."

In Sanchez's America in *We a BaddDDD People*, instead of whips and chains, most are tormented by greed, drugs, impossible gains. Black families are torn apart in poems like "—answer to yo/question / of am i not yo/woman / even if u went on shit again" where a Black woman watches her Black man disappear and return as someone else under the haze of drugs, though there is enduring, home-growing, proliferate love. She calls out the seedy, underhanded politics of capitalism, sexism, and pay-for-play sexual encounters in "Indianapolis/summer/1969/poem," where she admonishes families for not teaching their children that the revolution isn't about getting "coin." Sanchez speaks plainly and combs the streets for what she believes people need to hear, her candidness another tenet of the Black revolutionary artist. Sanchez shocks the stoic, prudish, and unaware with the hope of teaching some to know better or, perhaps, with the intention of moving some beyond indifference.

Sanchez's revolution is sometimes angry, sometimes celebratory; she chastises and idolizes in equal measure. She's a shape-shifter, a courier of love and hate. In short, she is all kinds of human. The work of the revolutionary artist/woman, on top of dealing with culture, is often most intentioned and piercing when motherhood is the topic. Layer upon layer of experience (caregiving, care-needing, assumed inadequacies, laborious conflicted histories, etc.) abound. In "summer words of a sistuh addict," a woman shoots dope on Sunday, making it her temple and God after church. The woman in the poem is not simply negligent or shooting up for recreation; she turns to drugs and explains she is self-medicating against the trauma from her mother. Her casual escape becomes a spiraling addiction, and only the women in her community know how to try to salvage her. The women are a sounding board and communal conscience, voices of reason and restraint. Their final query puts the onus on the daughter, on her part in this undoing. Their inquiry—an intervention, perhaps a saving grace—is followed by the chorus of women mingled with her own tears as she is broken and reborn.

In this work, losing the love of other women is immobilizing. Often, as the poem brings out, it is still the larger community of women who cry, chastise, and sing us through our mistakes. Letting abuse, anger, dirty laundry, and the like drive poems in this collection is revolutionary mining; not being afraid to show everyone, even kin, in all their unsightliness, their flawed living, even if the folks at home chastise you for telling it like it is. Who is at fault here—the mother, the daughter, society, the pusher, the preacher, the almost-absent God?

Sanchez's poems suggest what Walker praises in truly revolutionary art: that there is no summing up a life neatly. That we are sometimes the comfortable and sometimes the afflicted, but revolutionary Black women poets paint life with all its many spirals.

•◦● ● ●◦●◦ ◦ ●◦●◦ ◦ ●◦●◦ •

In the documentary, when asked about whether her work is personal, Sanchez talks about the Collective "I" in the way I think of it. She speaks for the communities of common folk. She is listener and medium. This duality reminds me of something I go back to in the revolutionary work of Elizabeth Alexander. She aligns with Sanchez's and Walker's theory that the artist must work for the people but also be *of them*. In Alexander's *The Black Interior*, published two and a half decades after *We a BaddDDD People*, there is a burrowing under the skin of Black America. Alexander's excavation, she explains, is done by means of "a metaphor, of what I call 'the Black interior,' that is, Black life and creativity behind the public face of stereotype and limited imagination . . . meant to envision: complex Black selves, real and enactable Black power, rampant and unfetishized Black beauty." Alexander climbs the shoulders of Walker and Sanchez by continuing to envisage the underlives of everyday Black folks. Her books of prose, *The Black Interior* and *Power and Possibility*, are both meant for a people she loves; admiration for the ancestors and their path winnowing on our behalf takes her to the page again and again.

Alexander's lifelong admonition is clear and has become the crux of my own work: *Honor the elders' voices. Honor your own.* But she is also writing about what Blackness is beneath its layers. She is looking at Black art and Black living through a meticulous, critical, and causal lens: she gives care where she has gotten it. She is planting seeds and growing those who grew her up by making them infinitely bigger.

Alexander is a model for my work and life. I think of her as a woman bearing grace, power, and reinvention, co-mutual force and spirit, siren and beacon. Her revolution carries me. At times, when I am supposed to be writing and I am drifting into some netherworld of inertia, I search for interviews she's done and let her voice play out on the speakers by my desk to remind me that lives should be spent doing something useful. Sometimes I don't even need her voice, just the picture of her that used to be on the home page of her website, where she sat clear-eyed (upright in the way my mother urges me to sit), near bright florid pillows, to the left of ancestors holding a wall and in front of floating shelves of books. (I made out the titles *Duke, Primo, The Big Sea,* and *Zion* at first glance.) She is all the things I am or want to be: mother, poet, worker, woman enough for herself, wide ocean for younger poets like me. Like Sanchez and Walker, Alexander knows the import of crafting the right words to illuminate her people, and this is my desire, my struggle too.

Sanchez in the '60s is undoubtedly speaking to and for the wild youth, those who may not yet be broken in entirely by racism's heavy yoke. Walker is speaking to those who are helping to usher the next generation into the mixed-up world. Alexander is heralding the ancestors and elders (like Sanchez and Walker, especially the Black woman's interior) who leave a trail for us could-be revolutionary artists to seek and follow. This revolutionary art is about culpable responsibility for Sanchez, hard labor for Walker, and authentic revisioning for Alexander.

Revolution is the rate of a working engine but also reincarnation or epoch; life's wheel turning. In geology, it is when a region, a mass, a mountain occurs. Are we a mountain? Us, here—the new working, living, Black women poets? Yes, of course, we have been made out of some shifting.

Race is not something you get out from under, nor should we be compelled to want to escape it—all three women agree. But there is no denying Alexander's truth about how pressure from the literary community can change the way we move professionally. This is an ongoing argument—being *solely* an artist versus being a *Black* artist versus being a *Black revolutionary* artist.

My second book of poems, *What We Ask of Flesh*—wherein a Biblical woman is cut into twelve pieces and sent into the tribes of Israel, a woman-child is burned and transformed, a Black woman becomes many women, and women are reborn—is a book about women lost to freedom and coming to revolution in spirit. I am asked about this work by an interviewer: "How aware are you, when writing, of adding another voice and layer to the historic record?" I muster an answer, but while watching the documentary, I continue to think about whether this work—this duality of a Black woman's living—is a burden. Can we ever make art for art's sake? Sanchez and Walker never seemed to think that was the reality—they never ignored the awareness of what is Truth. The antecedent of the Black community wedges (or opens) us into positions of disadvantage, and it takes all the bright bodies—the thinking, moving, painting, writing, singing, dancing, teaching, healing folks living in, around, of, and through us—to pull us all out.

In *Poems in Conversation and a Conversation*, a chapbook by Elizabeth Alexander and Lyrae Van Clief-Stefanon, Black art and artists work in tandem, moving through others, reexamining themselves. The poem "The Black Woman Speaks" is named after a graphic series by and written in the voice of sculptor/activist Elizabeth Catlett. In it, the task of the revolutionary—the cumbersome, all-encompassing, oft-inglorious, mindful mess—is made plain: this is heavy intellectual work that women artists do. We bear the weight of families, cultures, worlds. We mine the course. We're another layer of the archive but also on the humble, daily grind, keeping the engine turning as we can.

I realize so much of the work on this book of interviews and essays stopped when I got married and gained children. I wrote poems but barely managed this deep consideration—spiral and rabbit hole—into the work of others. Looking back, I believe I was just trying to get my bearings; love is so full and wide—like motherhood, also new—it covered everything. I hadn't learned how to handle the demands of a revolutionary life and am still learning. A seasoned revolutionary (one who understands the work *is* life) is an ever-turning apparatus. The work is a wellspring—this ceaseless taking care of home, the neighborhood, the living spaces, and spirits of people while singing the songs of the people. And isn't making a home *while* tending our history revolutionary?

Even if this is the case, I am under no illusion that revolution in the purest sense wasn't, for Sanchez and Walker, also a fight for an end to various injustices. It is less so for Alexander, but her coming of age in America was more blatantly turbulent—as in, sanctioned by public opinion as well as on-the-books law—than mine has been. So is the work of reconsidering the past revolutionary, without the same kind of consequence and weight as work done during the Black Arts Movement and just beyond it? Is there a continuing need for Black revolutionary art? What are we still chasing, still fleeing? When does the revolution end— meaning, when does it become a permanent fixture? When have we rolled the engine enough to keep it continuously turning, so that there will be a radical, inevitable reformation of society? I keep hearing the voice of Sanchez as a playwright in my head, intoning, "But how do it *free us?*"

This is not 1960s America, but, as I switch between CNN and the documentary, after the Obamas have visited Cuba, people are hunting Assata Shakur again. The blur of things warns me that we are still living in precarious times. We of another generation—what is our revolution?

What is revolutionary work in the age of a somewhat freer Blackness? Are hashtags revolutionary in their swiftness and necessity? Is my faith? Is having faith in the revolution, in revolutionary art, a radical act? And what is happening to those we bear, to the next *next* generation? Are our children getting freer? I was born in 1981; I have passed my Jesus year and am listening to talk radio as much as music, which means to me that I am as interested in learning as I am in feeling, and I don't remember this being the case ten years ago. It's certainly not the case for the students in my classes or the children blaring music in my house.

Behind us, the Sanchez documentary cuts to a poem about her father as my husband and I talk about this new kid, Chance the Rapper, and how he has piqued my soul music–loving husband's interest. He's an emcee devoted to being free from traditional signings and trappings of the business. This leads to a long tangent about how the internet is right, that we are just coming to know what free Black children look like and are learning how they will move around us in a way we weren't able to exist. "I do not dismiss the Collective 'I' on our back," I tell my husband. "We all had to carry the race, and some of them are getting free enough now to feel that they only carry themselves." When did this happen? When did revolution also start to mean you could be free of the yoke of the past? I am in wonder of it and them. I am proud and frightened about forgetting and forging into the tilting axis of a changing world.

•◦●◦●◦●◦●◦●◦●◦●◦●◦

After I have been informed that none of the new classes I design will be offered this term because "there might be a few too many courses on 'sensationalized' topics," the documentary ends with younger poets reading Sanchez's work, and I am cleaning house again. I have not been back to my son's closet in many months but the things I cannot allow him to wear to school or the bus stop are hardly there. His grandmother has snuck in a bandana that she bought at Dollar Tree because he said he wanted to play cowboys, but it is red and I must throw it away because I don't want someone to think he is a danger to them or himself. After Trayvon Martin, my husband and I sat in the kitchen deciding how to explain the Truth of all this to the child. I do the actual work of explaining, the actual work of pulling things out of his closet and putting them into the dumpster while he cries, and then I write:

OUR CHILD IS NOT YET TEN AND WE
ARE CLEARING HIS CLOSET
of do-rags, backpacks, hoo doo, hoorides, Black
magic, mysterious gadgets, misters and missus, the missing,
heretics, hearsay, heard-him-tell, run-and-tell-it,
snitches, stitches, sticks, saving, saviors, Toms, Dicks,
nightsticks, shanks, broken bottles, blunts, objects,
bullets, ballistics, crypt walks, autopsies, undergrounds,
jaywalking, gestures, gentrification, justifications, juries,
kickbacks, nickelbags, accessories, neverseen, dragging, drug
cartels, trafficking, riding while, driving while, looking while,
loudtalking, Mirandas, bandanas, the ash faultline,
blood in the streets, Bloods in these streets, gang-
banging, bass slanging, Ma-we-was-just-out-listening-to
at the wrong place, wrong time, tongue-tying, art-
iculation, relations, bad association, watch who you
know, love, bump into, fistbumping, fist fighting, forced
arrest, urban unrest, what it looks like, who coins it,
who sets up camp, who's pictured on those shirts,
why children are in these streets, what blisters
and buoys, *Boy, tie up those laces, unzip that hood*

I think about what Alexander says in her essay about Rodney King, which seems dated now, as my children do not recognize his name and cannot fathom how he comes back to us. Alexander forewarns us that our memories of seeing violence enacted influences our understanding of ourselves and the culture. This is well before the videos of Philando Castile or George Floyd and is one of the many things we are still trying to get free from. Not just police violence (a vestige of slavery and Jim Crow martial law) or of stereotyping (a vestige of ignorance, fear, slavery, propaganda, and sometimes our own making) but also of the weight of the lens that bends the actual, relevant Truth of our daily lives. This cleaning out of my son's closet is the thing I actually did, but that I *had* to and the *why* of this makes it political, perhaps revolutionary, though I'd never hoped that would be the case. I'd hoped one of my new classes would be offered because the import of the topics would seem undoubtable, undismissable to the powers that be—not fetishized, sensational, sexy, sassy, hip, nouveau, not yet part of the necessary canon of our American experiences. The *BaddDDD Sonia Sanchez* documentary credits roll as I pick myself up off of the floor near my son's closet and head to the table, where more work waits.

BINGHAM-RISHER: You recognized as poetry things you heard in everyday speech? But you were so young.

SANCHEZ: Yeah, I was young, but we had to sit in church and listen and, if you listen, at some point the ear becomes attuned to the musicality. . . . I think also, my dear sister, the music of my grandmother's speech. My grandmother spoke Black English, we did not. Quite often she would say something and I would repeat it. For a while my aunt—who was really my first cousin, but in the South when your first cousins are older, you call them aunts—she thought I was teasing. But Mama said, "No, just let her be." And the musicality of her words, how she said what she said, which I recognized, was much different than the way we talked. We talked, evidently, "proper English." She didn't talk "proper English," but Black English, and it was beautiful.

Forrest Hamer

GIRLS LOVING BEYONCÉ
AND THEIR NAMES

*[T]he power within us to make, to destroy, and to transform
moves us far beyond what we are able to consciously intend.*
—FORREST HAMER

*T**ell me the story of your name.*
Every semester, in every new class, this is where I begin. I ask the
students to share how their names came into being, what was desired for
them before they were born.

My mother had chosen another name for me, but it was stolen by her
sister. So now I have a cousin Lenika who's done well by my old name,
and my mother was forced to reinvent another.

When I asked Forrest Hamer to autograph his books, I had never seen
anyone so upset about such a small mistake. We were at the Callaloo
Creative Writing Workshop where he was teaching and, like all the other
students there, I became enamored with his work and unassuming na-
ture, wanting nothing more than to spend the last few nights surveying
his words. As he signed his books, he misspelled my name, and when I
crossed out one letter for another, he apologized to no end. He held me
there, despite the line forming behind us, repeating, "I'm so, so sorry
about that. Names are important. Please let me take care of things."

I was sorry to have pointed out the mistake in front of him, as he
seemed so deliberate in showing each student deference and care. In

addition to being a poet, he is a listener, a psychologist and psychoanalyst, the combination of which, he'd explain during our interview, were "twin efforts to discover mind through language merged." He said: "You have to be an avid listener, as a psychoanalyst, and an intense kind of listening has to happen to be a poet as well." After the signing mishap, he offered to buy me another set of books and was sincere in this, though I refused. But the fact that he was willing to do so told me that he is a poet, and human, of shrewd watchfulness and deep compassion; he hears what's singing in us and bears out our glory.

•◦ ◦ ◢◣◥◣ ◦ ◢◣◥◣ ◦ ◢◣◥◣ •

The first boys I fell in love with taught me to sing their names: *Ronnie, Bobby, Ricky, and Mike,* and especially Ralph, though he was singing lead and is left out of that particular refrain. New Edition, a group part Jackson 5, part pop-locking, falsetto-waving new R&B wonders. When I was four, my big cousins Delanya and Darveen—already in high school and too cool for most things—introduced me to New Edition, their walls plastered with *Right On!* magazine posters of the group, and my Walkman and heart were never the same.

When New Edition sang "Delicious," a distant cousin to Stevie Wonder's "Summer Soft," love appeared before and after the storm. Their voices looped and faded to just the inner part of the verses and what's almost unsayable lodged in the bursting heart. I played every New Edition cassette or album—my first record in my own collection was their third, *All For Love*—until the tape's ribbon wore down under incessant rewinding or until the album skipped. If anyone had listened to the New Edition catalog back to front, they'd have known most of my giddy hopes, the love language I carried with me, my glittering fears.

So, for a few weeks before I was married, I listened to Drake tracks looking for what my soon-to-be daughter found irresistible. I knew the deep love of boys singing soft and understood this was part of Drake's appeal (and what others often criticized), but I was scouting what kept Sonsoréa in the constant haze of what was blasting from her headphones in the back seat of the car.

Her four-year-old brother, Michael, was easy-peasy. I gave him his space in the first few weeks his father and I began dating. One night while I was visiting them in Phoenix, a group of us—ten or so grandmothers (or soon-to-be mothers-in-law depending on your angle), aunts, cousins, sundry and all—were at Poncho's Mexican Cantina, which I dragged them to three times a week. Milling around the benches and palm trees in the outdoor area, we waited for our number to be called. Michael was across the lot intertwined with his grandmother, twenty or so feet away from where I stood laughing with his father. With no coaxing or warning, Michael wiggled out from under his grandmother's arms and barrelled toward me. He didn't say a word, put his hand in mine, and I became his favorite thing. Easy-peasy, this love, it needed no deciphering.

Sonsoréa was a lot more like I might have been after my parents divorced, if either had chosen to remarry. Respectful, kind enough, but on guard always. Like her, I, too, was wary of love in real life—not the kind New Edition told me was possible, but the falling-apart kind that was unbearable if people who were supposed to be grown up, responsible, didn't actually know everything, even ruined things, barely listening to us or each other. At thirteen, my parents split up, I was the best soloist in middle school choir, and I met Sonsoréa's father, years before she was ever imagined.

·•♦ ♦ ♦•♦♦ ♦ ♦•♦♦ ♦ ♦•♦♦ ·

At the Callaloo Workshop, Hamer was quiet and observant. It seemed like most of the students there were extroverts or at least a bit eccentric, and he was just the opposite.* I worked with Natasha Trethewey

---

*Case in point: the night of the big student readings, we all gathered to hear the work we'd created during our time together. In lieu of a traditional introduction, I asked a favor of poet Douglas Kearney (who I'd taken to calling Big Brotha' Doug and who'd taken to calling me Peaches). Doug was endlessly kind, unabashed, and had an immense repository of song lyrics, experimentation, and "for the culture" detours at the ready. So I asked him to simply go to the stage and belt out an a cappella rendition of the first verse of Das EFX's "They Want EFX" to get the room hyped before I read a poem about my grandmother cooking meals for folks walking from Baltimore down to the March on Washington. Somehow, with all the quirky, whiz-kid Black writers in the room, it worked.

and Hamer had another set of poets, but I remember—in the large fo-
rums where we'd all meet together—feeling like Hamer was "reading"
us (maybe like patients?). He made us think of ourselves, and others, as
individual critical beings. We were all fully invested in his heart and eye
(as he was so "care/full," as Lucille Clifton might have put it), and we
hoped his keen observations would make us keener as well. By the end
of the workshop, a hush would fall over the room every time he started
to speak.

When I interviewed Hamer, he expressed that, as poets, we are "sur-
rendering to the process of discovery through language" and that he
hopes "by paying closer attention to what has been said we will be better
able to say what has yet to be imagined." But in his book *Middle Ear*,
most of the poems start in the middle of quiet, loss. I question why he
often mulls over what's missing and he explained: "I'm half-deaf and the
meanings of listening have been amplified by that fact of my constitution.
It highlights the idea that there is more sound than one can hear—re-
gardless of one's capacity—and another that sound is both an exterior
and interior matter." He said, thinking about himself as a therapist and
a reader, "I respond acutely to the tension between what is sounded and
what is not, and I try to listen for presence and absence at once."

•❧ ❂ ✒❧❂ ❂ ✒❧❂ ❂ ✒❧❂ ❂

What wasn't said between myself and my daughter—who turned thirteen
two days before I married her father—but what I've come to know for
sure is: thank God for Beyoncé (a sentence many have uttered in these
decades she's graced us). If it weren't for Beyoncé, another girl like us
with an untraceable name, we wouldn't have had much in common. What
my daughter doesn't say is plenty, so I must listen to the in-between. Of
course, a kid will never tell you you're cool; you're old, for heaven's sake.
If they did compliment you, you'd still make them clean their room, so
what would the point be? And anyway, it was clear to the children, to any-
one really, that I was on the nerdy side since I always had a book in hand.
Sonsoréa wasn't impressed until she discovered I, too, was a Beyoncé stan.

Though I wasn't fully convinced of Drake's powers—as I would point
out his dichotomy years later when I wrote the poem "Love in Stereo"—I

was polite about him, as I knew half his appeal, at least to my daughter, was that he felt so openly. He was not infallible; love still hurt him. He turned up, but also longed for trustworthy others. She said, "His music is more of a journal than anything else," and told me we could trust him because he went by his real name, more or less. He doesn't run from who he is and is wise enough to know "Girls Love Beyoncé," so we should give him credit for loving women who love the names they're given.

A few weeks after her father and I were married, Sonsoréa found me on a deep dive of live concert clips on YouTube. She was shocked and pleased to discover I knew half the routines and all the lyrics, in their right order and pitch, to the songs in King Bey's catalog. What Beyoncé does isn't easy, though critics posit about her angle (*But whose power is she enacting? Can we really call her a feminist?*) and range. I was just grateful for joyous conversation with a teenager who said little but went back and forth excitedly about Beyoncé's samples and footwork, outfits and lighting, how to reclaim our power and bodies, and the meaning of all our über-Black, made-up names.

∙•● ● ●•●● ● ●•●● ● ●•●● ∙

Hamer and I turned to music briefly when I asked about the blues myths and mythos that appear throughout *Middle Ear* in poems like "Arrival" and "Crossroads." He said he shunned the blues as a child, but living a bit more, growing up, gave him an acute understanding: "I could hear loss—of love, of hope, of security—in a way that let me hear the survival and the thriving implicit to the blues. So blues helped *Middle Ear* come into being with its repetitions, its worrying of lines, its holding of contradiction, its gut-uttering, and the meditation on what we do and do not bear to hear."

With my daughter, and cousins, and girlfriends, I ruminated on this idea—this "survival and thriving implicit" to the creation of the thing— when Beyoncé released *Lemonade*. It's not a blues album, it's a hybrid of sorts; not pop, not straight-up soul. It's an amalgamation of the embodied weight and wisdom of living: an accusation, a warning, a mingling of verse and reverb, what lies you've been told, and, despite this, what the body knows.

·•● ● ●●●● ● ●●●● ● ●●●● ·

Beyoncé's *Lemonade* appeared as I was researching my grandmother three times removed, born in 1859 and interviewed in 1937 for the Federal Writers' Project slave narratives. The album was as much relief as distraction, which I was grateful for. My work was traversing the wider (gaping) spaces held in the Black women's bodies I hold, and *Lemonade* was a deeply intimate and nuanced Black American women's narrative, tackling what grandmother love is, daughter love, mother love, how to breathe life into what's been broken, how to own your history, feast on it and birth what will carry you. This was what I was also looking to do, by tracing what my grandmother's life might have been in those years after Jubilee, when the enslaved were freed.

Looking for help finding variations of my grandmother's surname, Fulkes (to date I've found twelve), I read thousands of names taken on by those reinventing themselves, then reinventing themselves *and* their futures, giving new, bold, and stylized names to their children. Many took last names like Rich, Sharpe, King, and Freeman (free man) as an ample starting place. But I am most taken by how they stake a new claim, naming daughters such embellishments as Season, Autumn, or Starling, signaling new beginnings, Revelia (Biblical, short for Revelation) or Iona (I own her), meaning *This here God's* or *This here mine* or *Make no mistake: this here both.*

We go back to naming, legacy, and memory often in our house. When Sonsoréa was old enough to drive, like most teenagers (certainly like me at that age), she had surmised, for what felt to her like a long time, that someone's world should revolve around her.

So I was not surprised when she began proposing I write a poem with her name as the title. A few times a year, I explained that "It doesn't work that way. I'm not an 'occasional' poet per se. I don't choose my muses; they choose me." But, like most of what adults say that is out of line with teenage reasoning, these arguments were inconsequential to her.

I tried to appeal to her sense of justice to get me off the hook: "And what about your brother, Michael? Wouldn't I have to write a poem for him too?" But she was sixteen and cared little about who might immortalize her brother. Besides, she argued, "He doesn't have a very interesting"—I think the precise term she used was *poetic*—"name." Touché.

•◦● ● ●◦●● ● ●◦●● ● ●◦●● •

In *Rift*, as in the poem "Common Betrayal," change is a recurring theme often met with reluctance, so I asked Hamer about this and he said: "I'm surprised—though I really shouldn't be—by how much transformation is a subject of my work. . . . That we are also in a constant state of change does seem to make urgent the matter of paying attention to what we can, if only for the sake of addressing the awe of what has already been."

How do we capture children, milestones, admiration, the wide-open heart as they are? They are all fleeting and imperfect, most more wonderful (or unbearable) in theory, in the faint haze of distance growing wider over time.

Somewhere along the way, I realized Sonsoréa and I were both impressed with self-reinvention. How could we make ourselves over, even if the world around us was a swirling unknown haze? That was my world when my parents separated, when we traveled across the country to start another life. This was what Sonsoréa and her brother were asked to do, and in the wake of this, we all, in our own ways, looked for forces to help us reassess who and how we could be.

Beyoncé did this each time she emerged, and Sonsoréa and I have been impressed with the depth in her voice, her return to hardcore R&B since the album *4*. We were mesmerized by her vision and double-voiced ethereal bursting into her own womanhood on *Beyoncé* (and talked at length about this being her fifth solo work but the first eponymous one—when you grow up, you truly grow into your name, we decided). By the time one of our favorites, Prince—cool enough that he once refused to possess a name you could vocalize at all—died suddenly and *Lemonade* arrived, in part mirroring Prince's art of reinvention, Beyoncé had outpaced most others in her merging of Southern cultural roots, the gothic and pastoral, the personal and performative, the pain in your own house mirroring the pain in your world at large, and how you rebuild yourself to walk through fire, to be a phoenix on the other side.

•◦● ◦ ●◦●◦● ◦ ●◦●◦● ◦ ●◦●◦● •

I gave in to my daughter's request for an eponymous poem, but where would a poem like this begin? First, I thought much about what could have been the literal meaning of her name. (I tried to pin it down to one culture or root, but haven't found anything near it yet.) I thought instead of how she embodied her name, what she'd made it mean for me and others around her.

When writing, I engage in much research. I follow whatever maze my mind designs, turning from one idea to another. While on the journey to this piece about my daughter, I studied (in no particular order): bridges, chapels, the etymology of the word *teenager*, the origins of her birth parents' names, hatchlings, outer space, and a jumble of other phenomena. This research is coupled with the things I read or reread that somehow shifted what I envisioned: Toni Morrison's *A Mercy*, various books of the Bible, an essay by Chimamanda Ngozi Adichie from *Elle* magazine titled "Why Can't a Smart Woman Love Fashion?," several entries in the *Oxford English Dictionary* online, a poem called "Verge" by Mark Doty, and a *Science Daily* article titled "Two Planets Suffer Violent Collision." All of these forces worked to help mold my fragmented thoughts into one expansive idea—a stretched-out, zigzagging definition that is completely made up but based in many different kinds of truths.

•◦● ◦ ●◦●◦● ◦ ●◦●◦● ◦ ●◦●◦● •

At Sonsoréa's slumber party, we pumped Beyoncé loud enough for the neighbors to call, believing no parents were home. Sonsoréa and friends—Brezhanay, Jakara, Keziah, and April—sang like they believed they were all things possible, were a gift I was given, and gave.

I am a girl too, they are women too, and we are all cut from the same sparkling cloth as Beyoncé—fleet-footed, raucous, and wondrous.

My daughter and I had the same problem: we never had and never will find our names on those mugs they sell at airports or in trinket shops. Our names were created out of thin air just like us. This can initiate a kind of fascination and longing for the bearer of such a name. Hence, she was always writing her name on book covers and notepads, practicing her autograph. She was particularly impressed by the scope and flourishes of her capital *S*, which was most likely why her poem ended up looking something like a series of swirling *S*'s moving down the page, form following function, I guess.

As is usually the case for me, the poem's shape bloomed out of its content. I tried it in couplets, tercets, then finally double-spaced in labyrinthine arcs. I liked that the physiognomy of the poem echoed Sonsoréa but allowed room for my ideas about how she (and all children) are jagged, shimmying things—difficult to follow and lead, curved into our beds or secluded in their dark rooms, as far away from our reach as they can manage, trying to figure out who they are or capture what they most desire.

⋅•❀ ❀ ❀❀❀ ❀ ❀❀❀ ❀ ❀❀❀ ⋅

Revising the poem, I watched Hortense Spillers's lectures on YouTube, trying to augment what I knew of building family and intimacy. I glanced down at the comments as Spillers talked about the troubled paradox of touch or intimacy in Black living and saw one comment with a woman's name and image next to it that read *Please, get over it. Past is the past.* I wondered: what privilege is this? Is someone hiding behind a stolen face on the screen, or what woman in any world has the luxury of imagining every woman's body, in this or any time, is hers and hers alone?

If you are Black in this life, race informs everything. I frequently dream about being in paradise a few lifetimes from now where I'll explain this to the newly living and how bizarre they'll find it that all these generations, in every place we inhabited, had this obsession with skin/gender/color/names. *But why was it important?* they'll ask again and again. Those of us who lived through it will have to try to deconstruct history without making ourselves culpable or diminished.

While working on my daughter's poem, I was also studying Forrest Hamer. In each of his books, *Call & Response, Middle Ear,* and *Rift,* much like in life, race is a change agent that enters and often consumes. In Hamer's poem "Edge," the speaker and the landscape, even the onlookers, are changed by experience, fragmented by time. The speaker's mother, passed on into another life, recounts the painlessness to her daughter, then there is a flashback to bygone days: a homecoming parade. The Supremes are blaring and the speaker dreams it is the end and beginning of life as they know it. But an all-white cemetery looms across the street, so does the absence of people the speaker loved—his mother, the daughter, the eventual self—mean they weren't there, the joy never all-encompassing and everywhere?

What edge is this? The edge of innocence, of a life just before it ends? The edge of a street, a cemetery, the changing times? Is it nearer the edge of a sharpened knife, or more like the corner of a dresser protruding, or maybe the edge of the world as some of us know it? Hamer leaps and shifts, through hindsight, as the speaker finds himself marked by what he cannot know or name. This mother, who was and is no longer but is still in rumination, the joy that was a passing parade covering over hopelessness, the dire times and those who couldn't transcend them: all edges of what remains. Reading "Edge" underlined what a privilege it was to be a dark woman mother poet, in this day and space and time, to be able to sit with wonder and gaiety, then try to capture those moments as they are.

•ₒ♦ ♦ ♦ₒ♦ₒ♦ ₒ ♦ₒ♦ₒ♦ ₒ ♦ₒ♦ₒ♦ •

One season my brother-in-law and our kids were obsessed with getting us ready for the zombie apocalypse. I told them if the zombies were coming, I hoped they were the fast-paced haints from Michael Jackson's "Thriller" and I would be saved by my love of the lock and drop two-step. But I think what they were trying to assert was that we needed to be adaptable, that we had to know how to save ourselves.

If you are like Michael Jackson or Beyoncé, you have to command zombies with your voice, but mostly with high-kicks, so the kids and I practiced this religiously. We sang to the ceiling and danced wild daily. Call it what you will, in reluctance or prudishness, but a precision dirty wind can be a kind of brilliant command and act of resilience—deafening and disarming all at the same time.

•ₒ♦ ♦ ♦ₒ♦ₒ♦ ₒ ♦ₒ♦ₒ♦ ₒ ♦ₒ♦ₒ♦ •

While the children were preparing us for the apocalypse, I stumbled upon an article from the *New York Times* titled "A Zombie Is a Slave Forever," accentuating that race is an underpinning of almost everything in the culture. An offspring of the brutal French-ruled slave trade in Haiti, zombies emerged as a mélange of African religious belief and the fear that even death wouldn't let one be free. Home meant a paradise like Africa, meant heaven. The enslaved wouldn't reach it if they took their own lives, just writhe in a kind of undead limbo, re-mastered, cursed under the thumb of another.

I think about acceptance—the only thing most of us really desire—and what that means for young people, like my daughter, what it meant for a young person like me, who also had brown skin and an untraceable name. When Sonsoréa was young, after she'd introduce herself, rather than take the few necessary seconds to practice the pronunciation of her name, people would ask her, "And what do you like to be called?" She was a bit reticent to say what I did in a heartbeat: "She likes to be called *her name.*"

We're very different. She is much like her father—reserved, observant. I am outspoken, strident, and sometimes unforgiving. I was especially protective of her because of this difference, but mostly I noticed she didn't need my protection as much as she needed to know why I thought it was important to speak up for oneself, to have people hear you (how else will people learn to respect, remember, and care for your well-being?), and how that can spill over into every aspect of your life.

When Beyoncé was receiving the MTV Video Vanguard Award, I stayed up late to watch the performance once as it aired, then in the rebroadcast right after. This was no small feat for me, as I have never been a night owl, but the performance was electric, and I had to see our girl bear it out again in her mosaic bodysuit and sparkling Spanx. What impressed me the most was that she managed to fit every song from her surprise *Beyoncé* album, in snippets or undertone, into the sixteen-minute performance. She was the Black Madonna and street hustler, a mother and tease, but in the morning all my colleagues would only go back to the word "FEMINIST" emblazoned behind her as she stood atop a moving walkway and stared the ungodly down. Most of the intellectual set at the predominantly white institution where I work were enraged, but the few women of color I found scattered across the Department of Women's Studies, the Women's Center, the Office of Equity, Diversity and Inclusion were as hyped as I was about a Black woman coming into herself and bringing the feminists along to boot.

The term is not one I use; "womanist" is a better descriptor for my aesthetic, but since Beyoncé made it one of the largest parts of her performance, I got to hash out its fraught record and usefulness to my daughter, and I was overjoyed about this. I imagined young Black girls all over the world hearing something different than the intellectual set—this wasn't a pop queen playing at politics, for us it was a Black woman deciding she could claim whatever she needed to further design herself, to be woke, in control of her body, *and* revolutionary.

Were my colleagues and I hearing the same music, I wondered, the same musings? I flashed back to Hamer who, when I asked about awareness and human psychosis, explained that "entire realities become constructed inside people's minds" to the point that the "fantasies about who one is and who the other is" skew what we see, perhaps how we shape our own lives.

I am a bit mystified about the blowback (but shouldn't be, as history has taught us people will look for ways to discredit any Black woman with a little influence or power), but isn't this dynamic fullness, this free will, this freedom what we all want for ourselves, our daughters?

·•● ● ●•●● ● ●•●● ● ●•●● ·

The long and short of it is, I was new to parenting, so I was still breaking my neck to win my kids over and make them happy. This new life was blissful but strange. All along I'd written to question things, but love needs no explanation; I understand it as bursts of things I want in unending supply. I'd been writing about my husband and children because they'd become mostly all I saw and lived and did. I was fascinated by how, in such a short while, my family had become this intimate micro-cosm covering everything larger than itself. Poems like Sonsoréa's weren't about the things that haunted me; they functioned more as adulation, as acute love and listening, and aren't praise, homage, and joy worthy musings?

＊● ● ♦ ●ᴀ● ● ♦ ●ᴀ● ● ♦ ●ᴀ● ·

When crafting my name, my parents weren't trying to plant the flag for cultural diversity nor were they concerned with whether my name might make others uncomfortable, and I don't think Sonsoréa's mom was either, but this, too, is part of that collective struggle we were thrust into. Beyoncé is a family name, a ritual her mother wanted her firstborn to sustain. All our parents were trying to lay claim to what was and always would be theirs, which is what Black folks have in common in this country: an un-derlying longing for what is solely their own. Fortunately, we are past the time when children were sold off in daylight on auction blocks, but those wounds and others are ingrained in all (Black, white, red, yellow, purple, chartreuse, *all*) our psychic energies. That we are here is mostly miracu-lous, as is the fact that we help others and language come into being.

As much of Hamer's work has the tinge of the spiritual, I asked him about his poems in Kevin Simmonds's anthology *Collective Brightness: LGBTIQ Poets on Faith, Religion & Spirituality* and how reverence served as an impetus for his work. He said: "What I came to appreciate, and still do now, is how as humans we strive to articulate something of the awe we experience when we recognize the depth and breadth of ex-istence over time." He went on: "I think this address of that awe—and to it!—is inherent to the process of making, and I delight in how poetry offers me one of the most profound dwellings wherein to engage my awe of being alive as this one version of life I happen to be."

Part of naming is amazement and articulation, recognizing the won-der and seriousness of ushering another in. Naming is a way to honor this life, this particular elation, as is addressing the minutia of our whole human, complex selves in poetry.

In what some called "post-racial" America, my husband and I shared with our children the importance of stepping into their brimming selves, adding to what Hamer called "the mind we all share" by ensuring others saw them in their full light, learned their idiosyncrasies, how to pronounce their given names. We asked them: what does the silence take from us, what does it take from others? And what does disinterest in, even hatred or fear of self, keep us from examining or discovering? These are complex but vital lessons. This grappling led to what became a poem about my daughter's name, about us and our growing together. I hoped that, reading it in the distant future, she'd know the labor and joy all this brought to my life, but also that the road to a poem is a long, winding one, and how I'd learned the road to parenthood is often the same.

SON·SOR·ÉA (\SAHN-SOAR-RAY\)
Luminary of questions
formed from dust and inexperience.
Daughter of Sonia and Michael
who now, by fate, has come to me.
Reluctant bridge bearing the weight
of her untraceable name.

How could we have known
which planets would collide
and give rise to one who'd stray
the paths of our roaming,
boundless, growing wild, demanding
an answer for what's always asked.

Everyone wants to know how
to pronounce it, what it means.
It begins like a song we keep trying to sing
then ends in beckoning, like most things
we dream but can't pin down.
Code for *angle-voiced taunter of brother,*

laundry avoider, lover of saccharine and sleep,
synonym for teenager,
derivative of *in medias res*—
molding clay or cloudy mirror—
bird in want of nest and air.

It could mean *ray of the sun* in some native tongue,
what we've held thus far,
but more likely is   *young heart that yearns toward you,*
boyish, uncertain, like the myriad of us
given time to learn what we love.

We are tied together like this
in odd and fortunate symmetry:
our names invented, infinite
like the journey entire.
And what passage doesn't teach
each of us, stitched like a jagged seam—

and couldn't that be what it means: *all we haven't lost*
or broken, the possible gained?—

then, no matter how we arrive,
by what force or where or when,
who wouldn't remember
it was always beautiful?

When I asked poet Erica Hunt about innovation and writing to escape what others have made for you, she said: "You can't even think outside of what you don't have a word for. If you don't have the word for it, can you think about it? You're trying to language your experience all the time."

Sonsoréa and I have been given a word for our names. We've been invented in language, in intimacy, and have invented what will be.

In our interview, Hamer insisted that we can desire many things from invention: "[T]here are still other times when I want a poem to teach me something I don't yet know about my life in the future and my life in the past." This is also what I hoped my poem would teach my daughter: who we thought she was in those tender years, how she could make and unmake her becoming, who she still might be.

My daughter is grown now and has a son of her own. For a long time, she labored over what she'd call him and came to Naveen, meaning pleasant beginnings, or bright, or prince, depending on whom you ask. She knows now what I know, what the poets and entertainers and children have helped teach me. So I was not surprised when poet Mahogany L. Browne tweeted exactly what I want for my daughter, for us all: "I wish you the satisfaction of your name being spelled right, pronounced correctly, & remembered lovingly."

We are given names, given language, then reinvent what the world might know of us, what we might become. We decide what the language means, how we might be bodied in ourselves, how we'll be foreign in the mouths of others until we define our living, decide how to be free.

BINGHAM-RISHER: Do you remember your first encounter with poetry?

HAMER: I would guess it happened as my body responded to my mother's heartbeat, to lullabies or the Bible stories I heard each night before sleep, or to my grandfather's singing.

Erica Hunt

WHO RAISED YOU?

I had to invent this lineage,
or whatever I feel was lineage.

—ERICA HUNT

My earliest memory is of my mother holding me in her arms, pointing up at the stars. She was explaining God and even now doesn't understand how I can know this. She claims I describe it perfectly, but I was only eighteen months old at the time, so it's nearly impossible that I'd remember. And yet, I can't forget it.

I was in pale pink footie pajamas. We were on an American army base in Karlsruhe, Germany, where my father was stationed, and the cold had set in. But the nights were clear, so she began at the beginning, walking me under the wonder after dark and telling me who made the pinpricks of light, the snow, our hair, our eyes, maybe not the swing set in the nearby field, but the hands that fashioned it, and the hands that carried me.

I'm the only thing my mother ever made. I come to this realization when I have my own children and she has chastised me again for not calling each day. I'm sure my mother never thought that after she'd reached sixty, the tables would turn and she'd be running after me. I am wary of the phone—maybe it was all those years in the '90s when I spent countless hours with the receiver glued to my ear. Now, when I head home after the day's never-ending yammer, I just want peace. I understand that this, too, is a ridiculous longing because I live with a teenager who sings loudly enough to drown out the music Alexa sends blasting into our bathroom almost constantly. So by peace, I can't mean quiet, just a bit of time to and for myself.

My mother brought an only child into the world and suffers the consequences. Who knew as I approached forty I'd be so desperate for every piece of myself I could strangle away from others. I want to spend my whole life being a good daughter, as she has spent most of her life being a wonderful mother. But she's taught me to live how I want to live, so I call less and take the chiding when she scolds me about spending all my time with another.

• • • • • • • • •

For a keynote address, I was asked to answer this impossible question: Which of my identities—womanhood, motherhood, or race—affected my work the most? At the same time, I was preparing for an interview with Erica Hunt, studying her trajectory while wrestling with what shaped my own. I'd been hoping to sit with Hunt since Cave Canem, as during the workshops there, she was a real bulwark to me.

At the retreat, most fellows were scared out of our minds because the teachers were the "cream of the crop." People we'd only fantasized about being in the vicinity of were going to sit in a room, look at a new poem we'd written the night before, and—we assumed—tear it to bits. Erica Hunt especially intimidated some of us because she's considered a "language poet," one who veers away from the short-form narrative most of us were writing and more toward the lyric. Her writing is often abstract, a patchwork of images and ideas, an assemblage of fragments, like mothering, like most of our living.

We were afraid Hunt would hate our work, think it boring, without nuance, straitlaced. We thought she might eviscerate us in front of our peers, or let our peers nitpick our living to death, as had been the case in most of the workshops we'd attended before. Hunt and I discussed this during our interview and she commiserated: "I had some terrible workshops where I was sort of made to feel like my experience was shocking, or not poetic. And again, this had to do with the racial composition of the class." Being a poet of color, often the writing workshop is a difficult experience; craft is rarely the concern. For many, myself included, being misunderstood culturally and socially was the bent of any workshop.

But like my fellow participants, I was soon disabused of this notion entering the space with Hunt. I brought in a poem called "The Lost Gospel of Peter" for critique, all narrative vignettes about Peter giving his own account of walking alongside a pitiless Messiah. Not only did Hunt encourage constructive criticism of the work and the work only (not of our experiences, cultural or otherwise, that might have brought us to it), but she also carried a copy of my poem to other faculty, up and down the halls, showing it off in unabashed praise. She did this for other poets too.

I remember that being one of those moments when I felt like I could walk this path, could make myself into what I hoped to become, especially since I deemed our aesthetics to be very different. I asked Hunt why, as praise is rarely a part of any workshop or writing program, she made it a part of hers? She told me: "You know, when you wrote to me about that experience, it made me more conscious of my workshop practice. It made me conscious of two things. First, that experience you described reminded me of how discouragingly routine it was to be a Black person in a white workshop and realize the other students are often clueless about certain lived experiences or the poem's system of association—and how often the white students were either blank or incurious or a little bit shocked, even if the poem was to me ordinary, just not that strange. The feedback was either patronizing or not useful. I thought, 'They're not getting this; I'm not fitting in here.'

"The other thing is, yeah, I'm not interested in leading a workshop to reproduce me," she continued, "I'm using the workshop to actually understand what this person is trying to achieve in their poem and help that become their best poem." That poem, "The Lost Gospel of Peter," became an anchor, the final one in my first book, after having her eye on it. Also, that experience helped a lot of us who are now teaching to think about how we can be a bridge for our students. I've talked about this with other poets who were there, and we specifically go back to that moment when we were sitting in Hunt's workshop and were taken up by her encouragement. We learned we're not there to break or bruise anyone, and we don't have to build them in our image. Our job is to help them grow what's already taking root.

·•● ● ●●●● ● ●●●● ● ●●●● ·

Even when we were entering erratic, difficult phases in our lives, my mother read books. I could count on them being on the nightstand in her bedroom, on the schrank we'd gotten while we were in Germany meant for gold-trimmed china and other precious things, piled on shelves under the TV—almost anywhere I looked.

I don't remember a time she didn't read to me; I had my own little library by three years old. She sparked and fed my obsession for books and never faulted me for forgoing cookouts and gatherings to stay curled in some corner with a book in hand.

We had different tastes—she loved Danielle Steel and V. C. Andrews, almost any romance, any mystery, but love for me was seeing a Black girl on the cover. If I wasn't sure by the image on the front, I'd turn to the author photo on the back or inside flap, and seeing a Black woman there would shock and delight me. *It can be done!* I'd think. *That can be me.*

When I stumbled upon books like Terry McMillan's *Waiting to Exhale* or Toni Morrison's *Paradise* in my mother's collection, I was more than intrigued, if not in over my head as I snuck in to read those books when I was too young for the rowdy relationships, murderous families, white folks acting vicious, or whatever adult things she'd tried to shield me from.

Reading Margaret Wilkerson Sexton's *A Kind of Freedom,* I think of my mother. The year is 1986 in the novel and in my memory. My mother is almost thirty years old. Like Jackie, one of the novel's characters, my mother will suddenly find herself raising a child alone, after the perfect, upwardly mobile, doting man she married is swept up in the cocaine epidemic and begins losing everything. My mother took a series of jobs—the last I remember was Toys "R" Us, a place I loved because children of the associates got to choose items from the scratch and dent bin behind the Employees Only doors. It was there I found my Mother Goose, an animatronic, lullaby-singing storyteller; my first purse with a zipper and purple shoulder strap; and a host of other treasures.

My mother was always tired driving home in her red and white striped uniform, but she still read to me in it as we huddled in her bed. Soon we lost the brick house on Dahlia Drive, a long road in Augusta, Georgia, where my father had been stationed after Germany, the neighborhood perched between the Piggly Wiggly and my first school. It was in a new development with people who became friends, waved at us as we passed, and watched me from time to time when my mother had to run to the store.

After the loss, I remember making our way across the country with my aunt, her sister, who said, "You're so small," to my mother before saying hello when she came to drive us to our new life in Arizona. She meant, *you're tinier than you've ever been, you're wasting away, you're barely there.* When we left, the stars were as bright as streetlamps. No one came out to comfort us. We said nothing, leaving what was lost behind, locking the door for the last time.

·•● ● ●●●● ● ●●●● ● ●●●● ·

Reading Erica Hunt's work generates more questions than answers, and isn't this the goal of most artists? Her exploration of the avant-garde begs the question: as Black women poets, what are we allowed to be? Hunt's poems are an unconventional take on travelling toward home, as when she does (seemingly) turn to the personal, she does so with a careful distance.

While reading Hunt's chapbook *Time Slips Right Before Your Eyes*, I began linking my personal experiences to the poems therein as a means of surrendering to the text. In the poem, "Chapter 2: Back-Home," Hunt continues an unfinished story, putting me in the mind of parts of my own. The matriarch narrator is tunneling into memory but begins revealing (family?) secrets, stories she lets slip by mistake. In the past, it seemed, she had been able to keep her anger at bay, but due to time or dementia or intention (the reader has to assume or infer this), her stories have become undisciplined, uncouth. In other words: she is putting folks' business in the street.

When my grandmother began what would be the last decade of her life, her stories changed significantly. I was given glimpses of the past that had often unwelcome addendums: the girls she knew who were taken advantage of, the time she spent "up Petersburg" (code for a "colored" mental institution in her then-new homeplace, Virginia), the truth about children we all thought we knew to be blood. So much of her decorum and tact, an intricately woven set of untruths, went with age.

The truth came, ugly as it was, sparking new narratives of home for all of us. What happens to what you believe you know for sure when your mother, your mother's mother, your guides, your lineage, your path are riddled with holes? Does it unmake you? Do you piece together whatever you can, however you can, to make yourself whole?

⋅● ● ●●●● ● ●●●● ● ●●●● ⋅

It could be because I am an artist, but I daydream about how people will remember me. I've helped raise many children—my godson Rashad, my cousins Jasmin and Nicole, my brother-in-law Johnathan, my daughter and son. I think about how I speak to the children I'm housing or how I act when I'm upset about some trivial thing. I ask myself, *What have I done today that these children will be on the couch about in the future? What will the therapist I pray they have say about the kind of model I've been?*

During my time with Erica Hunt, we talked about her book *Arcade*, which, for me, reads differently from her earlier work because she understood the weight of having other people to take care of by the time she wrote it. *Arcade* is a collaboration with visual artist Alison Saar—"how you get multiple voices within the work," Hunt pointed out. The cover ("the woman whose body is a map," Hunt called it) influenced the poems and vice versa.

I went back to poems like "Coronary Artist 1" and "Biographical Suite" and asked if she thought that book was about shifting responsibilities. She was well into the thick of her life; her daughter was already six or seven when her first book, *Local History*, was released. Was *Arcade* a book about growing up and into? She said: "My son had come along, that's one thing. I think 'Coronary Artist' is, in a funny way, about mothering. It's that artist of the heart, so I called her Coronary." She continued: "I was feeling very full, and in some ways, a little uncertain about what to do here. I think I was about forty and thinking of what to do next."

I had *Arcade* sitting on my kitchen table and my son said, "That woman's all cut open!" I explained that the poems are about a woman coming into motherhood, adulthood, caring for others, so she's carrying different things. By the end of our conversation, he said, "That's brilliant!" and he was only nine. I told Hunt the story and she shared a warning: "I often have to remind my kids that it's sometimes not just the physical world tasks that absorb energy, it's your emotional work that fills you up and takes up bandwidth. How much can you take in?"

Reading Sharon Olds's poem "The Green Shirt," I am prodded about the fear of every parent: that we will break what was given us. What was handed to us empty, unsullied, will become overfull, irreversibly soiled. In the poem, the speaker's son has broken his elbow. The joint bruises and turns into a twisted remnant of itself, as does the boy sulking around the house in the same green shirt for a week, scared to remove the sling holding the damaged limb in place. The parents fear they've stunted his dexterity and potential ("and they said he would probably sometime be back to normal / sometime, probably, this boy with the long fingers of a surgeon . . . he was given to us perfect, we had sworn no harm"). I've read "The Green Shirt" countless times, and each time I come to the lines quoted above, I think of a Scripture at Zephaniah 2:3: "Seek Jehovah. . . . Seek righteousness, seek meekness. Probably you may be concealed in the day of [his] anger." Probably, maybe. Keep working at good and maybe you'll get it right. Maybe you won't ruin them. Probably, if you try not to hurt them, they'll remember you for good. Maybe you'll save them and yourself in the trying.

⁂

I am supposed to be in the office hashing out my keynote address but instead find myself enraptured by *The Light of the World*, Elizabeth Alexander's memoir about losing her husband, artist Ficre Ghebreyesus, to cardiac arrest four days after his fiftieth birthday. The morning after the book has arrived, my car sputters a bit, and I call in to work because the car is a good enough excuse for me to stay home and sit with this difficult beauty until I am spent through. Every fifty pages or so, I have to stop to be broken open. I weep so violently sitting in the car on this spring day split between sun and crisp wind that I move to different locations—my driveway, a coffeehouse, a nearby park—every hour or so, for fear someone might notice me and call for help. I can hear it now: *There's this woman on the street with her windows up and her car running. She's crying. I can definitely see her crying. She keeps looking down, I don't know what she might do.* And I cannot explain myself to the police if my grief has made me suspicious. I will only make the suspicion worse, I think. I am not dangerous, not wholly wrecked or reckless, but who can tell why we might put anyone in danger?

I turn on the radio about once an hour to make sure the world isn't falling apart while I'm falling apart and find *With Good Reason* coming across the airwaves. And I swear, the show, for no reason I can tie down, is about Lucille Clifton, my teacher, Alexander's elder poet whose name means *light*. I am listening to Clifton talk about Fred, her husband who also died early, then find myself driving to a Jamaican restaurant my husband loves. I buy us lunch and end up at the parking lot of his office. I know he is alright, I am not frightened he isn't alright any more than I am when he's not with me, but I don't want to be without him while there's so much grief in the air.

I am always scared to lose him after having just found him again, or him finding me. This makes me seem ridiculous in the wake of others. Lucille and Fred were married for thirty years and had six children; Elizabeth and Ficre, sixteen years and two boys. We have only five years and children I didn't birth, so I am the chaff in their lives. I am a wife and stepmother and those things stand in the gap of loneliness, sometimes for good, sometimes for bad. This is not self-pity but a reality for me, another odd burden. A colleague from an old job remarried, inherited sons and daughters, and I remember her calling them "the boneless children." Not from her body, not of her bones. This means that if my husband dies, my children will go, most likely returned to their rightful owner, and I would have to grieve twice or double, concurrent or one after another after another. This is another kind of knowledge, a blinding, humbling light. To know what we have is impermanent, it could go with the wind at any moment, as could they.

⋅⋅●⋅●⋅●⋅●⋅⋅●⋅●⋅⋅●⋅●⋅

During our interview, Hunt and I talk at length about improvisation. She has just the night before gone to a Jay Wright reading, which she spoke about like a religious experience, calling it "a revelation." ("I had had such a bad day Thursday. By the end of the day, after seeing this reading, I was like *Hallelujah!*") I told her I could spend the rest of my life reading Wright's book *Transfigurations*—it's like Marquez, or the Bible; it keeps opening itself up. She went on to explain how in his hour-long set, Wright shape-shifted—had no pattern, spoke three different languages, dipped in and out of the lyric "I," Egyptology, ornithology, threw in a coda, then sang. This made me think about how her work is often without a clear throughline but makes headway into the serpentine lines of communication, how we exchange histories, where we are headed.

Hunt explained how she took the collage of Wright's words in: "[A]ll I would do is select out the lines. I had to adjust my hearing to what I could notice. It's like picking out the color red in a painting. Or the red in your bookcase. Red here, red here, red here . . . and then to adjust to what he was doing, not a preconception." If she'd been working so hard to try to force a narrative, I said, think about how much she would have missed. She was so animated describing Wright's prowess, and I was excited because, while she was glorying in Wright's meandering, she was really explaining her life's work on the page to me. As she spoke, the light bulb went on. Every night I was reading her poems, highlighting lines, underlining in blue ink the things that really astonished me. Once I turned to my husband in bed and said, "Every line could be an epigraph!" Each held its own weight, or slick rediscovery, some disruption of a phrase or repurposing of a word. And each weighted line had its own trajectory in a poem, then taken together, the poems created a mishmash of life's questioning.

"And that's actually, if anything, a method," Hunt said about Wright and herself, when I point out their similarity. "It is a kind of collaging. And the collage, the chunks, the patches, last a line or sometimes six lines when you get into a story, because you know [Wright] gets you going, and it's the same thing with me—six lines, and then it jumps again. The collage. He does it, and I was particularly impressed, I'm harking back here, but I was impressed with the materials of it. The materials are like, as I said, Egypt, Yoruba, some Aztec stuff as far as I could tell, Robert Hayden. Probably more if you dig."

Wright is building a patchwork of archipelagos, as is Hunt, but she is also layering a radical examination of womanhood near each shore. In her poem "A Coronary Artist" she says: "Custom has it that a woman gets up first to solve the dilemma of / the burning moment." It is the thing that tethers and binds me to her work, as it is the thing about which I have the most to learn. These multilayered complications (i.e., mothering, separating one's self from motherhood, writing in spite of or through it) that are part of Hunt's "oppositional poetics," innovative railing against narrow perspectives, are also part of my remaking. I am relearning myself, wondering if one existence (Blackness, womanhood, artistry) defeats any other?

⁕ ⁕ ⁕

One night, all night, I dream of nursing twins. They are so new, they feel like nothing in my arms, almost weightless. Deep brown like my husband and me with crowns of black, silky almost-curls beneath soft cotton hats. I take turns putting them to each breast to quiet them, until I wake and am childless again.

Childlessness, like singleness, is a slippery word. Everyone's definition of singleness is defined by their own terms, sometimes in the moment, unbeknownst to anyone on the other side of the equation. If my definition of single is *not being married*, then if I have been living with the same person for fifteen years but we haven't taken vows, I can in good conscience tell someone I'm single. If my definition of single is *being married to someone I love*, then if I am married but I have fallen out of love with the person, I can in good conscience claim to be single. Given context, most listeners would object to my singleness in both situations, but singleness, like motherhood, is malleable and can be riddled with holes, as it is made in our own hands.

I have never birthed a child, but I am raising a son. He has become twelve overnight and I've been raising him for seven years. When I was married, he was part of a sweet package deal. I loved him from the second I met him, though, depending on the terms, this doesn't make me his mother. He calls me Mom half the time, the other half he just calls me my first name. I clean his room, I learn new math he has forgotten, I talk in detail to the doctor about his sleeping habits, growth rate, and his ravenous eating of late. If anything keeps me up at night, it is usually "worry from the boy," as my husband puts it, which is mostly worry from the world housing a growing Black boy and everyone out of our purview maybe misunderstanding his antics. But this being consumed by daily fear and love and knowledge of him, depending on who's defining it, still doesn't make me a mother. Perhaps this is why I dream of children.

∙•●●●●●●∙∙●●●∙∙●●●∙

My son has been carting my book *Starlight & Error* to school each day since it was released. I think he fancies himself a little famous, though he won't say as much. Each day when we empty his book bag, it tumbles out, a little more worn for the wear, among his half-pencils, crumpled homework sheets, tangerine peels, and other unknowable things. We are on our way to Bible study one night when he asks me about a poem called "Our child is not yet ten and we are clearing his closet." "This is about me, right?" he inquires, and I say yes. "But what does it mean?"

The poem is a litany, a list, it's an exercise I give my students, one long rant held together by the title and, in this case, racial and family chronicles. "Bring your book," I say, meaning bring your beat-up copy of my book, as we head for the door. It is summer and there is plenty of evening light to read by. "Read it to me," I say as I drive. He sits in the back seat diagonal to me and I can look into the rearview and watch him take the words line by line. He is a wonder—he pauses at each em dash, pronounces almost every word right, and waits for me to interject if he wants something clarified. We don't read poems in the house very much; every once in a while, he is given poems at school. He doesn't especially love reading (he's told me this, so I won't push books on him as much as I might have—"Mom, reading is your thing, not mine," he said, when I got a bit too excited about a reading challenge over winter break a few months ago). But he reads the Bible aloud for our congregation, long winding genealogies and all, so I should be less surprised at his deft work with the poems. It is such a rarity to hear anyone read your own work aloud that I go on giving brief explanations between each poem and tell him, "Read another," for the whole ride.

He has read ten or so poems—a few about himself, one about his sister, one about his dad and some others with titles from musicians he knows. And unlike other times I've been given a gift, it doesn't seem to fly by. All the lights turned red just as we approached them; the traffic was slow but not altogether stopped—a perfect ride. When I pull into the parking lot, I tell him what I'm feeling: "That was one of the best moments of my whole life, you giving my words back to me," and he blushes a little as he unhooks his seat belt and scurries ahead of me.

Hearing a child full of skepticism and wonder step into my longing one word at a time, ask, "But why did you say it like that?," then letting me explain metaphors is something I never dreamed. His pursed lips signal *Okay, I get it*, or a vigorous nod with high eyebrows means I've done or said something better than he expects. What artist doesn't jump at the chance to tell someone, anyone, about all those hours of labor, about what brought you here, about care and the point of the line. What mother doesn't want this, what daughter, what lover, what every person doesn't hope someone, anyone—when they've tried to color in their hopes and difficulties—will say, *Tell me everything*, then, *I think you did it right*.

• • • • • • • •

My students were the children I tended for a long time, as I was teaching well before I was married. I taught an online course, African American Literature and Its Cultural Traditions, for the first time the winter the world came apart. I never saw most of my students face to face. I met a few who ventured into my office to learn about class technologies, rally for grade changes, or wax poetic about Black life if they were Black. I inundated them with work from Phillis Wheatley to Walter Mosley, and they had to study the country's racial history as well as its literary one. I assigned *Ethnic Notions*, the documentary about racial stereotypes, and connected the dots between it, Jim Crow, and Obama's America. In their closing reflections, most were shocked to find how little they knew about the world they lived in and how it got this way. They were already working on their exams when my friend was killed by police and the last correspondence they received from me was a final grade. This is not my usual style. In most courses I ended with Derek Walcott's poem "Love After Love" and Lucille Clifton's "won't you celebrate with me," but I couldn't bring myself to a hopeful farewell. Though I knew they were on break and had already begun to forget what they'd been made aware of, I thought about writing them a note to explain my abrupt silence. If I had written that last note to my students, it would have gone something like this:

Dec. 15, 2014

Dear Radiant Minds:

Just a short note of farewell and a little context for some of the things, I hope, we'll all continue learning. The last entry you added to our class timeline was about Trayvon Martin; it could have easily been about Mike Brown, Eric Garner, or one of my dearest friends, Rumain Brisbon, who was unarmed, killed by police in Phoenix on December 2nd, and who has become the latest rallying cry in the protests still erupting as I type. I've learned much looking for ways to teach you from a distance this term, but I didn't imagine I'd be looking, in the end, back to the works I assigned for some understanding myself.

I hope that, if nothing else, you've learned two things in our class: 1.) that African American literature, music, and art can't ever be separated from the historical movements surrounding them, and 2.) that humanizing a people shouldn't be left to its artists, and shouldn't be a point of history or reflection. Instead, we should work to make that true without intense scrutiny and examination: human is human, just like struggle and fear and love are human, and it shouldn't take art to teach us that, though sometimes it still does.

What makes us mothers? What makes us the children of others? Are teachers stand-in mothers? Are students like our children, are poems? Attentiveness, deep consideration, thoughtfulness: each a different kind of love.

•ﾐ ● ﾐﾐﾐ ● ﾐﾐﾐ ● ﾐﾐﾐ •

When discussing Wright's massive scope with Hunt, what I would call research she calls his "materials for building." I asked about her own materials, and she cited photos and music, but mostly what *isn't* collected: "I'm also interested in the silences," she said. "Sometimes an article out of the newspaper or a news story that I hear." Then she turned to her own crafting: "There's a poem I'm writing now, it's a long poem. You know, it's about the world we're in right now, about me as a mother. It's called 'Veronica.' She's my double. She talks about her son, I talk to her about my son, about our sons, and daughters. Trying to really come to grips with the world as it is, and the world as we'd like it to be. And the poem as a critique of this world that we're given. And then how do we reconstruct it?" She went on: "Jay Wright was really helpful. He reminded me again of how, I believe it is Ra, who dies and is dismembered and goes into the Nile. And then Isis comes and re-members him, re-constructs him. I think that's going to be very important to understand how to envision a world where we are not in the grip of death cults, that really mean to harm us and harm our children."

I am at a gas station near home and I know something is wrong the moment I slip out of the driver's seat. A few boys—teenagers maybe one or two years older than my son—look around wildly, enter the store, leave it, then circle a car in the parking lot. By the time I return the nozzle to its holder, the boys are bolting toward the surrounding neighborhood, and a cop comes out of thin air it seems, screaming into his radio that he is in pursuit. There are other Black folks scattered about and we all make frenzied eye contact before buckling into our seats. As I drive in the direction they ran, I am quiet and frantic. I am so scared for the boys running for who knows what.

We are all complicit in Gwendolyn Brooks's poem "The Boy Died in My Alley." I recall it, watching the boys disappear into the neighborhood with the police following. If they are harmed, the questions will be put before all of us, some of the same questions asked of the poem's speaker after a boy is shot and dies in the alley near her home—*Did you know him? Did you see anything out of the ordinary?* And what can we say to this? Brooks does not know him but has watched the violence mount, the motherless and fatherless grow in her city and she does little to extend a hand. The truth of the matter is, often, as is the case with the boys in front of me with the police close on their heels, *I have seen the boy before, running into the street with no regard for cars and their jarring horns. He may have known my son, they rode the school bus together. He may have been with him.* Brooks, too, is tormented by her knowing, once the boy has been taken from the Earth but his body calls to her from the alley floor.

We warn our son not to run from the police—*They will shoot if you run and say they had a reason,* my husband and I explain. *Don't get into trouble. Don't do anything that could make you seem suspicious, wrecked, reckless.* But his skin makes him seem troublesome in this life. When I get a call from the school about some fleeting incident, I'm racked by the unforgivable and write:

THE PRINCIPAL CALLS AND I UNDERSTAND
I WILL BE HELD ACCOUNTABLE
Will mothers ever be anything other than tired?
Will I ever be a mother, other, not tired?

Will mother be tied to other forever?
Will ever be other and mothers be never?

Never tired, ever mother. Always other, only never.
I am ever other, ever mother, always tired, never done.

Only son, only daughter, always tied to forever.
I am an only daughter, I have an only son, we are ever other, one and one.

My mother is virtuous, self-reliant; a sounding board to all her sisters, nieces and nephews, and friends; a meticulous caregiver and saver. She worked hard to show she knew how deeply I was affected by and cherished words. She gave me hundreds, if not thousands, of greeting cards throughout life that I've saved. In a card she wrote me when I was seventeen, she said, "How many times have I told you that you make a mother's heart rejoice?"—a compliment, admonition, and unwitting burden mothers lay on us. (In another card given when I was twenty, she said, "You've turned out to be a fine young woman, which means all my guidance, discipline, and love paid off, just like I planned"—did I mention she was funny? Though maybe not as humble as she could have been when bragging about how well she shaped me). She was always concerned with who I was becoming. Most of her lessons revolved around being independent, seeking God, showing empathy. Maybe this was why, though we often had little money, she invested in books and me. Perhaps she saw, in my obsession with climbing into the worlds created by others, the intimate lesson I could glean: you can always make something for yourself, if you don't find standing at the ready all that you might need.

Hunt didn't quite fit in, in some spaces people dreamed for her: "I was both inspired by and also a little bit intimidated by [the Black Arts Movement]. It was very male. And I can remember thinking a little ferocious for me too. . . . I did spend some time in San Francisco with the Language Poets, from about 1976 to 1981. That's another place where I was drawn into conversations about the material aspects of language, the progression from imagism to the Objectivists, Modernism and Post-Modernism, and so forth. But I also kept saying, *It's not me completely either.*

"So while the Black Arts Movement fed me," she continued, "grounded me in adamantly oppositional skepticism, excited me through its liberatory goals, as a young Black woman, my very being knew more needed to be said, written, 'rehearsed' to make sayable and possible the 'impossibility' of me. I wanted to go for the full expression of me towards what, a North Star."

Hunt was asking what all artists, and mothers, and children, ask while cobbling their lives together, making it up as they go: What allows for the full expression of me? Which identity feels most like a warm and wanted skin?

After her self-exploration, Hunt's first book, *Local History*, was a long time coming. I was taken with a poem in it called "Second Voice," where the speaker asserts self-identity above all others. The poem ends with, "No / strings and anything might happen." So, I asked Hunt, what was she trying to escape? Was she trying to move out of formal verse, Modernism, this fixed legacy of other writers with that first book? And she explained: "Well, the strings are the puppet strings, right. So does language work you, or do you work the language?"

For Hunt, the larger question is about what the limitations of our language allow us: are we free if we don't have the language to free ourselves from any one identity? She said: "We let commercial language structure the ways in which we can even imagine ourselves being free, or what it would be to be an independent woman or man. A person of our own, pursuing art as Black people, pursuing my interests as a woman. We can't even think that way because we are confronted, shaped, and molded by the language that is handed to us. I'm always scratching my head about that."

Her work was labeled experimental in most circles, and she said her writing created its own lane because music was her biggest influence: "My sister is in college and she introduces me to John Coltrane. I became a very avid fan. . . . Other jazz musicians as well, other musicians coming out of the Black Arts Movement. So to me, that's actually the stronger influence, in some ways. It's a more direct influence on my writing, and my sense of freedom within the writing. Their sense of freedom and experimentation."

Improvisation is Hunt's aesthetic, like Coltrane or Byrd, and she also found writers who spoke to her imaginative sensibility.* "I got excited, I remember, early on by the hyperbolic, world-building poetry of Aimé Césaire. I must have been twenty, and I said, *Oh!* I was so very excited. I said, *Well, who is this?* This surrealist, this Martiniquan word-rivering surrealist. And Nicolás Guillén, the Cuban poet. And [Kamau] Brathwaite, and so on." Those poets spoke to her family's background, she'd explained earlier: "[M]y family is Caribbean. Second generation. My mother was born in Harlem, but her parents were born in Jamaica. They came in 1914, the beginning of World War One." So these poets speaking out of familiar cultural experiences expanded her materials and range. She continued: "[A]ll those things began to feed me in a different way. I could get out of the little trap of the United States canon. . . . Taking freely from every era, from every vocabulary, and from every culture and saying, *It's coming through me, and it's coming through an African-descended sensibility.* So it's coming through me and through my experience, and through the collective experience too. Then we're talking to each other and so forth, all of those things."

I asked, if she had to define the term *avant-garde*, what would it mean for her and her work? She wouldn't exactly tie it (or herself) down: "It's so tricky. I don't know if I use it strictly enough. But if I were to use it in a very strict way, it would be about artistic and writing practices, which stretch or somehow break through or interrupt predetermined boundaries. . . . It's almost a laboratory. . . . People have different ways about

---

*Improvisation is also about play, Hunt reminded me. There can be joy and humor embedded into deep digging and discovery. She said, "I'm trying to constantly coax new understanding and new meaning. Stuff that may have been given, and from more conventional and more typical observations. I love a pun. And I love trying to coax meaning out of old sayings. That's why I admire the brilliance of Harryette Mullen's poetry. She loves that too. Trying to coax new meaning, new resonance out of stuff that's been around, that you almost don't even notice it anymore, but how do you make it noticeable again?" This, too, led me back to what is possible on the page and in mothering. How do we step outside of our mothers to coax what's new out of what we've always known? Can we laugh and learn, can play be our method, or do we let ourselves be overreached by the thought of failing?

being innovative. I would hope that innovative writing is done by people who use a lot of tools from different tool kits. They have a tool kit they would bring from the avant-garde practice, maybe they bring it from folk culture or blues culture, or they bring it from their grandma's chest, but innovative would be fluid practice."

Mothering is fluid practice. Poeting is fluid practice. Sometimes, you are so small and the world is so big that you have to write your own history and hold onto it. In "A Coronary Artist," Hunt says: "One becomes an adult without / knowing the details of how it was done." Every time I put pen to page, I am hoping to save myself from forgetting, maybe save others the trouble of lying about what happened later. Worry haunts me now. With age comes responsibility and the assurance that people are nothing if not hungry and misguided. I'm writing for my children's sake more than for my own, just like my mother worked the night shift for many years mostly because I was born. Only grace lets poetry put food on a table, fill a classroom with unexpected fervor, or make us feel as useful as our mothers in our strained, imperfect art. This work lets me take back the dead and rile the living. It's what keeps many of us from shouting every minute of the day.

My mother read books, and in books, she came back to me. She reassembled on all those pages in ways that altered my understanding of mother-love, mother-wit, a woman's longing, the brilliance of the body and who I was becoming. Her tending was the yoke hung heavy about my shoulders, and the gift. My mother and books taught me that other Black women—friends, aunts, cousins, lovers—would be varied, have their own joy and pain, but could still carry me.

This is how I would begin my keynote address. Mostly, I spoke about trying to be as steadfast as my mother with a bit less of my will over my children than her will over me. I also work to send my students into the world with context and empathy. I am still trying to balance the identities

I contain—some I choose, some I inherit or am handed and told to handle gingerly.

I thread the myriads of me into the words I'll fashion; I'll reframe what isn't a clear throughline into a shimmying road. I'm a daughter, a teacher, now, a mother, eternally, a poet, the red unsown, a patchwork of students and mothers and children who raised me.

BINGHAM-RISHER: Were you trying
to move away from this fixed legacy
of other writers? Was improvising
language a kind of freedom?

HUNT: I have to say that I've always had
an interest in philosophy of language. . . .
And I always will play with that, it's
a constant. That is actually that thing
that drives, compels me, to say why I'm
interested in experimental or innovative
methods, because in a way I think we
need to *think* better. I think part of why
we are so un-free, and why we consent
to our lack of liberty is because we
haven't practiced being free enough.

Natasha Trethewey

THE TERROR OF
BEING DESTROYED

The thing that was important was the necessity of
remembering, of rescuing things from historical amnesia.
—NATASHA TRETHEWEY

In Toni Morrison's collection of essays *The Source of Self-Regard*, she explains: "I have been told that there are two human responses to the perception of chaos: naming and violence." So we—especially those of us who are poets—invent language to try to explicate madness, or fight like mad to free ourselves of it.

In one essay, Morrison asks, "The slavebody was dead, wasn't it? The Blackbody was alive, wasn't it?" meaning, *Isn't the slavebody finished and the Blackbody still becoming?*, which is a luminous way to say, despite what we imagine, isn't history still gripping us, and isn't the present the place where we find ourselves most confronted with it?

The morning after Toni Morrison left the Earth, all the world was grieving, especially Black writer women like me. I felt a real hollow, a low point in the belly, an emptying, and I was insatiable in my trying to collect her pieces in any way I could. I read every pop-up article and looked at the myriad photographs of her thick silver-gray dreadlocks. I began reading *Song of Solomon* again (after having camped out in front of my local used bookstore twenty minutes before they opened to buy all the Morrison on the shelves. I needed doubles of all I had, so I could annotate them with full vigor and keep my copies—some of which are signed, actually signed—in their best condition). I began to laugh five lines into the novel when I realized Morrison had warned us about the damage she'd do when *Song of Solomon* began. In it, an agent is about to fly and leaves notice for those who might want to witness the spectacle. The note reads:

> At 3:00 p.m. on Wednesday, the 18th of February,
> 1931, I will take off from Mercy and fly away on
> my own wings. Please forgive me. I loved you all.

Not only do these look like lines of a poem instead of prose now that I've typed them—which attests that Morrison had the gifts of a poet and chose to use them differently—but I also realize she is firing off a warning shot about how her living will overtake us in the years to come. She, Morrison, is *actually* born on February 18, 1931, which actually was a Wednesday. She does take off from Mercy (i.e., she is flung from the bosom of a particular God) and flies away on her own wings (i.e., takes every advantage of her singular gifts in the world and ransacks it with her meticulous invention of beauty and race and grief, things most others barely scratch the surface of). And because, while doing this she will wreck us all (i.e., confounding us with her mounting complexity, forcing us to confront the country's inequities and horrors as well as see our selves in sharp light), she begs forgiveness in advance. She reminds us she'd only done it (i.e., wrote what the world can't do without, though it has tried repeatedly to lessen or unknow it) because she loved each and every one who would come to hold her in regard.

Morrison's milieu throughout her career has been to sit with violences and their inflictions and also to paint Black as humanness while forcing us to wrangle with our intricacies. I didn't discover Morrison until I was an undergrad in college. So when my daughter, a sophomore in high school, came home with *The Bluest Eye* as the text for her first quarter, I was ecstatic, almost too excited, as there was nothing less cool than thinking you'd been given something graphic enough to be banned, then having your parents be happy about it. So as not to blow it completely, I offered to reread the book along with her. "It's been a long time since I've seen it, but it's never a bad time to go back to Morrison," I mentioned as casually as I could. My daughter agreed (mostly because I'm good at helping with big assignments, which she knows must follow or else her teacher has made her read something she says from the onset is "disturbing" for absolutely no reason at all), so we spent a few weeks with Pecola Breedlove in our house.

As I fell deeper into the book's beauty, my daughter became more sullen by the minute—not to mention my husband and son who had to hear all the Morrison talk at the dinner table, in the car, at the park. I walked through the house cornering folks at random doing "brilliant line drive-bys," and my son or husband or daughter, whomever I'd captured, nodded and rolled their eyes. "Isn't it beautiful?" I asked over dinner, and they began telling me what I didn't yet seem to understand about myself:

"You know you like terrifying books, don't you?" said my husband.

My daughter chimed in, "Her daddy raped her. She's a kid who loses a baby and everybody in her family is mean. She hates herself and wants to be white. But you keep saying it's beautiful. What's beautiful about that?"

My eight-year-old son concurred. "You'd never let me watch a movie like this. It's rated R, R, R but you lo-o-ove it."

As they made their arguments, I was dumbfounded but starting to get a better grasp of the things I am drawn to and how they might seem horrible on the surface. *The Bluest Eye*, Morrison's first novel, is an unflinching look at a fractured child and an examination of how we can all play into one's brokenness. Despite its terror, I had fallen in love with Morrison's language, the way she bears the story out, and am intrigued by her ability, and the ability of others, to make beautiful something so ugly.

It wasn't until I was asked to speak on a panel about Morrison and saw a stage play of *The Bluest Eye* that I began to understand my family's reservations. It's one thing to read about horrific living and altogether another to watch one's dissolution play out in front of you (this would explain my aversion to rated-R movies, as my son emphatically pointed out). On seeing the play, I realized that Morrison is perhaps the most revered and celebrated American novelist of the twenty-first century because in her writing she was most like a poet—layering metaphor into every square inch of dialogue. Every mark of God's creatures and God himself are dissected and demanded an answer of: marigolds hold the town's secrets and tongue, Soaphead does the work God refuses with little power other than people's need to believe in something, an old dog is harmless, helpless, turned inside-out like Pecola, blue eyes are a doll's downfall, a girl's wish, every unturned head in a sea of longing. Still, I admitted to my husband after I saw the play with girlfriends, "You might be right: *The Bluest Eye* might be the saddest book ever written." Of course this is hyperbole, but for someone with my experiences—living as a young Black thinker in America—there may be no sadder story than a boundless girl full of nothing but potential irrefutably, irreversibly broken by the culmination of her circumstances, all of which are made outside of her being, and none of which she or any of the adults around her seem to be able to control.

An added layer to my fascination with the horrific is articulated well by David Pilgrim, scholar and founder of the Jim Crow Museum at Ferris State University, when he told *HuffPost*: "To be Black in this country is to be surrounded by, and even gutted by, premature death." Part of the "slavebody's" clear existence when you are Black in America is that you grow up, like Pecola Breedlove, facing loss. There is real fear, emanating from the parents, grandparents, siblings, and extended families who hold you in their care, that you will be taken from them without ceremony, with little consequence, by any person or entity who does not regard your importance or humanity.

I attended the Callaloo Creative Writing Workshop one summer after reading the magazine it was named after, then known as "the premier journal of literature, art, and culture of the African Diaspora." The two poets teaching that summer were Forrest Hamer and Natasha Trethewey, and I found myself in Trethewey's group of eager students. We'd all read her first book, *Domestic Work*. It won the inaugural Cave Canem Poetry Prize, which was a huge deal to those of us who were still trying to get into the retreat. Rumor was they were getting three hundred to five hundred applications a year for the thirty or so spots for new students; Black poets were turning out in droves for the chance to study with Black poetry stars. So the Callaloo Workshop was a welcome stepping-stone of sorts—competitive, twice as long (two weeks), and intensive study with a poet we admired.

Trethewey came in with history on the brain. On day one, she brought us poems by Eavan Boland and Martín Espada's "The River Will Not Testify" and asked us to make a list of historical events we could research in our hometowns, however we defined home. The things I loved the most about her book *Domestic Work* were her use of forms and the way she salvaged her own history.

There were poems about her grandmother leading her own kind of rebellion as a factory worker in Gulfport, Mississippi (putting a used Kotex in her bag the uppers searched every evening, though none of the Black women were stealing). A poem called "Flounder," a narrative around the metaphor of the double-sided fish—one side white, one side black—which told the story of her mixed-race heritage, how she would reckon with it and it would reckon with her in childhood and beyond. Later, during our interview, she would tell me she was reading Theodore Roethke's "My Papa's Waltz" when writing the poem and how she landed on it being a ballad, a repeating poetic form. Like Roethke's poem that also used rhyme and syllable counts to shelter each line, "Flounder" was built as a poem-story about children and family but would catch most off guard, as it sounded like a song with a gut punch built in.

I was so taken with her in-depth study of the overlooked and underseen that I bought her second book, *Bellocq's Ophelia*, about a brothel of fair-skinned women in New Orleans, photographed by E. J. Bellocq, immortalized in their misunderstood light. She gave them voice, memories, backstories. She used sonnets to raise Black women's layered perception and gave me permission to see around shadows, to scavenge in

the underlight.* Trethewey came to these poems in a similar fever, run-
ning toward a flicker of light she was given unsuspectingly: "I remember
seeing one of Bellocq's photographs and being taken with it because it
reminded me of the cover of my ninth-grade Hamlet text. It looked very
much to me like Ophelia at the brook. I left class, ran through the snow
to the library, and found a book of his photographs. Then I found that
image and sat right down there in the stacks and started writing the title
poem of *Bellocq's Ophelia*."

She went on: "I didn't know yet anything else about why I was drawn
to it, and that became my research project for the semester. Of course, in
doing that research, I learned that a good number of those photographs
had been taken in the mixed-race brothels. So these women who looked
very white in the photographs, in our contemporary gaze, probably were
not. At that time, I was looking for a way to write about my own experi-
ence growing up biracial in the Deep South and being told by professors
to let it go."

With Trethewey as a sage, I wrote poems about the unsung places
that shift and shelter us. I wrote sonnets, sestinas, villanelles. I was alive
with the burgeoning lives of everyday heroes, misunderstood misfits,
hometown missives, finding form for them, making them sing.

Trethewey's *Native Guard* is a book that changed me irrevocably.
There are lines in poems—like "Myth" and "Genus Narcissus"— that
I still quote to students and roll over in my head when I am reexamin-
ing sharp whittling, double entendre, subtlety. When I am writing for-
mal verse, when I am writing about photographs, when I am writing the

---

*When Trethewey and I spoke, we lingered on photography for a long while, as I was
just discovering ekphrastic writing and some use for my obsession with Gordon Parks
and Carrie Mae Weems. Trethewey saw each image she was drawn to as "an impetus
to expand the moment of the photograph to see what else is happening just beyond
it or behind it or before it." She mentioned, "That's sort of what Roland Barthes was
talking about when he coined the phrase *punctum*. It is that thing in a photograph
that draws your attention to it and makes you think about what has gone on outside
of the frame. It's the thing that carries you away from that still moment." Photographs
stayed with her because, as she put it, "this is the way people from the past refuse to
remain in the past."

history of the missing, I am writing what Trethewey taught me, what she continues to refine and perfect in her own musings.

In Philip Gourevitch's *We Wish to Inform You That Tomorrow We Will Be Killed With Our Families*, essays about the Rwandan genocide and its aftermath, he says we're beholden to our own perceptions as well as how others perceive us. I imagine myself all the time in the boxes that have been imagined for me: Black, woman, poor, child—all the disenfranchised, abused, most traditionally powerless through time, most in danger always. And I wonder about what danger might come to devour me. Maybe this fascination is linked to what James Baldwin calls "the terror of being destroyed" in *The Evidence of Things Not Seen*—his book about the Atlanta child murders—as the inevitability of our own mortality is magnified in the face of immeasurable evil.

In the book, Baldwin outlines why memory fails us in the face of tribulation and why we still come back to examine it. That is quite possibly why, in my reading life over time, I've found myself drawn to accounts of terror—acts of historically perpetuated, abysmal violence or destruction. Books like *The Bluest Eye* and many others I've turned to over the years help me make sense of the senseless.

At a reading I attended once, a man asked a group of historical novelists if anyone could really create a compelling account that didn't have tragedy at the center. This started a long debate, but, in the end, no one in the audience could come up with an answer. Surely many wonderful books are written without tragedy as their core, but do they illumine the resilience of the human spirit as well as texts emphasizing that even the unthinkable hasn't broken us entirely, that a large part of our humanness is enduring? I read about these things to bolster myself, to try to fathom the ugliness of our anger, our bloodlust, our free will. I could be reading to try to clamor against destruction, or it could be because I have few means of explaining these acts to myself and settling them in my spirit.

·•❧ ❧ ❧❧❧ ❧ ❧❧❧ ❧ ❧❧❧ ·

In my poem "What We Ask of Flesh," I examine a child developing from girl to woman-in-progress. The poem is for my cousin who was burned badly when we were both children. I was there, another young cousin was there, and all of us were powerless when she stepped into an electric pan with hot oil that had been plugged in and stationed on the floor.

What I didn't expect, coming into my own womanhood, before writing this poem and others about my own trauma, is how much I'd have to suppress to thrive (some things that came back to me and came out in those first two books were things like practicing for drive-bys on my block with friends in elementary school, my father holding the head of a friend who'd been hit by a car, etc.). In order not to be overtaken by pain or contrition, there were a great many things I chose to forget or else lumped together into one homogenous glimpse into my past. The actual memories that spawned this poem, I had suppressed for years.

In the kitchen, learning to cook, I splashed myself with drops of oil and, in a flash, I remembered everything about that day. I lost a bit more of my childhood, writing this. I think the innocence we manage to hold on to is chipped away, bit by bit, when we must start answering the questions of others who can no longer be children themselves. And what does forgiveness and guilt mean, when you long to be forgiven for something for which you are not fully responsible? What happens when an almost-child witnesses the abandonment or neglect of another?

When I asked Trethewey about writing and creating silences around the forbidden trauma of the past, she said, "I think of it as restraint, but being restrained means withholding something and creating that silence that you're talking about. . . . I think of the things that I've been given to write (this is a thing that also comes out of my graduate school experience) and I remember turning in a poem when I was, early on, trying to grapple with my mother's death in poems. Someone in the class said, 'This just seems so sensational. It seems like something that came out of a newspaper,' and I was just sitting there thinking, for some people, these things are real life."

Trethewey was only nineteen when her mother was murdered by her former stepfather and had just begun imagining herself a poet. It took years, decades, for her to write poems about what she called the "shared culpability" she feels, though she wasn't there and none of us can be blamed for anyone else's violence. But, decades after, she found enough distance to pen a memoir, *Memorial Drive*, about life with her mother before and after the incident. Trethewey's challenge for herself and for other writers is not to sacrifice craft for the suffering: "The question is how do we write about things that are possibly sensational that happen in real life, but also have a kind of restraint so that the thing—or the occurrence—isn't what guides the poem, but that the means of the telling does?"

I am overcome by Morrison's ability to frame the unspeakable, to mete out its temperament and harness it. While she was the first novelist that forced me to face the forbidden, in poetry, it was stumbling upon the likes of Ai's new and selected tome *Vice*. I poured over it during my junior year in college, reading all three hundred pages end to end one winter night. It scared me witless and convinced me poets could do the work of journalists, memoirists, and novelists in their embodiment of the unthinkable (what most would assume unknowable) as Ai set out to do.

Most of my family's experiences were inconsequential to those in the ivory tower I'd decided to climb. So throughout my time as a first-generation college student, I spent most of my school breaks looking for images and voices that were relevant and familiar to me. That was usually the voice of the disenfranchised, those taken for granted, often exploited, sometimes successful, but always outside of the majority. There are generally two ways to paint this picture or draw a direct line to the working class: by focusing on the triumphant spirit or by illuminating the gritty underbelly of this oft-violent, systematic oppression and where it may lead. Ai readily chose the latter. Her work wasn't just voyeuristic; her writing about evil was compelling because she created fully fleshed, flawed, and improbably normal human beings who cause atrocities. Ai certainly wasn't the only poet to have ever breached malevolence in this way, but she was the first poet I'd found who gave singular, unaffected, first-person voice to those causing destruction, and I was stricken with her uncanny ability to cast violence in such unaffected light.

Ai's *Vice* opens and readers are soon faced with an aborted fetus in wax paper, slaughtering and hanging, children beaten and led with leashes, headliners plotting and persevering, and lightning enrapturing bodies as they perish. At times crass and witty, then eerily reverent to all the wrong gods—power, poison, prestige—*Vice* changed what I thought was possible in poems. These murderers and harbingers were everyday people; they could be next to me at the DMV, teaching my children woodshop someday, guiding me into a funeral pew, or helping me price check at the grocery store.

Part of the poet's job is to illuminate the extraordinary in the ordinary. When Ai does this, she magnifies our cruelty and fears. In "Hitchhiker," a woman picks up a man who swelters in the Arizona heat, and before she drives anywhere far, the stranger becomes the thing of nightmares, burying a blade in her chest and singing an upbeat Dean Martin song. In "Life Story," an eight-page opus about a priest accused of sexual abuse, the speaker foreshadows his double-living, double-talks to God with one mouth and coos to trap little boys on the other side of the same hollow. After luring a boy in the dark, he ignores the child's pleas, calling himself "Daddy," touting how he'll continue, then finds countless others to terrorize. When talking about her book *Cruelty* with Lawrence Kearney and Michael Cuddihy, Ai said, "I wanted people to see how they treated each other and themselves." She believed in this responsibility and in tethering, she explained: "I'm irrevocably tied to the lives of all people, both in and out of time."

What more is there to being human, being flesh, than the interconnectedness of our lives and hopes and dreams? I was brought into this world by the patchwork of coincidence and plans, and I will leave this world tethered to as many lives that tether me. So when people come back and reenter, I am not frightened, just full and parched and eager.

This is not to say that I believe in reincarnation. I don't believe Jehovah God is unimaginative, but I do believe that we often see glimpses of other lives in our own, even that we relive what others have endured. This could be why I find solace in 1 Corinthians 10:13: "No temptation has taken you except what is common to men. But God is faithful, and he will not let you be tempted beyond what you can bear, but along with the temptation he will also make the way out in order for you to be able to endure it." The standout idea for me isn't the faithfulness of God, but this concept of commonality. Here, all trials are ordinary. Every day, someone has already endured what we find unbearable. Every day, we must walk the path— whether it be to bury our loved ones, to fight an indiscriminate disease, to lose a friend or lover—that we know others have crossed but still seems incomprehensible. The fact that we continue on—sometimes succeeding, sometimes enabled by spirit or might or time and unforeseen occurrence, to surmount the impossible—is what makes us fascinating. And so, I write.

I teach Ai's and Trethewey's poems in a craft lesson I call The Forbidden (after Louise Glück's essay of the same name from the book *Proofs & Theories: Essays on Poetry*), where I have students dissect subjects considered reprehensible. Ai's "The Good Shepherd: Atlanta, 1981" is an excellent example of pop culture headline, persona, extended metaphor, and voice. In it, the infamous conductor of the Atlanta child murders speaks. In Glück's essay, she says what I know to be true: "the forbidden exerts over the susceptible human mind irresistible allure." In the craft lesson, we explore poets who dare to tangle with the tension and historicity of the forbidden in our public and personal lives.

One of the benefits of reading about the inconceivable is that this examination helps charge us with wisdom that must—if we are to think of ourselves as reasonable, intelligent, critical beings—breed empathy in us. I ask my students to not only expand their idea of what poetry might be able to house, but also to expand their ideas about the human condition, their own misconceptions, mistakes, and unease, and how as readers and writers of poetry we might help wrestle some of this terror to the ground.

Ai's "The Good Shepherd: Atlanta, 1981" is included in the packet of poems students must read in this lesson. Maybe it struck me because I was born in 1981 and, after a few years in Germany, my father was stationed at Fort Gordon army base in Augusta, Georgia, about two hours east of Atlanta. I started kindergarten in Augusta and, though the murders had ended a few years before, my parents—and the parents of the friends around me—were still leery of a place so near where close to thirty Black children (and at least two adults) had been abducted and murdered. Though Wayne Williams had been arrested for the killings, much mystery and angst still surrounded the case—all those Black children gone missing and so little done about it. I was an only child, my parents were new to the area, knew no one and nothing about the place except that it had been splayed all over the news for years as the site of this fear, and now they were tasked with yet more impossible odds about keeping their Black child safe in America.

In Ai's poem, after killing another boy and pushing his body off an embankment into the cold water of the river, the speaker thinks of a new coat, calling his victims "lambs" after slaughter, then goes home to drink hot cocoa. He scrubs the evidence of the killing, little boy's blood and remnants, from all over the bathroom and calls this covering up "joy" for the sake of those who might know what dirt he's done. He goes on to intone that his killing, his leading them like "a good shepherd," is providence; he is a god that can't be satisfied, but for their little bodies devoured time and again under his guiding hand.

I have my students—some first-generation college students, some legacy with alumni parents, most from insular homes and neighborhoods—examine The Forbidden so they are forced to talk in mixed company, outside the gaze of the various communities that raised them, about long-held falsehoods they hold about others and how those harbored and honed falsehoods could, in time, lead us to the unthinkable. I vie with this terror in my own work as well.

By the time I began writing my second book, *What We Ask of Flesh*, I'd bought my first house and discovered the new multifold anxiety of being a woman living on my own. I dreamt constantly of what dangers might come for me and started writing poems about the worst things I'd found that women have endured. The book is hinged on a twelve-part poem called

"The Body Speaks" about an account in the Book of Judges in which a woman is gang-raped by townsmen and left for dead on a stranger's doorstep while her husband sleeps. When he rises to find her, her husband, in his anger, cuts her into pieces and sends her body parts to each of the twelve tribes of Israel to begin a bloody war. In *What We Ask of Flesh*, all my horrors are on display: missing children are found riddled with bullets, a young girl is burned and loses herself, mothers are buried, a house is given the ten plagues reincarnate, and voices sing well into the afterlife. The Forbidden makes its way into my work as I am grappling with fear of the unknown: Do we transcend death or dread? Can we save ourselves from any coming disaster? Will disaster break or bind us? Can we be reborn?

Ai died in 2010. Three swift losses (Lucile Clifton, Ai, and Carolyn Rodgers) happened for me and lovers of Black women's poetry (though I'm under no illusion that Ai would have wanted to be counted simply as a writer of note with race attached to her identity). But she was a Black woman writing to me and this I cherished. For a long while, I didn't know that to be a contemporary Black woman poet was a real-life possibility. Finding her work continued to assure me it was and also that I could write anything, *anything* that suited me whether others were disturbed by it or not as long as I wrote it *well*. This freedom was a real gift, a sacrosanct fact, and I counted her among my sheroes. Others felt similarly, like Major Jackson, who, in his essay "Assuming the Mask: Persona and Identity in Ai's Poetry," said: "In interviews and at public forums, Ai was quick to point to her multiracial background, even going so far as to remark upon percentages of her ethnic amalgamation: Japanese, Irish, Choctaw, and Black. Despite how existentially important her mixed heritage was to her, I read her simply as a poet with an inner complexity and perceptiveness that felt truly American *because* she was Black." So when Ai died in swift succession along with two other heroes of mine, I wrote their voices in imitation and elegy. *What We Ask of Flesh* ends with a three-part poem in the voices of each. Ai's section reads in part:

> even the forgotten and unutterable
> thank me for bearing their children,
> naming them and giving voice.

They nod recalling our offspring—
wife-murderers, child-beaters,
cannibals—hearkened to light.

In his book about the genocide, Gourevitch says something worth pondering about violence: that Rwandans now refer to the leaders of the genocide as its "authors." In order to get the majority of folks, the other powerless, to join them, they recognized that they had to address the desire all the powerless have to be powerful. As a girl trying to make my way into full-fledged adulthood and later as a woman trying to help usher other humans—my students, my children—into the world, my questions for myself always were: How do we foster *power* (inner strength, fortitude, awareness in and of ourselves) without it being at the expense of others? Is power belief? Is it knowledge that we are all more similar than different? And how do we make this knowledge and belief, this power, *stick*, when we are confronted head-on with terror?

My writer girlfriends and I decided to visit Thomas Jefferson's Monticello because we were in Charlottesville for the Virginia Festival of the Book on the one day a week the estate had begun offering a tour on the Hemings family. It was my first time there, and I was already in awe and incensed by the time we made it to the parking lot, after driving the long winding road uphill carved out, much like the mansion, by the hands of the enslaved almost from nothing. I had never looked out at the thousands of acres on the mountain overlooking the city that, a year and a half earlier, was all over the news. The Unite the Right Rally marched through the streets and a white supremacist rammed his car into a crowd of counterprotesters, killing one woman and injuring a dozen or so others.

The Monticello tour guide, a white man, educator, and botanist who only did these tours on the weekend, was set on being clear and focused on honesty. I was shocked at how well he didn't dance around the ugliness the house had seen, that Sally Hemings was Jefferson's wife's half-sister, that they might have favored each other, that he might have been drawn to her for this and other things. Our tour guide began by having the large group of us meditate on privilege and agency. What kind of agency did the enslaved have? What bartering could be done to relieve some of their children's suffering? To keep the family intact? To acquire a skillful hand, to free themselves (in mind if not in body), to house and become something? What faith was there in exodus on the horizon? What faith in hands that winnowed wood and bent iron, in ingenuity and sought-after craftsmanship, in Black creation? I felt the weight of this as we walked the plotted land, grand gardens, the underground tunnels, the large room where many were auctioned away from each other when Jefferson died in debt.

After the tour, my friends and I strolled a cobblestone street dotted with artisans and bookstores, one block from the street where protestors clashed that would soon be renamed to honor the woman killed there. We stepped inside a packed house where I would read, where there was standing room only for poetry. People were looking for peace and I was straining against history, the utter folly and impossibility that is Monticello and the city of intellect sloped down from this excavated hill on the outskirts of the city. But this room of people gave me faith. There was every age, every background, people were waiting for the word, for what reflection and hope words could make.

Silence is a kind of destruction. How dare we waste what has been carved out for us, excavated in shards of glass, saved stones, letters from the past?

Destruction is what we've inherited and keep trying to disinherit. These are the facts of our lives and what we find ourselves battling as readers, parents, teachers, and citizens of the world. In Ai's poem "Elegy," the speaker, a guilt-ridden, dying soldier, says what I feel while reading these horrors: with him are the others from killing camps, victims of atom bombs, so many. Like him, I believe we carry each other. We carry our deeds, our pillaging, our mistakes in the same way that we carry our loves and successes. I believe if we see these failures and destruction in the living of others (even in books), we will be less likely to act out this horror and, hence, to harbor it in our own lives. The in-depth study of unfathomable brutality might save us from being accomplices in it in some distant or not-so-distant time or—at least this is the case in most of my own work—we ultimately turn to illumining pain in order to move through it, beyond it, where we can. As a writer, my philosophy is that beauty transcends terror. Capturing our resilience and totality makes us more prepared to move through the world, more empathetic and perceptive toward those enduring trauma, to everyone—past or present—looking for ways to escape and survive. In *The Art of Death*, Edwidge Danticat says we write our pain in hopes that we serve a higher calling by illuminating this horror. What faith we must have to face this terror and keep going.

BINGHAM-RISHER: What do you think the job of women writers is, especially writers of color, as artists in this millennium?

TRETHEWEY: I can't remember who said that poets are charged with the collective memory of a people, but I think that we are. The duty is to create work that values the human spirit and dignifies humanity, in that it is willing to speak to and for, as much as possible, all of us.

Patricia Smith

STANDING IN THE
SHADOWS OF LOVE

Basically, a lightning bolt comes down and says,
The life you thought you had, you don't have anymore.
—PATRICIA SMITH

Desire is obsession, the things we keep going back to that dig in us, that we dig into. It is always present. No matter the time or distance, it is always in front of you. Poetry is about mining—extracting the things that come back to us—reexamining love and shadows.

When I married, I inherited extended families and became obsessed with reevaluating my upbringing. I started interrogating what I learned about love throughout my childhood and how I'd let those lessons move through me. The book that came from all this, *Starlight & Error*, grapples with how we collide and come to be, how the mass of what we are—the stars, songs, and voices that guide us—lead to our own essentiality. As obsessions always will, several rose to the surface of this work: music, domesticity, God, cosmos, progeny.

All the things that converge the night Rumain is killed.

As I am revising, contending with the overt sweetness of *Starlight & Error* (one-sided nostalgia and sappy romance stacked chronologically), I am knocked back into reality when one of my oldest and dearest friends is shot by police.

On December 2, 2014, on his doorstep with a pill bottle in his pocket and a Happy Meal in hand for his daughter beyond the door, Rumain is next in a long line of the taken.

One headline reads, "Eric Garner, Mike Brown and now, Rumain Brisbon: White Officer In Arizona Shoots And Kills Unarmed Black Man."

That day in December, Rumain becomes one more on the growing list of Black men gunned down (mostly by police) that leads to the Black Lives Matter movement:

July—Eric Garner
August—Mike Brown
October—Laquan McDonald
November—Tamir Rice
December—Rumain Brisbon

Boy who journeyed with me from middle school, through three states, past college, his phone calls and thick letters filled with photographs, Chicago love, and wild chuckling; boy close as kin, now gone.

I lay sleepless in the chaos of the following weeks. I try not to wake my husband, who is lying closer than usual. He is worried for me, I am frightened for him, and we are both anxious for our son sleeping in the next room. I wear headphones awake in bed, letting music spin, voices move in and out of focus.

As soul music is an obsession fixed in me, I am frequently writing in the voices of those who drifted from vinyl each Saturday morning in my parents' homes. In Patricia Smith's introduction to my second book, *What We Ask of Flesh*, she calls colored girls a definitive, lost tribe, then names me among those who honor Black nostalgia, saying: "She gravitates toward the addictive sugar of soul music, follows the gospel of Smokey and the Temps until she realizes how gorgeous their lies were." This is maybe the greatest compliment I have been given in all my natural life.

I am almost sure I bonded with Smith coming down a *Soul Train* line. Not long after, I'd find myself sitting with several other writers on a windowsill in a nightclub in Austin, Texas, listening to Smith recite verses from memory for a man who has bought a round of drinks in return for poems. There is music blaring in the club (which we will later dance to for hours, and which we leave only to sample Sam's BBQ, a legendary barbecue joint Smith has heard about across town), but everyone in a ten-foot radius is enraptured by the way she births and voices others, bringing fears and fantasies to life.

When Smith has released the crowd, waving her hands and shimmying toward the dance floor, even those of us who've witnessed her work for years put our drinks down and beg for more. This is a poet capturing others, enrapturing us in the crux of her arms, under her skin, leading us anywhere she wants us to go. And on and on into the night, and in our writing lives, we do nothing but follow.

·•● ● ∂•⁀● ● ∂•⁀● ● ∂•⁀● ·

Music informs much of my work and I turn to other poets—like Patricia Smith (especially her "Motown Crown" of sonnets)—as models for how to embody the electric energy of soul and, of course, I turn to song because it usually soothes me. Assonance, sparse enjambment, repetition, and end rhyme make their way into much of *Starlight & Error* because, in subtle ways, I am trying to emulate what the soul singers are doing.

This lifelong obsession with music haunts Smith as well. She told me about writing a poem when she was only eight because of her instinct to think of music as poetry: "You know [I wrote a poem] with that hard bad rhyme, the June/moon type stuff. I think there's something inherent. Like I was just telling someone, I have this tremendous bad song memory. My husband tells me, 'We could quit our jobs and travel the country making bets in bars that you will know the next song on the jukebox.' I mean white, Black, country, rock, anything, you name it . . ."

I told her I thought I was the only one who worried about how much of my brain matter is used up by old song lyrics and she joked, "When I can't find my keys, I think, *Oh, but I know the words to that song.* So getting back, I do think, when people ask, 'How did you know poetry?,' I think there's something inherent in the way you hear and perceive language . . . from early on, I would listen to my mother's records, the song lyrics, back when songs were narratives, it wasn't just one hook over and over and over." She continued, "They told a story, they rhymed, and I think my love of that played into it. I wanted to be romantic in that way or I love the way that sounds, so let me see if I can make words sound like that."

Like Smith, much of my work has its roots in the music that formed me and formed my perceptions of love. There's an early poem in *Starlight*

& Error where I'm really just trying to champion and channel one of the greatest soul musicians to ever grace us, Stevie Wonder:

IF IT'S MAGIC

When I find the *Songs in the Key of Life* 45s
I marvel at the messages my parents inscribed:

Sweet Dee and Junior Bee—In Love '79
their marks on the sheath's concentric circles,

inside, on the lyrics booklet, worn smooth
their scratches on the grooves.

I spend a year playing the set
enthralled every few days by some new epithet—

a background voice trailing,
a tone's shift or timbre—

my mother counts the years since their beginning,
how I interrupt their ending,

heartache and revelry,
what each of us remembers.

Such strange obsessions I inherit:
their soulful cinders, indecipherable

refrains, this awful insistence
on fraught and ordinary pain.

Long before she was writing about Motown, Smith found her way to journalism and an assignment led her to a slam poetry night that changed her forever. She said: "[T]hey had college poets and they had Gwendolyn Brooks, who was sitting in her seat waiting her turn. I knew who she was, but she was just sitting and waiting, not saying, 'Hi, I'm here. I need to read and leave,' like they do now, she was sitting and listening to everybody, applauding, giving people feedback on their poems, signing her books, whatever." She went on: "The poet and the poems themselves were accessible, immediate. There were a lot of poems about stuff we'd talked about yesterday, things on the news. There were people kind of processing their own life."

Poetry, much like music, would give her another entry point into the intimate, would provide another voice for what might come barreling toward you in the night, as it did for me.

When Rumain dies, no matter what book I bring to bed or which tracks blare through my headphones, I am restless and afraid. I am so new to being a mother, so new to living with the double fear that Black men carry as a weight balanced atop my own young Black woman's already triple fear. Not to mention having to balance this with hope and a brave face for my small son's sake who is still, as Smith puts it, "sweet in that space between knowing and not knowing." One poem in *Starlight & Error*, "Benediction," bears the line: "Bless the boys who loved us before they were forced / to be men." It is a prayer, a pleading, a wish for some grace in the face of childhood. In other words, I am asking the world to give Black boys time to be silly and abundant, to grow into men, not be pushed into adulthood. It's a petition for the sanctity of youth, as if that will solve anything.

A real hopelessness, a great fear, wells up in me when Rumain is killed. His death is altogether ordinary and sensational, common and outrageous.

Smith found the same kinds of violence in the city around her, in the stories she'd craft daily. Those notes and news clippings showed up in her poetry, from her first book, *Life According to Motown*, on down to others like *Teahouse of the Almighty*. She said finding the poets gave her license to wrestle with this haunting: "Once I found that community, it sort of gave me permission to write about things that I was writing about in the newspaper, things that bug you and bother you long after the story's done. You can then flip that coin over and write a poem from any aspect of that story. . . . It's such fertile ground, you know?"

As a poet, I found I could tackle the sensational with a degree of distance. I could step into another life and ask questions without the answers having much consequence for me. Like Smith, poetry gave me another set of pipes, other shoes to fill. Her whole career, Smith has been compared to writers like Ai and Stephen Dobyns because of her skill with persona, but she may have been the best at embodying others because she is turned on her heels when the violence comes for her too. She explained: "When I was about twenty-one years old, my father was murdered. . . . I was my father's baby; I loved my father, everything my father did was golden. He'd take me to the candy factory where he used to work and put the little hard hat on my head. My father got to hear me talk about what I wanted to do, but never got to see it. So, to have a single, really stark act of violence take away so much so quickly, and my mother didn't really have the skill to get me through that, I was on my own."

She continued: "The slam was a recreational activity for a while, but then when I saw people coming up and saying, 'That happened to me,' then a real responsibility comes. . . . There are people who are always arguing about this, [they say], 'You're doing this to be sensationalistic,' but where else are you going to see this? Let me tell you, the life you're living right now, boom, just like that, it could be changed. I know because it happened to me."

How strange it is to realize in the days after Rumain's death that, once and for always, we are no longer children.

Sometimes I forget how many seasons have passed between experience and memory. Amidst my grief, I write about losing time. In the poem "Solstice," I am a still point and my children—like me—have lost their trust in anything, anyone:

When you discover you are old enough
that nothing has novelty

you live with teenagers
who've learned

little more than to abhor everything—*I hate Daylight Savings Time. I hate Virginia. I hate being here.*

. . .

If we can steal their light and time
without warning

what joy is there to be had,
what can they love without fear?

I met Rumain when I was thirteen. That year I kept a journal, every day for 365 days. Since then, I'd rarely looked at the massive blue binder on the lowest shelf of my bookcase. When Rumain is killed, I crack the binder open, looking for remnants of who we were, who he was, as opposed to what people begin imagining.

Rumain was the closest friend I had from seventh grade until college. He moved from Chicago to Phoenix and landed at Challenger Middle School. A year older and infinitely wiser, he laughed when I'd strut over to make an inquiry no one else would (was my fearlessness boldness or naïveté? Even now, I can't be sure). The girls sent me to find out who the cute boy in the Bulls jacket was the first day he arrived.

Reading my journal, I find so much happened that year: my uncle died, I prepared for high school, I loved a boy (the man I would later marry) and lied to him about it, Rumain and I became best friends. He watched over me like a brother, asked about my chorus recitals, gave me teasing nicknames, rapped Tupac's "Dear Mama" to his mother on Mother's Day. Our marathon phone calls got me grounded more than once—our inside jokes and late-night meandering, the both of us equally boy- and girl-crazy, trying to figure out who we'd like to become. We whispered in the dark behind our mothers' backs for countless hours that year and many years thereafter; we grew up together and in spite of ourselves.

Tucked into the pages of that old journal are letters and photographs we sent back and forth for at least a decade. I lay them on my living room floor and cry most of the night after he is killed. In the morning, when I am brave enough to read them, I find Rumain was all the light I remembered—silly and solemn, funny and cocky as any teenage boy with all his natural insecurities can be—very little of the myth people quickly begin to craft.

•◦○ ♦◦◦◦ ○ ♦◦◦◦ ○ ♦◦◦◦ ○

Once he dies, I am consumed with trying to pin down the last time I saw him. I think it was around 2005, nine years before. That winter was an arduous one for a mutual friend of ours, whom we'd known since we all met at Challenger Middle School. Her grandmother had been suffering with dementia and had drowned in the family pool not long before Thanksgiving. I'd been trying to reach her for weeks before her birthday (we'd always spoken on her birthday, which was four days before Rumain's—November 20 and 24). When she finally had the energy to call, I could tell something terrible had happened. I flew out to Phoenix to spend a week with her and do some searching of my own.

When I was sixteen, I left Phoenix and had since become a writer. I'd finished graduate school and was working on my first book. I dreaded going back because everything about it reiterated how difficult and scattered the years there had been, when my parents separated and we moved two thousand miles away from the life I'd known, running, it seemed, from our demons. The mountains and flatland made an imposing tableau.

When I got off the plane, I went to the address on Rumain's last letter and knocked on the door. He blinked a few times when he saw me, standing across the threshold with my hands on my hips, then laughed and said, "What you doing here, Shorty? You bum-rushing people like the police now?" before he hugged me and let me in. We walked around his apartment, with little furniture and an unmade bed, baseball caps and tennis shoe boxes stacked in the corners. He was just as thin as he was in high school, maybe thinner in an undershirt and oversized jeans. We sat on the couch and talked for hours about how Phoenix had changed, old stomping grounds full of new people. I don't remember much of what we said. His oldest daughter had been born. He showed me pictures. Were children's things—bottles and blankets—scattered about as well?

On the flight to Phoenix, I'd been reading Joan Didion's *The Year of Magical Thinking* at the suggestion of friends. I remember reaching a passage about Didion and her husband, John Gregory Dunne, writing as a team. *Did he know I wrote it?* she intoned when friends asked her about a column where she mentioned the possibility of divorce. Her husband had not only seen the column but had edited it, a fact that surprised her friends but never escaped her, even after he'd died and left her there alone. As I read during the flight's turbulence, I was, all at once, ruined by its beauty. I cried so fiercely that a stranger sitting next to me offered a tissue and airsickness bag while telling me, *It will be alright, we'll land alright,* but I'd barely noticed the plane's lurching. We were beginning our descent before I could calm myself to thank him.

That's how the trip began, with me being ransacked by the recollection of what death takes from us. After Rumain dies, when I am trying to pin down the last time we were together, I find *The Year of Magical Thinking* on my office bookshelf. I remember it distinctly, of course, but don't realize yet it is the book I had on the last trip to Phoenix that would find me knocking on his door.

After a series of long, awkward messages, our friend calls to confirm her grandmother did pass away the year I suspected. A few days later, I am rereading Didion and stumble across a poem I've scribbled on the blank pages at the back of the book, a habit I've worked my way into after something bowls me over, most often forgetting to date it, a bad habit wrapped into the good. So I am surprised to find these fragments, and the date I'd struggled to remember, waiting for me like a gift:

11/23/05
I found yesterday
in the pocket of an unworn jacket.*
Three nights ago—the evening
when truth slipped in the

---

*As I went back to *The Year of Magical Thinking* while writing this essay, I realized that the first two lines of this poem are actually Didion's. She didn't enjamb them, like I did, and wasn't thinking about them figuratively. It was just a chance sentence structure (she wrote: "I found yesterday in the pocket of an unworn jacket a used metro ticket . . .") but I heard the line and was struck by how odd it might be to find our past in our pocket, or any other place we least expect it.

sheets between us—
was stuffed into the toe
of an old shoe.
1985—the year my grandfather
died, the year my grandmother
told us of the three lights
that followed her up the
stairs to their bedroom—
was sitting cross-legged
in the back of the closet,
a quiet child waiting.
The months I spent
lugging clothes in a shopping
cart, past the corner store
to the laundromat that
charged 25 cents to dry, were
in the cupboard this morning
not far from the
years I spent as a
child staring into the
Arizona horizon with
empty hands, the nights
I went in search
of words to sober my
(wasn't himself) father, the
evenings I found them,
but did not stir from the
length of warmth
that coursed the space between
the neck and shoulder
of my mother.

All those lines, then this:

(In literature, everything is forgiven.)

I'm still not sure what it meant.

When your friend becomes a flash point, with the public clamoring for one side of the story or the other, what's strangest is most everything people say about them is myth. Back in Phoenix, my husband's cousin calls to tell us, "They're making your boy out to be Scarface or somebody," which is to say, we are in the twenty-first century, but it is still better to eviscerate some men than for anyone to admit *we've made a mistake* or say *we're sorry for what we imagined.*

One letter Rumain wrote to me is from 1997, a few months after we'd both left Phoenix for a time. In it, I find what's left of his voice:

> *Are you missing me yet? Cause I'm missing you like crazy. It's like ever since I left Phx I haven't had any one to talk to, and knowing that when I do go back you won't be there just hurts my feelings. But you know what, I ain't gon' trip cause I know at least one day before this life ends we will see each other again. I really don't have much to say besides I miss you and I can't wait 'til I see you again, and that I love you with all my heart. Shorty, I hope you like the picture.*
>
> *P.S. Don't get too close to your new homies cause can't nobody replace me. Do you want to know why? Well I'll tell you why cause you ain't never had a friend like me.*

The world is mourning a man and I am mourning a little boy, an almost-man, a man becoming. I search for pieces of him everywhere. What I find is never enough.

A few days after he is killed, I am back on the living room floor, rereading letters. Laying against a shelf, mouthing the words I'm reading, my son finds me, puts his hand on my shoulder, and asks, "Mom, are you alright?"

I must look something like Hannah to Eli, drunk with grief. He is perplexed, so earnest and confused. I do this infrequently—wallow in sadness out in the open—so it must seem to him like something has gone very wrong. I feel terrible putting on a smile and saying I'm alright, but what else can you tell a nine-year-old who is in between video games and has found you here so unlike yourself?

Like most parents, I worry that I might be ruining him. I write the lines "no child has ever learned / by anything other than mimicry" in a poem that will become "Skipping Stones" in *Starlight & Error*. I can count on one hand the times my son has had to be grown up, and I am weary the world will force him to this sooner than I want it to.

Once when I was around his age, my parents were screaming in the living room, something they rarely did. When I couldn't stand it anymore, I rushed in with my fists clenched and yelled, "Stop it! You're killing me!" and it startled them so completely they began apologizing, first to me, then to each other, but the damage was done: I'd already seen them for part of who they were—flawed and helpless—and they'd already recognized who I might become: a growing mirror, unsteady and gazing, like my son.

•••••• • •••• • •••• •

Do our flaws make or unmake us? The world is being told every flaw Rumain ever had in an attempt to unmake him, to make him—like many others—an unworthy footnote, a victim of his own living.

In the midst of violence and skewing that violence, spinning it to water down intention, I want to write something, so my children will know no one is perfect, so Rumain's children will know there are other lenses, other lives wrapped up in our complexities. I turn back to Smith, as she is putting poems in the world that will be part of her book *Incendiary Art*, about the violence that takes Rumain's life and many others. She is rebuilding their lives brick by brick and this is no small task because, after violence and errors, she's had to rebuild her own.

By 1998, Smith was everywhere. She was a four-time individual champion of the National Poetry Slam, the most successful poet in the competition's history, winning in 1990, 1992, 1993, and 1995. Kurt Heinz said of her work, "Smith coined a kind of performance poetry which defined slam."

She'd published three books of poetry, all in multiple printings. She'd begun working in other mediums (collaborating with musicians, she'd done a successful run of her theater piece produced by Derek Walcott), and she was a celebrated columnist at the *Boston Globe*. In an article titled "Shall We Meditate on Truth?" Bob Holman said, "Patricia Smith's career as a journalist is over. Her career as a poet is just beginning."

When she resigned from the *Boston Globe* (after writing four columns that included fabricated material), Smith said her life as a poet was the only thing that saved her: "It took me years of therapy, one marriage breaking up . . . What it did for me, the blowtorch, it blew me over here, and it's going to take you a while, but you're going to come out of it doing the type of writing you were supposed to be doing in the first place. [It said], 'I tried to tell you, but you were so busy trying to get your little picture in the paper. Okay, go right ahead. We gon' burn you *and* the paper.'"

She went on: "And the community that helped [was the poets] . . . that and the fact that I had a *way* to process it. . . . You know, I went through the fire; I moonwalked back into the fire; I went under the fire; I lit two matches, like Richard Pryor, and pretended I was the fire. Once the slate has been cleaned in that way, it really is ludicrous to me to stop and say, 'I would write about that *but* . . .'" Her life was unmade and the poems gave her a way to steady herself, to keep moving, to burrow into the difficulty and find a way to walk the fiery coals.

⁕•⊛ ⊙ ⊛⊶⊛ ⊛ ⊛⊶⊛ ⊛ ⊛⊶⊛ •

When the Four Tops' rendering of "Standing in the Shadows of Love" spins from the shuffling on my playlist in those weeks of mourning, it is no wonder I hear their rough pleading and I get stuck. Amidst the police brutality and rioting, the odd disturbance looming over my own house, I suddenly hear this familiar not as a man longing for his woman, but as a woman in need, a mother supplicating her fallen son:

> Didn't I treat you right, now baby, didn't I?
> Didn't I do the best I could now, didn't I?
> So don't you leave me
> Standing in the shadows of love
> I'm getting ready for the heartaches to come

I let the song repeat for hours, then *days*; I am obsessed with the ugliness of desire to the point of suffering.

Like Smith and others, when writing I've found it best to fight obsession by trying to climb into it at its core. Hence, while my boys are sleeping, Rumain's family is making plans to lay him to rest, and the Four Tops' missive is still spinning, I scour the online *Oxford English Dictionary* for the etymology of the word *shadow* and, among other things, I find:

- Comparative darkness
- A phantom; a faintly surviving renown
- What is fleeting or ephemeral
- Image cast by a body intercepting light

Throughout *Starlight & Error*, I write inside and around these ideas. In the poem "Regents Prompt: What are the best ways for step-parents to deal with the special problems they face?," children are haint and harboring, mothers are "bound by the weight [they]'ll cradle." In the poem "Noble & Webster, Shadow Sculptures," "Our house is a mess of musk and sawdust— / . . . keels and scrim and kin / caught in the net of our limbs / . . . illusions stacked into a kind of mortality."

I am stuck on the confounding things: how do we keep living beyond our mistakes and fear? How do we save what's coming? How do we transcend the errors of those who made us? Can music save us? Can the stars?

I write a poem in hopes of getting inside this obsession. This helplessness that accompanies mothering and ageing is the underlying foundation of grief. We worry for what we didn't say to, and for, the missing. Poems are also the place I can continue to question God, in my faith and the persistent intricacy of maintaining it in such a violent world. As with Smith, poetry allows me to tell my story and others', to find the rhythm of another door, another skin.

In the poem I eventually write about Rumain, and in the book as a whole, I try to do many things: enact the horror that accompanies death, the oft-unmentioned ugliness and marring of a perfectly good body. I move from metaphor to literal to lyric trying to encapsulate the many roadblocks to keeping the living. I address how death transforms the mothers too—how they are blamed for what happens to their children by our judgment and questioning. This is truer in the case of these "martyr children," like Trayvon or Mike Brown or Rumain. These "martyrs," created by the social upheaval that surrounds their deaths, then demand activist mothers, women who must rearrange their whole lives to keep "doing" for children they no longer get to keep.

And what of the generations who haul the weight of all this?

I could not turn to persona, could not step into the shoes of others because I am one throbbing bluster of questions, so I write:

GETTING READY FOR THE HEARTACHE TO COME
OR A BODY INTERCEPTING LIGHT
Psalm 39:6 – *Surely every man walks about like a shadow.*

Grief is a half-sung ballad
   the mothers I've known are bellowing
into stilled ears or stitches
   in the sewn up backs of blue-Black boys.
There are various sites of trauma:
   wombs, needles, pipes, badges,
ropes unraveling, all wavelengths of visible light,
   prison fights, the Devil's busy hands.
Bodies aimed when they leave
   like bullets or planes, rarely become letters,
tulips, fireworks, any welcome opening,
   rarely live as good, as free, as long
as we hope. The women enduring this
   must become: saints or blameworthy,
miracles or memories. The Bible says men
   are gods or gleaning but mothers shelter
the in-between: ghost-children wandering the streets
   of every generation—father-god, son-god, holy-

spirit—flexing in photo albums, toys in the curio,
     lighters, guns and flasks carved
with initials, all the left-behind things
     gathered around a table, mothers
singing, *Didn't I do the best I could, didn't I?*

Once the poem is written, I am at least freed from the Four Tops and move on to other fixations. My overarching hope for *Starlight & Error* becomes a desire—an obsession—with proving, in our work and life, LOVE (layered and crafted memory that faces the truth of the thing) CONQUERS FEAR.

Truth be told, you are reading this now because, after learning from Smith, being married, being a mom, losing a best friend, and trying to be ready to guide others through losses that will come, I've realized how important it is to be free to say what I'm afraid of out loud, to dispel it, to show my children that even in unimaginable times, we can create our own way out of fear. In living and writing, there is ultimately nowhere else to turn but my eternal conviction in things bigger than all of us and our desires.

Smith closed her introduction to *What We Ask of Flesh* by saying: "Colored girls know one thing more than they know anything else, and that is that a God is real and present, hurtling through our blood, blessing us every dawn with a blank canvas upon which to sing."

I sing in this shadow; in every desire, I hope to be a body intercepting light.

BINGHAM-RISHER: Your poem "Building Nicole's Mama" illustrates how much our work can change the lives of our students. What have your students taught you?

SMITH: They have taught me to go into every situation seeking to learn. . . . Some of the best things that have happened to me have been outside of the setting, when the class itself is over and there's a kid who hasn't said anything in the back of the room, so you say, "Come over here and have lunch with me. So what's going on?" Then I tell them, I want you to write about that and I'm not going to pass judgment on it. They might say, "My English isn't good," or "I can't write." How important it is to convince everyone that their voices are legitimate and that I'm not doing anything you can't do.

Tim Seibles

REVISION AS LABYRINTH

I believe the essential thing is to recognize the possibilities
of the Divine, to be more and more awed by this life—more
kind, more loving of the world and its inhabitants. What
does belief mean if it doesn't transform you, if it doesn't
make you behave with more reverence for everything?

—TIM SEIBLES

For a long while, I sing. I think, for a time, this is what I will be. I'll go to Broadway, where the real singers are, then be part of an earth-shattering show like *Rent*, record a cast album, and party with Stevie Wonder at the Grammys. I have it all figured out until I'm about fifteen.

Reality starts to set in when I sing an entirely broken note, loud and wrong, at the Desert Willow Nursing Home as a soloist with the school choir in the middle of "Georgia On My Mind." Everyone is nice enough about it, but I know then I can sing in the shower and be happy, and less embarrassed when things go wrong on the fly, but writing can make me a life. I can pore over words, again and again, until they take shape, have resonance, bend and bind them until they take flight.

When I was a junior in high school, I found Tim Seibles's book *Hurdy-Gurdy* in a local thrift store. I was hammered by its deft music. I remember, so clearly, reading the poem "Trying For Fire," about someone being lost, disillusioned with all the spinning, ornate world whirling. Reading it, sitting up in my bed, I felt a little faint, a little dizzy. My head was blaring, heart banging, I couldn't breathe. I'd never had that kind of re-action to anything, certainly no book, and I'd read plenty by then—many that I loved beyond telling—but none moved me like the work of Tim Seibles in that moment. That poem, that book, awash with ornament and tenderness, told me there were contemporary poets wading through the parts of the world that bewildered them, dissecting it and piecing together the fragments like a collage to say: we can go on, this I believe.

•●○●•●○●•●○●•

Revising poems—salvaging music in phrases, sharpening images, vacu-uming out the inessential or, perhaps, letting the piece go entirely—is a metaphor for how we might handle the work of shifting, redirecting our own habits, recharting our path (or abandoning a course altogether) to get on with a new life. In her essay "When We Dead Awaken: Writing as Re-Vision," Adrienne Rich maintains that "the act of looking back, of seeing with fresh eyes, of entering an old text from a new critical direc-tion—is for women more than a chapter in cultural history: it is an act of survival." So when I'm asked, in one way or another, what is your basis for revision? When do you know to let a poem go and what does this letting go entail? To answer, I must begin with fragments, and my father.

I am small as nothing but armed
with intimate knowledge
of flawed and mammoth exemplars

A fragment of my father appeared on the other side of the glass as I stared out of the kitchen window into the twilight of our backyard as a child. He came out of darkness, soundless, almost a shadow—I barely knew him, as he had begun disappearing, going missing for days at a time when I was seven years old. It's not my earliest memory of him but the sharpest. Who was he then, and how would I grow into who I was be-coming in his wake? Those were the strangest, hardest days when his ad-diction started to take hold of us. How young my mother was, just thirty, in a town far from either of their mothers, grandmothers, siblings—any familiar safe havens—with a seven-year-old and house note to think of.

My father, then, was even younger, twenty-seven or twenty-eight, still no doubt believing he'd be invincible in the face of anything.

·•● ● ●●● ● ●●● ● ●●●·

I believe in wonder, in God putting something in my hands while I was in the right place, at the right time, in need. Only someone omniscient, outside myself and peering in, would know how it could spark my belief and devotion. So when I found *Hurdy-Gurdy* nestled between a host of *National Geographics* and romance novels, the only slim volume of poetry on the packed shelf, I thought the book was a gift, something that larger Being knew I'd value, and that's why it had come to me.

I wasn't savvy enough to realize I'd just moved two thousand miles from Phoenix to Norfolk, so my mother and I were broke as ever—she couldn't afford much so we went to thrift stores after she got paid every other week. She let me get four books at a time because they were four for a dollar on Fridays only, and that thrift store was in the same city Tim Seibles called home. He'd probably taken the book there himself, as he left copies in all the local used bookstores or on any shelf where the curious lover of words might find them. We were a few miles from Old Dominion University, where he'd been teaching fewer than five of an eventual twenty-five years, where I would find him among the English faculty on their website and think, *It's a sign*, and follow him there.

I wrote all through elementary school. I started a literary journal and poetry club in high school, loved song, loved poems, but thought I'd be a journalist because it seemed a safer choice as a first-generation student going off to college. But Tim Seibles knocked me back into the danger of knowing that what may be most difficult may also be what's meant for you. You may be faced with Frost's "road less traveled" that demands a leap and long view, the throwing caution to the wind that is revision. Sometimes, even when you don't yet know what you want, you have to manifest faith in your possibility.

In college, I took creative writing courses with Seibles, classes like Introduction to Forms, Searching the Harlem Renaissance, and Craft of

Poetry. I weaseled my way onto the list of students he advised throughout their time in their major, so I could sit with him once a semester to inevitably talk poems, but also to ask where I should go, what I should read, how I might begin the artist's journey. During our interview, we talked about him going to Southern Methodist University in Texas to play football then being bowled over by poetry in the classroom unexpectedly and following this path. I asked, so at nineteen you decided *I'm going to be a poet and this is what I'll do for the rest of my life*, or just that you were going to start writing poetry? And he said, "That's part of the beauty of youth: passionate ignorance that assumes the future awaits with open arms."

I was not given over to ignorance; I saw the path—*he was the path!* On campus he was everyone's favorite word-slinging professor and the ardent sage called on in spirited or solemn times. People knew his life was poetry—when he leapt those years before, he'd never strayed the undergrowth.

In his book *Fast Animal*, Seibles sculpts the voice of a Black vampire, pens sweeping odes to the ordinary, and deifies ghosts of his past. He elegizes childhood friends and firsts with unabashed erotica and nostalgia for the wild recklessness of innocence. When we discussed it, he said revision is about our own volition and meandering: "There's what one does intentionally as a poet and what one stumbles into that works, intuitions that seem to instruct us as we write."

Most often, I let the spark of a poem—the flash of inspiration that leads to a furious draft scribbled in minutes—lead me wherever it wants to go. I am grateful to arrive at an end, to have any travelling thought followed through, but the real work of the poem does not come in that moment. It comes after I've let that breakneck draft sit for a day or so, then amble back to it with keener vision. Once revision begins, I'm trying to get out of the way of the poem. When I return, it is my job to rid the poem of its vague fogginess, the things clarion only in the mind of the one who experienced the moment or dreamed it first. Craft is what helps me salvage the spark that led me to the page in the first place; research helps grow it up and give it a face. To add precision and build tension, this is where I begin, with hope that I will redeem and transform what undoes me.

In poems, in my hands, my father is a shape-shifter. He battled his addiction for much of my childhood. My parents were separated, but not divorced, until I was twelve, and my father would do his best to get clean and come back intermittently. This was hard on all of us—my parents, who had never fallen out of love, just lost trust and some dignity; and me, their only child, too smart, bullheaded, and ravaged by the loss of what I knew, trying to hold a grudge and his gifts simultaneously.

The hardest part was, before the shifting, he was a successful, brilliant, jack-of-all-trades, a devout husband and father. In short, he could do everything and he adored me. I thought he called me Little Face because I carry his cheekbones and eyes, all his expressions, but when I asked, he said it's because in baby pictures I was so beautiful to him, I looked just like my mother. Anyone who has seen us together understands that he has convinced me, despite any of my mistakes, that I am nearly perfect and he will move the Earth for me. There is mountainous evidence of his far-reaching love that stands out in my memory:

- the not-birthday evening he snuck into the living room with a Cabbage Patch doll (nearly impossible to find where we were in Germany), made in my image, tucked under his fatigue jacket when I am three
- when I decided at the last minute that I did, in fact, want to be in the Third Grade Parade of Animals, and he pulled an all-nighter, making me a hand-painted peacock mask (he is an artist who eventually paints the cover of my first book) in swirling cerulean and green-gold shimmer
- my middle school chorus concert when he cried openly in front of my swooning classmates, the other fathers, my giddy chorus teacher, my mother, aunt, and cousin, after I picked through his record collection and learned his favorite Táta Vega song, "Come In Heaven (Earth Is Calling)," for my solo
- when I told him I was creating a poetry club at Booker T. Washington High School, he introduced me to Gil Scott-Heron's "Whitey on the Moon," in which white people get to reinvent

themselves, or at least take a few steps toward reshaping the fu-
ture, while Black folks are stuck in a kind of inimitable throbbing
sealed by poverty, much like what we were living through, and he
said, "Now, write what's true to you"
- the morning of my college graduation, when he quit smoking cig-
arettes, his last and longest twenty-five-year habit, when I asked
for this as my gift, so we went to buy Nicorette patches, gum, and
too many stand-in sweets from the store, he in his suit and tie and
I in my cap and gown, on our way to the ceremony
- after I was grown enough to buy my first house but still called
when a rat made its way inside that winter and he left his office in
the middle of the workday, rolled up his white dress shirt sleeves,
and killed it while I hid upstairs

These anecdotes go on and on. They span time and space, his coming
and going. Sometimes they bounce around my mind like fireworks, spar-
kling, boundless, then vanish under all the dark.

•ๅ● ● ●๚● ● ●๚● ● ●๚● •

The luxury of children is that they'll soon disappear

In art, half the work is unburdening yourself of what you can't hold
onto. But this is the fortune of creation too. Sometimes in revision, I find
several poems lurking where I thought there was just one. I find different
people inhabiting the same frame; who they are depends much on when
they appear in the web of memory, or what kind of nostalgia—melan-
choly or ebullient—I'm trying to trace.

I am dipping into experience and memory, even if I'm channeling
someone else's point of view. I asked Tim Seibles about this, as he writes
in the voices of others, but does one—the person or what's cast—out-
weigh the other? He said, "The personas are, of course, inventions, and I
love to simply hit the gas on my imagination just to travel to new visions
and strange places, but everything you do is an extension of your own
sense of things." He continued: "Other poems are more of a combination
of truth and fiction. You know the old idea about making up things so

that you might bring a clearer focus to what is actual—lying your way to the truth . . ."

The job of poets, at least what I set out to do, is to aim for allure and clarity. Clarity presents the most difficulty. Sometimes, I can make a poem beautiful—chock it full of phrases that excite me, but find its motive, its narrative, isn't clear. Other times, even if a piece is finished and effective—perhaps polished and compelling—it still doesn't make its way into a larger body of work because it may be too redundant in theme (the same is true of the memories and errors we harbor or glean). So to winnow what you've made is a skill all artists, all humans, do well to cultivate. Rich says, "[I]f the imagination is to transcend and transform experience it has to question, to challenge, to conceive of alternatives, perhaps to the very life you are living at that moment." How do you let the poem speak beyond your passion or grief? How do you devise your own understanding, sometimes in spite of what seems like the strange living of others? How do you remake yourself, as an artist and a human being?

· ·•◦ ● ◦•◦ ● ◦•◦ ● ◦•◦·

When I was around twelve, my father lived in a motel in Eatontown, New Jersey, that had been converted into a kind of halfway house for those who'd gone through months of rehabilitation and were trying to make themselves viable again. I visited him in the summer. My Nana (his mother), aunts, uncles, cousins, and play cousins were also in Jersey, and they all reminded me who he really was. I mostly stayed with Nana, as all the cousins did each summer, but a few nights a week, I'd crash with Daddy in his one room. One Saturday morning, the sun was barely coming through the blinds, but in my sleep I heard knocking every few minutes on the front door. I was just turning over, but Daddy had been up for at least an hour (an old army habit, he said, when I asked him about his getting up before dawn). In the bed, I faced the door. It cracked open and a little girl, no more than five, was smiling there. "It's Saturday!" she said, and my father ambled over to a dresser under the window, pulled open the bottom drawer, and she darted inside to pick something from it. "Thank you, Mr. B!" she said, as she ran back toward who knows where.

"Daddy, who was that? What'd you give her?"

"Someone's awake, I see," he said and waved me over to the drawer. In its wide mouth, there were bags of snacks: candies, chips, Fruit Roll-Ups, cookies, granola bars, bubblegum packs.

"What is all this?" I asked.

"There are lots of parents here. Kids too. Some have just enough to get by. When I have extra, I tell everyone if they had a good week, Saturday they can come and grab a treat. Mostly the kids take me up on it, but just giving a little, a bit of normalcy, makes everybody feel good."

My father—once an army sergeant, head of household, sole provider—testified that, even when we're in a place we might not have pictured, we can find some gifts to impart, some kindness to ourselves and others. When we went to visit Nana that afternoon and I told her about his junk food drawer, she laughed and said, "He always did have a sweet tooth; no matter where he is, he finds ways to make something worthwhile too."

I teach the same Derek Walcott poem, "Love After Love," at the very end of every poetry class, and a line there has become an adage in my life: "You will love again the stranger who was your self." In this, my father, too, taught me you can always start again.

In revision, I'm asking: How do I use what's left of this ordeal to repurpose it? After years have passed, what weight does this still hold, what will be freed by breaking myself open a bit to burrow into it?

My Aunt says Now the real work begins
the night of my wedding and some years later
I begin to understand:
children are their own kind of labor,
as are our imperfections, often weapons,
aimed at the other through the night.

Trauma changes us, but the grace of adversity is that it can be forged into some beauty. We can only do this pruning well by not dismissing the hard times altogether. We should turn them over, examine them from a new angle or not be afraid to tuck them away temporarily and dig them back up when we have the capacity to balance and refine them.

When working to open a poem up, this revisioning is imperative. Carl Phillips, in his book *The Art of Daring*, says, "To be resonant *is* to resist absolute closure" in a poem. Otherwise, why would we ever return to it? These poems, like our lives, are often collages. Your job as a poet is to only save the essential and to use everything on the page (diction, line breaks, punctuation, title) to your benefit as economically as possible.

In an essay on Sonia Sanchez's poem "Summer Words of a Sistuh Addict," poet Yona Harvey asks: "What's the measure of a poem's hold on you? It's inexact, of course. But it must have something to do with rereading that poem after a long time and feeling your breath catch in all the same places." Poems that resist closure hold me beyond the first reading and bring me back to examine the poet's technique. I'll read a beloved poem silently twice then aloud two more times. I write the syllable count at the end of each line, underline the assonance in stanzas in one color and the slant or hard rhymes in another. I circle unknown words and write the definitions in the margin nearest them to try to trace the poem's tension and resonance. This delving into the poem's inner workings, inside the experience of another, helps me chisel my own.

Poems are an extension of our living. The way I problem-solve in life is much the way I revise poems: I begin with information gathering, then keep only what's most useful. The process is rarely swift. I might let a complex idea sit for years until I have more skill as a writer (or more distance) and return with hope that I'll be able to tame it. Other times, the original idea wanes but I poach a line or stanza and generate something new. Sometimes, I have to come to terms with simply letting the poem go, stopping the work and moving on to others that are further along. But giving up is a last resort. There are plenty of things to try before abandoning the poem altogether.

First, I check for "poem killers," modifiers like adjectives (the *skinny, shy* girl ran down the *long, dark* hallway) and adverbs (he lunged *hastily* as she flung her arms laughing *maniacally*), which are usually filler in first drafts. I highlight them, then vacuum most out by asking: Does the line work without it? Are there clichés? How do they add to the meaning and possible understandings? Is there a word whose sounds add to the music of the poem that does the same work here? Do the words' meanings work in service of the poem or against it?

And what of shape? Seibles said about this: "The white space is about timing, silence, and emphasis, as are the line breaks." Work on seeing the space as silence and only filling it with what music the composition needs. I try to exorcise vague language, words so general they can have superabundant meanings, or phrases that amount to little more than emotional spillage. To heighten the imagery, ask: Are there comparisons (metaphor, symbolism) that can be made to illustrate the ideas? What senses or memories can I tap into to paint a picture of this experience for the reader? How do I fold in my intention—as a thinker and citizen—my leaning toward complexity and empathy?

•◦●◦◦●◦◦◦●◦◦◦●◦◦◦●◦

During our interview, Seibles and I often returned to the larger questions: what is life without reflection? What is freedom? How do we honor the body? The Divine? He explained: "Ultimately, the thing that drew me to writing and sustains my love for it is the freedom it makes possible. I will never be as free in the world as I am on the page." And, of course, we go back to the problem of race, as he does in poems like "After All" and "Really Breathing."*

In addition to how we "read" race, he wants to reenvision how people encounter what's sacred, to rewrite our casting of sex and violence in the same light. I mentioned being confounded by capturing the truth of sensuality. Why is it so hard to explain how people love and make love, make others, hold each other and find all manner of spirit in the uses for the body, in coming to each other to stave off pain, to multiply pleasure?

---

*He echoed Jeffers's sentiment when discussing how race can limit how people approach the work of artists, how they read you: "[A]s a Black author, sometimes you feel some aspects of your work will not be fully appreciated. Race involves myriad levels of complication. . . . I'm Black, but my humanity predates the construct of race. *Race* is imposed upon our lives."

He'd set a lofty goal for himself in this regard: "I want to rescue sexuality and restore it to a celebrated place. It is an expression of the *spiritual* in us as well as a feature of the *raw animal* in us. I make no apology for either of those aspects of our humanity. For me, the erotic realm is one place where those apparent opposites are beautifully reconciled." He ventured on: "In sex, we share companionship—a mutual interest in each other's deepest longings—and physical pleasure becomes a sort of text, a manifestation of another language, perhaps a prayer *to* the body *for* the body."

I, too, am working to reclaim the body in my reenvisioning of poems. I don't want to obscure any part of the sacred. I go back to Seibles's work, poems like "Someone Else" and "Donna James," where the speaker finds himself on the couch with a young woman who leads him into discovery of the unknown. After her foreign touch, he is transformed—a possession, reconfigured in a lover's hands. Because we have such limited language about sex and sensuality, the erotic is difficult terrain to maneuver for most. But the poets remake it. And isn't the body itself political? Doesn't desire often cover everything—good sense, prejudice, difference and anything beyond it? Don't intimacy and love change us irrevocably?

·•● ● ●●●● ● ●●●● ● ●●●● ·

When I was twenty, my parents asked me to remake myself in their image, as they decided to remarry after having been divorced for eight years and separated for many more. They wanted my blessing and asked me to sing Stevie Wonder's "Ribbon in the Sky" at their second wedding. I'd worked so hard to hold a grudge against love in general and let go of the childhood dream of them being together that I was furious. They'd spent much of their lives circling each other, tethered by me and their past until they found their way back. How dare they ask me to let them live as they were, to be eminently flexible, to keep the past as a lesson and little more?

The planets keep spinning
even as the worlds we know fracture,
despite our forming others
who'll pass through us or we'll consume

When my parents came to me, I was in college and had just decided that I wanted to forgo all my good sense and become a poet. This was risky business but I was in a perfect position to try, thanks to my father and, now, to my parents on the whole. When your parents have screwed up royally and you have managed, for the most part, to become a well-functioning adult, it's quite freeing. You get to be the one who triumphs *in spite of*, and almost any path you take—as long as it leads to some semblance of self-reliance—is thought of as praiseworthy, if not miraculous, by your parents and others. I was freed by my father's errors, not because they allowed me to act with cautionless, reckless abandon, but because looking at my father, and my parents as complements of each other, incited me to live with the questions: What, if anything, should stop you from walking into an uncharted course, toward whatever passion calls you? What could ever stop you from making mistakes, then starting over and remaking yourself again?

•••••••••••••••••

Each time I write a book, I am tasked with being honest about how much I've learned. How well can I capture experience anew? What have I come to love enough to let go of? Much of putting together a complete living is culling obsessions and dead weight.

I tend to write my way into a manuscript, so once I have fifty or so poems, I notice patterns or themes. Inevitably I find things to start removing; there are several poems with a few great lines but not much depth, so I use the lines elsewhere, as a starting point or to flesh out the imagery in other pieces. Then there are poems I keep rewriting (all are about the same subject, approached much in the same way, so I'll have to choose which one does the work most effectively). I have a scrap pile of "poem pieces" and keep everything from epigraphs to floating stanzas and old drafts there. I revisit those scraps when I feel like I'm struggling with writer's block.

For instance, I returned to the electronic folder I made for my book *Starlight & Error* and found more than four hundred files saved there. There are at least thirty different versions of the manuscript, and over the course of five years or so, I wrote more than one hundred poems for the project, though only forty ever made the cut. But those other poems aren't lost to me; in one way or another, that mining and harvest will come back around.

I agree with Seibles when he explained why poetry is an ongoing life's work, his pursuit of the beautiful, difficult fragility of us, and who we can thank for his relentlessness. "If my writing has seemed boldly out of bounds at times," he said, "it is, at least in part, due to the fearlessness my parents instilled in me." In this, we are one and the same.

⋅❀ ❀❀❀ ❀ ❀❀❀ ❀ ❀❀❀ ⋅

Some years after my parents' second wedding, my father walked me down the aisle at my own. We paced ourselves moving toward the altar along the long marble floor lined with paintings and folk art in the gallery. As we hit our mark, he turned to look at me and asked, "You ready?" then after I nodded, he said, "I love you," and guided me out among our friends and family.

I got misty not because of what he said, but because it was obvious he'd practiced this, and not just once. He had gone over, in his mind or his mirror, how to affirm his love and walk me into another life. He had practiced this perfect posture, a little stiffer than his usual cool, practiced looking over at me on his right, wearing a dress with a six-foot train he insisted on paying for, practiced what to say and how to say it, so that he didn't waste what I'm sure he imagined, for many years, might be a moment missed. But we'd come to this.

I'm fortunate to have my father. His life defines revision for me (*to amend or alter; to make corrections; to rise*). What I've learned now is you're trying so hard all the time as a parent, but you still falter. Just as when you're a poet, there's a constant effort to move your creations forward, but you hit a wall, you can't get them past their initial inspiration, can't do anything perfectly. This is the work of artists—the work of parenting, the work of growing up—to make process a habit, to mold, to nurture, then let what you bring into the world go where it wills or leave it to the wind.

I will never forget my father appearing at that window (I wrote about this in my first book, *Conversion*, in the poem "Sighting"). I had the memory and the distance then to craft it, bring it to the page. I will also never forget my father walking me down the aisle. I started that poem too, but didn't have the distance or skill to produce it. Maybe it will come to light, maybe not. I try not to fret about this, as this is just another way to stifle yourself—to worry endlessly over your temperament, your penchant for troublesome memories over joyful ones, what you are able to reclaim and what you miss.

My father and I lost some years, but from another angle, we've gained so many. Our lives are more than the things we lose. You are surely more than the slivers you'll come back to or free or discard over time. Revision, then, must ultimately be about care. How do we frame ourselves—in the past, in the future, in the current moment where we have hindsight and the power to mold how we've emerged in our hands?

How can we peer into another reality or scrutinize it through new eyes? Often art is the only way. Revision can be inventing our existence where we stand:

I GO BACK TO SEPTEMBER 1975
Here in the distance I am armed with intimate knowledge.

When my parents meet, they are strange in their certainty
and haughty, imagining they'll be able to withstand anything.

I interrupt to tell them I am the thing they've made
and they smile at the wonder of it then turn back to each other.

Neither is distracted by my ugly disfiguration—
Look at my hands *I say, to which they reply* Beautiful, just beautiful

barely glancing at the overgrown skin, knotted and outstretched,
how it adapts to flood and fire, saving itself to come back as it will.

The work, on yourself and your art, is never wasted. It is useful, necessary tending. At some point you will learn to be your own best, constructive critic. You will interrogate privilege and agency, the temptation to lean toward ease over laboring, humor as bridge or distraction, and how the kind of writer you are becomes tantamount to what kind of human you want to be.

I'm a girl who maybe should be broken, who should find it difficult to weather false starts, but my father has saved me from this paralysis. He has started life after life—and for that matter, so has my mother, forced as she was to learn to care for all she loved in the thick of the ever-changing moment. Now that we've seen the bottom, we are not entirely afraid to straddle the edges of the barrel; we slide down past the rim and inch our way up again. This is how the writing comes, like the living, in fits and starts, in possibility. Sometimes the tinkering leads little further than the spark. Sometimes it must be extinguished altogether. Sometimes it is just kindling enough to help steady another. When all the journey is valued, none of the learning discarded, its usefulness can be built into another kind of story.

All of the italicized lines that appear in this essay, for instance, are from old poems that I couldn't finish, except the last piece (a poem written after Sharon Olds's "I Go Back to May 1937"), which was whole but didn't find a place in any book. Though those are lines you'll probably never see in a collection, revision allowed me to sift and repurpose them. These fragments of memory, tracks of the past, become an undercurrent leading to the future—a map, a maze, a lesson in forgiveness, the groundwork for imagining.

BINGHAM-RISHER: In Muriel Rukeyser's *The Life of Poetry*, she talks about poetry melding what we feel with what we believe. It's a door to newness and possibility. Do you agree?

SEIBLES: I think—in contrast to the *money and power first* sense of life—poetry, by and large, invites us to make a saner, more humane world in which we measure the value of our actions by the truth of the feelings that accompany them. I mean, why are people afraid to feel? Because if you listen to your guts, you must change your life.

COME THROUGH

Every other summer, my mother and I host *The Color Purple* breakfast on the Sunday morning of the Knight–Hyman family reunion filled with folks from her side, when we've all managed to stay in touch, raise money, fuss about who's not coming, who's bringing what, and order the T-shirts on time. We call it *The Color Purple* breakfast because of Alice Walker's novel, of course, but mostly because we cook as much food as Celie does, rectifying Mister's mistakes and wooing Shug in the film. We make Belgian waffles, pancakes by the dozen, slab bacon, beef bacon, turkey bacon (people have gotten fancy over the years), chicken-apple sausage, French toast with strawberries and whipped cream, crates of eggs—scrambled, boiled, omelets with peppers—fried potatoes with onions, buttery grits. Anything we can think of, it seems to multiply like fish and loaves; whatever folks bring when they come through the door, we add it to the pile and make more.

People keep coming for hours. Little ones appear out of nowhere, the uncles crowd into my father's man cave, the aunts take up the sitting and dining rooms. Kids run the backyard with water guns or badminton racquets, unless we are at my house instead of my parents', in which case the kids are all changing into swimsuits, impatient for the beach up the road. We stay at the griddle and on the stove, the house gets no bigger, but we are loudest and happiest when it is full to bursting, when young and old are eating, when there are many thundering rooms.

This, too, is Black poetry—we are hungry, have many facets, and welcome folks in.

At *The Color Purple* breakfast, everybody likes something different, but they're all ready to be filled. We pile onto plates whatever each one requests—*Yeah, let me get a little bit of that burnt sausage from the bottom of the pan. Lots of cheese made into my eggs please. Can I have jelly for my toast and hot sauce for my fish?* Odd pairings, it seems for some, but everybody can come asking for what they want to get fed.

What do I want from poems, what feeds me? All kinds of things. During our interview, Forrest Hamer said it more clearly that I could have: "There are times I want to be moved by poems, other times when I want my experience of language to be upended and my ideas about reality to be upset, even other times when all I want is to hum along with the hum lying deep under the Earth."

There's much I love in poems, but what feeds me, makes them come through and stick to my ribs? I love a hybrid—an invented form; work steeped in music (whether in the rhythm of the poem or as a theme); extended metaphor; tension sustained throughout (i.e., it never gets boring, what comes after each line break is unpredictable); surprise—a shift in perspective or direction, a Volta, a turn, especially one tied so seamlessly to what's around it that the whole work becomes revelatory in the last line; capturing voices as they are, the plain speech of elders and children; making double or triple meaning of words, and, overall, poems that teach me something about human resilience, paring down experience into a compact thing. These kinds of poems come through me, open me up, teach me something about the beauty of existing.

I'm often asked by students trying to make their way into the writing life, How do you know when poems are "good" (though I'd argue "effective" is a more precise term)? When poets trying to make their way into the wider world ask me, How do you know when a book is really "finished" (effective/good)? I give them all the same questions: *What's the sound like? Is there rhythm as well as tension? Are there holes in the narrative? Is the title a help, hindrance, or spoiler? What are the "aha" moments? Is the ending an opening or only a closing?*

The most important thing to ask yourself, then, is what opens you up, what feeds you?

At *The Color Purple* breakfast, though we eat good, the food is secondary. We're really there to be with the people, to hold them for a time and savor what we'll need when we're inevitably apart. This, too, is the story of Black poetry, how community is a haven for us, small or large.

From my comrades in arms, what could I hope for? Mostly a few sets of eyes and ears I can trust with my work, my path, my yearning. Someone to meet for dinner when I have a reading in their home city. Or a few folks who'll come to a conference, see other Black poets in the lobby, drop their bags, and jump in cabs. We head to the nearest multiplex because we have arrived the night they begin showing the film on James Baldwin, *I Am Not Your Negro*, and we need to get some of that good wisdom and talk about it loud while sharing food and libations after. Sometimes I just need folks to be savvy and untangle the nuance of what we're doing, like this exchange with one of my dearests, Dante Micheaux, while I was working on edits for my first book, *Conversion*:

Sent: Monday, August 28, 2006 2:24 PM EDT
To: Dante Micheaux
Subject: In need of your brilliance

Hey Dante,

Remember when you were explaining why we can stick words together in English like "tenderflesh," etc.? Can you please explain that to me one more time?

Love,
Remica

From: Dante Micheaux
Sent: Monday, August 28, 2006 3:02 PM EDT
To: Remica Bingham
Subject: RE: In need of your brilliance

It's very simple: the language (being a Germanic derivation) allows for "compounding." So one can put two nouns together to create a new word (the definition of which is a combination of the definitions from each of the component words). In English, it is most common to use nouns for compounding but we also use other parts of speech (like adjectives)—you just don't realize because we use hyphens. Example: well-respected.

Compounding is probably the most lucrative process for anthimeria (something else we discussed in our workshop: when one part of speech is converted into another part of speech).

Hope this helps,
Dante

Sent: August 28, 2006 at 3:26 PM EDT
To: Dante Micheaux
Subject: RE: RE: In need of your brilliance

You see what I mean? Very well put. Thanks, Sugar(Nasty).

That nickname for Micheaux stuck because it's a phrase from his book-length poem *Circus* that I fell in love with. After hearing it, I started thinking about ways to expand my own poems; hence, the twenty-page-long pieces, albeit broken up by sections, that appear in my second book, *What We Ask of Flesh*. There is a direct iconography to my work from Micheaux's expansive amalgamations and broadening, as is the case for so many poets who come through me. So, as a poet, I look for ways to augment what I know, some new way to be changed.

Most times, the artist's life is an isolated one. For years, I knew no poets in real life, but their words, their bodies of work, sustained me. When I lose a loved one, I go back to Cornelius Eady's prose poems *You Don't Miss Your Water* or Matt Rasmussen's *Black Aperture*. When I need inspiration or innovation, I go to Tyehimba Jess's *Olio*, Douglas Kearney's *Patter*, Evie Shockley's *the new black*, or Vievee Francis's *Forest Primeval*.

And sometimes, if I am fortunate, a book gets stuck in me.

Many days in these difficult times, I have gone back to Ross Gay's *Catalog of Unabashed Gratitude* and Jericho Brown's *The Tradition*. I have not been driven to the page as tenderly and fiercely by any books of poems as I was by these two, in tandem. In my mind they speak to and around each other, but it could be because I remember Gay and Brown cutting up coming down the same aisle, spinning and shimmying, at a reading once, and this brings me joy.

Catalog of Unabashed Gratitude (and Gay's *The Book of Delights* that came a few years after) is about noticing life's little beauties. The poems warble the minutiae of everything—public fig trees, buttonholes, hummingbirds, decomposition and deflowering—what we, in our incessant rushing, have begun to overlook.

The book is a garden of thanks; plot after plot is full of wonder. There are compliments about things that make us most self-conscious. There is kindness multiplied. There's shared sleep and scratch biscuits in the house of a friend, and how we—the irises, bees, humans, and all—have continued to survive in a mean and wasteful world.

I push the book into the hands of students who are taught or have come to believe brooding is poetry's primary use. I'll admit that sometimes, even when I am working in earnest to write joy, the closest I get is nostalgia, maybe a light version of melancholy. But Gay, in vast poems, some that build for a hundred lines or more, pulls everyone into the community of longing, attention, not ignoring life's disruptions and brevity, but calling out for a witness to the boundless remarkableness of our presence in the world and the insatiable hum of what moves us.

Reading Brown's *The Tradition*, I am overwhelmed with the weight of responsibility. I am a Black American poet, there is a tradition of witness and preservation, of truth-telling and oratory, of sly-tongue and candor. All of which we—those walking in the tradition—are then called to keep. In his duplex poems, an invented form of Brown's design, it's like he is trying to outsmart and outplay himself in Spades; he keeps upping the bid and slapping the table. There's a slight variation of each repeated line building to a familiar yet heightened, resonant end: a portico in a delicate house.

I appreciate the crystalline simplicity. The night I receive a galley of the book, one of my best girlfriends has dropped by and sees it on my kitchen table. She is drawn to L. Ralph Burgess's artwork of a dark-skinned boy in a flower crown gracing the cover and opens to the Mari Evans epigraph about how we'll bring our full selves and love to each other.

My friend is not a poet, though she's an avid reader. My poems are probably the last she's read and mostly because she knows the cast of characters. I tell her: "You wouldn't believe how gorgeous it is, only two poems in. Let me read this to you." And she listens while I read "As a Human Being," where a mother chooses her battered husband over her bruised son and breaks him (or frees him, depending on your lens) indefinitely. "You know how people complain about poems not being clear," she says, "this book, right now, this book is negating all of that," and I agree.

This careful attention coupled with joy, this tradition of clarity, tenderness, and preservation, these are the rituals I want to see come through us again and again. I work for them in the poems I seek out and the poems I craft. Also, these ten poets I've interviewed, whose reminders I've lived with for decades, tell me my job is not to dream the same dream for all of us; my job is to keep making a way for words, for hunger, and to be open to many rooms.

·•● ● ●•●● ● ●•●● ● ●•●● ·

We sit around telling stories most of the morning at *The Color Purple* breakfast. We do this long after the food is gone. We remember great-uncles who shaped whole neighborhoods running numbers and old apartments we all passed through on Thirty-Fifth Street. It's important to remember our history, that when it seemed there was no mass of folks making a place for us, they lived and were.

What happened in the years between the Black Arts Movement and Cave Canem to sustain Black poetry? An innumerable mass of things: organizations burgeoned like the Hurston/Wright Foundation and Furious Flower Poetry Center along with their awards and gatherings; the Dark Room and the Baobab Collectives and Affrilachian Poets came together; journals like *Callaloo*, *Obsidian*, and *African American Review* began.

The world nodded in the direction of Black creatives when Derek Walcott and Toni Morrison won back-to-back Nobel Prizes and in the span of fewer than ten years Rita Dove and Yusef Komunyakaa won the Pulitzer. Hip-hop emerged and progressed from party anthems to social commentary to international cultural movement. Then there was the rise of performance poetry, slam, and spoken word, and the emergence and influx of graduate programs in creative writing was something Tim Seibles and I discussed during our interview. I wondered why more people seemed to be invested in the study of writing and art (though all the signs point to it being a thankless and not very lucrative endeavor) and he said "[the] proliferation of MFA programs reflects a felt need in this culture. People want meanings, visions, voices that reflect their actual lives." This is what Black poetry provides for me and many others.

I'm not a historian, and this list wasn't meant to be exhaustive, as an abundance is missing. But no matter how many details we'd add, we could never capture all the on-the-ground, under-the-radar work that is, for the artists, life-sustaining. The things you will barely find in the larger literary archive are the pockets of community—the two or three fast friends that tended to each other's work and love and sorrow for decades, in living rooms, cafés, and makeshift writer's spaces for countless hours.

Even when critics say nothing was happening, something always was, folks were always coming through, always creating. So, if you fancy yourself any kind of artist, to persevere, you must tap into community, however small or large. Community is what keeps the work going, what feeds. Their convergence might not be given a name, but their movement is what sustains us.

·● ● ●●● ● ●●● ● ●●● ·

When my aunts, mother, and I are cooking, some folks are just standing near the doorway, out of the kitchen, watching others work. Some are cousins growing into themselves and this tradition, itching to put heat to oil and simmer. If they are careful, we call them in and let them flip the pancakes on the griddle, season the grits, or make plates. These are our students, but also our kin. They ensure someone will bear these rituals in the future, then stir the pot all over again.

And the students who find their way to me, what else do I try to teach them? Poems and poets are often given a bad rap of being flighty or useless, but this is an ugly untruth I try to dispel, as poets are called to the fore always to synthesize and commemorate, whether in mourning or reverence or jubilation. In addition to teaching them about what I believe makes a good poem, I ask them to ruminate on how they might be called to use poetry in the real world. On a midterm, I might ask them to choose one of the following tasks:

- Writers are often asked to compose or at least find occasional poems (i.e., a love poem for your best friend's wedding, for a loved one's funeral, to give to a lover on an anniversary, to read as a toast at a graduation party).* Pretend you have been asked to do one of these things and either write an original poem or find an appropriate poem for the event. In a mini-essay, include the poem, then explain why it is relevant, what complex craft devices are at work, and how/why it would have an impact on the audience who asked you to find or create it.
- Go to an area museum and find one piece of art that piques your interest. Compose an ekphrastic poem (a poem in response to or about a piece of art) that even those who have never seen the artwork will be able to understand. Next, write a museum object label with a few sentences about how you felt encountering the

---

*This is also where I let students review several drafts of a poem I had to write for my grandfather's funeral, which at the time seemed like an impossible task, as I had to eulogize one I deeply loved but also do it in a few days' time and I am a notoriously slow reviser. I let my students see how the writing and remembering begins as a reply to an email from my grandmother, his second wife, and how the litany grows, in scope and detail, trying to encompass all those tendrils of family, our varying beloved over time. Then, finally, what I stand up to read in the church full of people mostly older and wiser than me, who knew his meticulous living, who nod and "uh-huh" all through the telling. I stress that, most times, the only way to get this right, to make a poem useful, especially in elegy, is to lean on detail and honesty, to craft with intention, a singular life.

artwork and a bit about the background of the poem you were inspired to write.

- Go to the poetry section of a local bookstore and write an inventory review about what kinds of patterns you see there. Include answers to the following questions: What publishers do you see most frequently? What is the ratio of male poets versus female poets? Poets of color versus others? Older, more established poets versus younger poets? Where is the poetry section in the store? About how large/small is the poetry section compared to other sections? How do these things influence your work/life choice to try to have a career as a poet or a champion of poets and poetry, and why?

What is poetry's use to us—in the real world, on any normal day? I am listening to *The Stacks* podcast about the anthology *Four Hundred Souls: A Community History of African America, 1619–2019*, and one of the editors, historian Keisha N. Blain, explains that at the end of each section spanning eighty years in American history, there's a culminating poem. The poets therein were called to synthesize the time, to bring all of the scholars' words and ideas together succinctly and creatively, "as a breather," she says, which means beauty and craft can be an education, an "aha" moment, but also a release and relief for all who encounter it.

⋅❋ ◦ ❋❋❋ ◦ ❋❋❋ ◦ ❋❋❋ ⋅

At the head of the table at *The Color Purple* breakfast, there's someone who's lived a bit more than others, usually aunties who have, through the years, fed and cleaned, even housed, many of us. The younger folks wait in a growing line, until we bring the elders a heaping plate. We pile on extra, though they never ask for it. But we know their breaking bread with us is a gift and want them made to feel like they've made us feel—"Happy and full as a tick," the elders might say; in other words: cared for, catered to, never without a place.

In Black poetry, the elders have made a place for us, so now, in their wake, what are we trying to build? My hope is to build a bridge of memory, to draw a line from the work of others to the work that will surely be what Erica Hunt, during our interview, called "letters to the future," to the readers we haven't imagined yet, who will need us in our fullness and hold us as we've held others in our pockets and backpacks, in our difficult hours and snatches of joy.

So much of the artist's life is a solitary litany of no's—you come to the page in the quiet of morning, when you can steal time, and wrestle with crafting a life all alone. When you fling your efforts out into the world, much will be lost to indifference or rigidity, many will say your interior life is insignificant, on the fringes, or superabundant, too much, too heavy, peculiar, more than what they consider enough. Every poet who grew me up was told the same, in one way or another. Every dreamer, every dancer, every painter, every drummer, every one stepping out on faith in art.

And yet. Here we are.

I've chosen to spend my life reading and writing poetry because it continues to introduce me to myself, and to beauty. I write as a way of tussling with what I can't answer in myself and—sometimes—the finished poem (the years-long process of sifting and casting) helps me get invaluably closer to that understanding.

For many of us, poetry is about clarifying questions we have about the world, asking those questions with as much precision as we can. Much of our work as writers is to help spotlight what is unseen or underseen. My belief in Black voices, this long-standing love of Black voices, is part of the vibrant fabric of the literary canon long overlooked. This work saved me and will save plenty others left in our hands.

Our work in the world is not only to craft what hasn't been foreseen, but also to pull others along, keep making room. How do poets pull up and come through? Carve out a place for those coming behind. Guard the lives and work of some who might otherwise be left to obscurity. Champion others. Find your people, soak up all you can, then begin to write.

ACKNOWLEDGMENTS

Some pieces were previously published (in other forms) in the following journals and anthologies: *Writer's Chronicle, Mosaic, New Letters, Gulf Coast, PoemMemoirStory, Critical Flame, Langston Hughes Review, Poems and Their Making: A Conversation Anthology,* and *Of Color: Poets' Ways of Making: An Anthology of Essays on Transformative Poetics.*

All thanks goes to Jehovah God for inspiring Acts 17:28: "For by him we have life and move and exist, even as certain ones of the poets among you have said, 'For we are also his progeny,'" and for every hope.

I'm so grateful to all the writers who shared their time and insight with me. My family, especially the Knight, Bingham, and Anderson clans, who hold me up always.

My graduate students, who were invaluable: Lucian Mattison, Robbie Ciara, Sarah McCall, Nishat Ahmed, Courtney Tala, and Kelsey Orsini, who helped me edit down to the wire.

Cave Canem—Toi Derricotte and Cornelius Eady, Sarah Micklem, and especially Carolyn Micklem, who ushered so many of us in. Thanks, too, to Alison Meyers and Nicole Sealey, who held down the fort after. And to all sustaining the sacred space.

To the friends who've continuously encouraged me: Matilda Cox, Princess Joy L. Perry, L. Lamar Wilson, Christian Campbell, Amanda Jonhston, Reginald Dwayne Betts, Linda Janet Holmes, Mahogany L. Browne, DéLana Dameron, DaMaris Hill, Phillip Williams, Myron Michael Hardy, Jericho Brown, Ross Gay, Aracelis Girmay, John Murillo, Rachel Eliza Griffiths, Frank X. Walker, Shauna Morgan, and especially

Honorée Fanonne Jeffers, for all the reasons herein. Dante Micheaux, who read every word and trusted my instincts long ago.

The Bennington Bitch Club: Jeannie Kim-McPherson, Ada Ude-chukwu, David Harbilas, Kari Ruth, Sarai Walker, William Vandegrift, Alexis Perlmutter, and honorary member Alice Mattison, for camaraderie and love. Most especially Anita Darcel Taylor, who read each of these essays then told me I was on the right track (or how I might get there). My Bennington teachers: E. Ethelbert Miller, Ed Ochester, Jason Shinder, and Amy Gerstler.

For lifetime friends, who always encourage me, many thanks: Jane Ahn, Veronica Gordon Murphy, Eugene Calloway, and Monica Black.

Natasha Taylor, sister-friend, mom-in-arms, best of the besties. Thank you for Orange Rooms talks, for love, and for everything in between. Prov. 17:17.

The Watering Hole fam, especially Monifa Lemons and Candace Wiley: I see you, Tribe.

Lotus, Etruscan, and Diode for having faith in the word.

All my students and colleagues who helped me on this journey at Norfolk State and Old Dominion Universities.

Sidney, Gillian, and Alexia Clifton—Daughters of Light, Keepers of Light. Thank you for continuing to share Ms. Lucille with us.

Jennifer Fish, for faith in spirit and for seeing.

For early encouragement about the publishing process, many thanks: Sarah Johnson, Meta DuEwa Jones, Mesha Maren, Camille Dungy, and Amy Cherry, who took time to read this work, give feedback and encouragement, then set me off to make it sharper.

Larissa Melo Pienkowski, agent of my dreams, thank you for your faith in and care for this work from our beginning. Haley Lynch, editor extraordinaire, who saw the promise in this work and understood the import of sharing stories of the Black interior. Helene Atwan, for support from the beginning and keeping the flame for countless essential voices. The entire Beacon Press team, thank you for seeing this work and ushering it in with a guiding hand.

Thanks to Beyoncé's film *Homecoming*, and just to Beyoncé in general, who I go back to, to remind myself what crafted, joyful excellence can look like on a dazzling scale and how you can center your folks, no matter who's watching.

The Parentals: Robert Bingham and Doris Knight-Bingham, for love after love after love.

For my Nana, Shirley Bingham, for all her stories and encouragement. Also, Rosie and Radeem Ellington, for always giving us all a soft place to land. And to Loretta Bingham, for having those words mounted on silk those years ago.

My Cute Sweet Husband, Michael, who loves and compliments my mind (and all the other things), who tells me passion is a gift, and gathers me.

My mother-in-law and brother-in law, Alesia Anderson and Johnathan Chambers, for all their love and care.

My kids, Sonsoréa (and grandbaby Naveen) and Michael, I'm so grateful for you. I hope you'll look back on this one day and know how much you've changed me.

Sonia (and Phalaan), thank you for trusting me and for cheering me on without knowing how badly I needed it. For emojis, flowers, and for love.

To all those who continually sustain me: light and love.

SOURCES

INTRODUCTION

Bingham-Risher, Remica. "Training or a Weapon." In *Starlight & Error*. Doha, Qatar: Diode Editions, 2017.

Cave Canem, "Mission & History," 2015. https://cavecanempoets.org /mission-history/.

Cisewski, Paula. "5×5: Diode Poets in Conversation." *Diode Poetry Journal*, March 6, 2018. diodepoetry.com/5x5.

Greenfield, Eloise. "Things." In *Honey, I Love and Other Love Poems*. New York: Crowell, 1978.

Hudson, Wade and Valerie Wilson Wesley. *AFRO-BETS Book of Black Heroes from A to Z*. Orange, NJ: Just Us Books, 1988.

IMAGINING HOME

Chandler, Davis, interview by Robin Young, *Here & Now*, March 20, 2015. "Investigation Ongoing into Black Man Found Hanging in Mississippi." NPR. https://radio.wpsu.org/2015-03-20/investigation-ongoing-into -black-man-found-hanging-in-mississippi.

Dungy, Camille T. ed. *Black Nature: Four Centuries of African American Nature Poetry*. Athens: University of Georgia Press, 2009.

Earle, Carville. "The Price of Precocity: Technical Choice and Ecological Constraint in the Cotton South, 1840–1890." *Agricultural History* 66, no. 3 (1992): 25–60.

Hamer, Forrest. Personal interview, via email. April 24, 2015.

Hayes, Isaac. "By the Time I Get to Phoenix." Track 4 on *Hot Buttered Soul*. Enterprise, 1969, album.

Hermann, William. "School Learns a Tough Lesson in Deceit." *Arizona Republic*, 1994.

Hughes, Langston. "Mother to Son." In *The Collected Poems of Langston Hughes*. New York: Vintage, 1995.

———. "The Negro Artist and the Racial Mountain." In *The Collected Works of Langston Hughes*. Columbia: University of Missouri Press, 2002.

Jordan, June. "Poem about My Rights." In *Directed by Desire: The Collected Poems of June Jordan*. Port Townsend, WA: Copper Canyon Press, 2007.

Lee, Michelle Ye Hee. "Recalling Arizona's Struggle for MLK Holiday." AZCentral.com, January 16, 2012. azcentral.com/arizonarepublic/news/articles/20120112martin-luther-king-holiday-dilemma.html.

Miller, E. Ethelbert. "October 31." In *First Light: New and Selected Poems*. Baltimore: Black Classic Press, 1994.

———., ed. *In Search of Color Everywhere: A Collection of African-American Poetry*. New York: Harry N. Abrams, 1996.

———. Personal interview. Miller's home, Washington, DC, April 24, 2004.

———. *Season of Hunger/Cry of Rain*. Detroit: Broadside Lotus Press, 1982.

———. *Whispers, Secrets and Promises*. Baltimore: Black Classic Press, 1998.

"Phoenix, Ariz." Infoplease, n.d. www.infoplease.com/world/us-cities/phoenix-ariz.

Randall, Dudley, ed. *The Black Poets*. New York: Bantam Books, 1988.

Ross, Diana. "Missing You." Track 1 on *Swept Away*. RCA, 1984, album.

Sanchez, Sonia. Personal interview. Modern Language Association Conference, Philadelphia, PA, December 27, 2006.

Terkenli, Theano S. "Home as a Region." *Geographical Review* 85, no. 3 (1995): 324–34. Accessed February 25, 2021. doi:10.2307/215276.

US Department of Commerce, Economics and Statistics Administration, Bureau of the Census. "1990 Census of Population: General Population Characteristics: Arizona." www2.census.gov/library/publications/decennial/1990/cp-1/cp-1-4.pdf.

ON FAITH

Bingham-Risher, Remica. "Young, small, and growing, often violently." In *Starlight & Error*. Doha: Diode Editions, 2017.

Franklin, Aretha. "Ain't No Way." Track 5 (B side) on *Lady Soul*. Atlantic, 1968, album.

Jackson, Major. "Urban Renewal—Block Party." *Leaving Saturn*. Athens, GA: University of Georgia Press, 2002.

Jeffers, Honorée Fanonne. "Giving Thanks for Water." In *Red Clay Suite*. Carbondale, IL: Southern Illinois University Press, 2007.

———. "I End in Winter" and "Singing Counter." In *The Glory Gets*. Middletown, CT: Wesleyan University Press, 2015.

———. "Incident at Cross Plains (The Lynching of William Luke, 1870)." In *Outlandish Blues*. Middletown, CT: Wesleyan University Press, 2003.

———. Personal interview, via video conference. March 20, 2015.

———. "The Gospel of Barbecue," "What Grief Is," and "Where the Song Stops." In *The Gospel of Barbecue*. Kent, OH: Kent State University Press, 2000.

———. "The Subjective Briar Patch: Contemporary American Poetry." *Virginia Quarterly Review Online*, May 29, 2015. https://www.vqronline .org/vqr-symposium/subjective-briar-patch-contemporary-american-poetry.

Marshall, Paule. "From the Poets in the Kitchen." *New York Times*, January 9, 1983. https://www.nytimes.com/1983/01/09/books/from-the -poets-in-the-kitchen.html.

NASA. "Hubble eXtreme Deep Field (XDF)." HubbleSite.org. September 15, 2012. https://hubblesite.org/contents/media/images/2012/37/3098 -Image.html?keyword=extreme%20deep%20field.

New World Translation of the Holy Scriptures—With References. Warwick, NY: Watch Tower Bible and Tract Society of Pennsylvania, 1984.

Peter, Paul and Mary. "Leaving on a Jet Plane." Track 2 on *Album 1700*. Warner Bros., 1967, album.

Smith, Patricia. "Terrell's Take on Things." *Close to Death*. Cambridge, MA: Zoland Books, 1998.

INTIMATE TENDING

Bingham, Remica L. "Adam's Conversion" and "Genesis." In *Conversion*. Detroit: Lotus Press, 2007.

———. "Finding the Myth in the Human and the Human in the Myth: Midrash and Mythos in the Work of Lucille Clifton." *Langston Hughes Review* 22 (2008): 27–35. Accessed March 13, 2021. http://www.jstor .org/stable/26434650.

———. "The Body Speaks." In *What We Ask of Flesh*. Wilkes-Barre, PA: Etruscan Press, 2013.

Clifton, Lucille. *Blessing the Boats: New and Selected Poems, 1988–2000*. 1st ed. American Poets Continuum Series, v. 60. Rochester, NY: BOA Editions, 2000.

———. "eve's version" and "fat fat water rat." *Quilting: Poems, 1987–1990*. Rochester, NY: BOA Editions, 1991.

———. *Good Times: Poems*. New York: Random House, 1969.

———. *Mercy: Poems*. Rochester, NY: BOA Editions, 2004.

———. Personal interview. Geraldine R. Dodge Poetry Festival, Stanhope, NJ, September 29, 2006.

———. "poem in praise of menstruation," "poem to my uterus," "surely i am able to write poems," and "wishes for sons" *The Collected Poems of Lucille Clifton 1965–2010*. Rochester, NY: BOA Editions, 2012.

———. "*won't you celebrate with me*." *The Book of Light*. Port Townsend, WA: Copper Canyon Press, 1993.

Derricotte, Toi. "Brother," "Clitoris," "Family Secrets," "Invisible Dreams," "Preface," and "When My Father Was Beating Me." In *Tender*. Pittsburgh: University of Pittsburgh Press, 1997.

COURTING PARADISE

Bingham-Risher, Remica L. "Distant Lover." In *Starlight & Error*. Doha, Qatar: Diode Editions, 2017.

Butler, Octavia E. *The Parable of the Talents*. New York: Seven Stories Press, 1998.

Coleman, Monica A. *Making A Way Out of No Way: Womanist Theology*. Minneapolis: Fortress Press, 2008.

Gaye, Marvin. "Distant Lover." Track 5 on *Marvin Gaye Live!* Tamla, 1974, album.

Jordan, A. Van. *M-A-C-N-O-L-I-A*. New York: W. W. Norton, 2004.

———. Personal interview. Greensboro, NC, May 1, 2004.

———. *Rise*. Sylmar, CA: Tia Chucha, 2001.

———. "Thought Experiment #1: E=MC²." In *Quantum Lyrics*. New York: W. W. Norton, 2009.

———. *The Cineaste*. New York: W. W. Norton, 2014.

Lee, Spike, dir. *Do the Right Thing*. 1989; New York, NY: The Criterion Collection, 2001. DVD.

Lordi, Emily. *The Meaning of Soul: Black Music and Resilience Since the 1960s*. Durham, NC: Duke University Press, 2020.

Rodriguez, Oz, dir. *Michael Che Matters*. 2016; New York, NY: Broadway Video. Netflix, 2016.

BLK/WOOOMEN REVOLUTION

Alexander, Elizabeth. *The Black Interior: Essays*. Minneapolis: Graywolf, 2004.

Alexander, Elizabeth and Lyrae Van Clief-Stefanon. "The Black Woman Speaks." In *Poems in Conversation and a Conversation*. Sleepy Hollow, NY: Slapering Hol Press, 2008.

Attie, Barbara, Janet Goldwater, and Sabrina Schmidt Gordon, dirs. *BaddDDD Sonia Sanchez*. Bala Cynwyd, PA: Attie & Goldwater Productions, 2015.

Bingham, Remica L. "Remica L. Bingham Interview." By Michelle Lesko. *Ithaca Lit*, December 31, 2013. https://ithacalitarchives.com/remica-l -bingham.html.

———. *What We Ask of Flesh*. Wilkes-Barre, PA: Etruscan Press, 2013.

Bingham-Risher, Remica L. "Our child is not yet ten and we are clearing his closet." In *Starlight & Error*. Doha, Qatar: Diode Editions, 2017.

Randall, Dudley. "Introduction." In *We a BaddDDD People*, by Sonia Sanchez. Detroit: Broadside Press, 1970. 1–5.

Sanchez, Sonia. "—answer to yo/question / of am i not yo/woman / even if u went on shit again," "blk/rhetoric," "Indianapolis/summer/1969/poem," and "summer words of a sistuh addict." In *We a BaddDDD People*. Detroit: Broadside Press, 1970.

———. *Morning Haiku*. Boston: Beacon Press, 2010.

———. *I've Been a Woman: New and Selected Poems*. Ann Arbor, MI: Bell & Howell Information and Learning Company, 2000.

———. Personal interview. Modern Language Association Conference, Philadelphia, December 27, 2006.

Walker, Alice. "The Unglamorous but Worthwhile Duties of the Black Revolutionary Artist, or of the Black Writer Who Simply Works and Writes." In *In Search of Our Mothers' Gardens*. San Diego: Harcourt, 1983.

GIRLS LOVING BEYONCÉ AND THEIR NAMES

Beyoncé. *4*. Parkwood Entertainment/Columbia Records, 2011, album.

———. *Beyoncé*. Parkwood Entertainment/Columbia Records, 2013, visual album.

———. *Lemonade*. Parkwood Entertainment/Columbia Records, 2016, visual album.

Bingham-Risher, Remica L. "Love in Stereo" and "Son·sor·éa (\ sahn-soar-ray\)." In *Starlight & Error*. Doha, Qatar: Diode Editions, 2017.

Browne, Mahogany L. (@mobrowne). "I wish you the satisfaction . . ." Twitter. February 16, 2021, 2:34 PM. https://twitter.com/mobrowne /status/1361760827561361418.

Clifton, Lucille. "jonah." In *Good Woman*. Rochester, NY: BOA Editions, 1991.

Hamer, Forrest. "Arrival," "Crossroads," and "Edge." In *Middle Ear*. Berkeley, CA: Roundhouse Press, 2000.

———. "Common Betrayal." In *Rift: Poems*. Berkeley, CA: Four Way, 2007.

———. *Hear, Hear: Occasional Posts on Poetry & Psychoanalysis* (blog), September 1, 2013, http://forresthamer.blogspot.com/2013/09.

———. Personal interview, via email. April 24, 2015.

Hunt, Erica. Personal interview, via video conference. April 4, 2015.

New Edition. "Delicious." Track 5 on *New Edition*. MCA, 1984, cassette.

Oxford English Dictionary. Online ed. Oxford: Oxford University Press, 2015.

Studium Generale Rietveld Academie. "To the Bone: Some Speculations on Touch, Hortense Spillers." YouTube video, June 27, 2018: 51:38. https://www.youtube.com/watch?v=AvL4wUKIfpo&t=1431s.

Wilentz, Amy. "A Zombie Is a Slave Forever." *New York Times*, October 30, 2012. https://www.nytimes.com/2012/10/31/opinion/a-zombie -is-a-slave-forever.html?referringSource=articleShare.

WHO RAISED YOU?

Alexander, Elizabeth. *The Light of the World*. New York: Grand Central Publishing, 2015.

Bingham, Remica L. "The Lost Gospel of Peter." In *Conversion*. Detroit: Lotus Press, 2007.

Bingham-Risher, Remica L. "Our child is not yet ten and we are clearing his closet." In *Starlight & Error*. Doha, Qatar: Diode Editions, 2017.

Brooks, Gwendolyn, "The Boy Died in My Alley." In *The Essential Gwendolyn Brooks: Selected Poems*, ed. Elizabeth Alexander. New York: Library of America, 2005.

Clifton, Lucille. "A Conversation with Lucille Clifton." *With Good Reason*, WHRO/NPR, Norfolk, VA: July 11, 2009, rebroadcast April 18, 2015.

———. "won't you celebrate with me." In *Book of Light*. Port Townsend, WA: Copper Canyon Press, 1993.

Riggs, Marlon, dir. *Ethnic Notions*. California Newsreel, 1986.

Hunt, Erica. "A Coronary Artist" and "Second Voice." In *Local History*. New York: Roof Books, 1993.

———. "Chapter 2: Back-Home." In *Time Slips Right Before Your Eyes*. Brooklyn: Belladonna, 2015.

———. "Notes for an Oppositional Poetics." In *The Politics of Poetic Form: Poetry and Public Policy*, ed. Charles Bernstein. New York: Roof Books, 1990.

———. Personal interview, via video conference. April 4, 2015.

Hunt, Erica, and Alison Saar. "Biographical Suite" and "Coronary Artist
1." In *Arcade*. Berkeley, CA: Kelsey St. Press, 1996.

New World Translation of the Holy Scriptures — With References. Warwick,
NY: Watch Tower Bible and Tract Society of Pennsylvania, 1984.

Olds, Sharon. "The Green Shirt." In *The Gold Cell*. 1st ed. Knopf Poetry
Series. New York: Knopf, 1987.

Sexton, Margaret Wilkerson. *A Kind of Freedom*. Berkeley, CA: Counter-
point, 2017.

Walcott, Derek. "Love After Love." In *Derek Walcott Collected Poems
1948–1984*. New York: Farrar, Straus and Giroux, 1987.

THE TERROR OF BEING DESTROYED

Ai. "Elegy," "Hitchhiker," "Life Story," and "The Good Shepherd: Atlanta,
1981." In *Vice: New and Selected Poems*. New York: W. W. Norton,
2000.

Baldwin, James. *The Evidence of Things Not Seen*. New York: Holt, Rine-
hart and Winston, 1985.

Bingham, Remica L. "How I Crossed Over," "The Body Speaks," and
"What We Ask of Flesh." In *What We Ask of Flesh*. Wilkes-Barre, PA:
Etruscan Press, 2013.

Craven, Julia. "Donald Glover's 'This Is America,' Through the Eyes of a
Jim Crow Historian." *HuffPost*, May 9, 2018. https://www.huffpost
.com/entry/donald-glover-this-is-america-jim-crow-history_n_5af31588
e4b00a3224efcc40.

Danticat, Edwidge. *The Art of Death: Writing the Final Story*. Minneapolis:
Graywolf Press, 2017.

Glück, Louise. "The Forbidden." In *Proofs & Theories: Essays on Poetry*.
Hopewell, NJ: Ecco Press, 1995.

Gourevitch, Philip. *We Wish to Inform You That Tomorrow We Will Be Killed
with Our Families: Stories from Rwanda*. New York: Picador, 1998.

Jackson, Major. "Assuming the Mask: Persona and Identity in Ai's Poetry."
Poets.org. September 30, 2018. https://poets.org/text/assuming-mask
-persona-and-identity-ais-poetry.

Kearney, Lawrence, and Michael Cuddihy. "Ai." In *American Poetry Ob-
served: Poets on Their Work*, ed. Joe David Bellamy. Urbana: University
of Illinois Press, 1984. 1–8.

Morrison, Toni. *Song of Solomon*. New York: Alfred A. Knopf, 1977.

———. *The Bluest Eye*. New York: Holt McDougal, 1970.

———. *The Source of Self-Regard: Selected Essays, Speeches, and Medita-
tions*. New York: Alfred A. Knopf, 2019.

New World Translation of the Holy Scriptures—With References. Warwick, NY: Watch Tower Bible and Tract Society of Pennsylvania, 1984.

Trethewey, Natasha. *Bellocq's Ophelia.* Minneapolis: Graywolf Press, 2002.

———. "Flounder." In *Domestic Work.* Minneapolis: Graywolf Press, 2000.

———. *Memorial Drive: A Daughter's Memoir.* New York: Ecco, 2020.

———. *Native Guard.* New York: Houghton Mifflin, 2006.

———. Personal interview. Decatur Book Festival, Atlanta, GA, August 31, 2007.

STANDING IN THE SHADOWS OF LOVE

Bingham, Remica L. *What We Ask of Flesh: Poems.* Wilkes-Barre, PA: Etruscan Press, 2013.

Bingham-Risher, Remica L. "Benediction," "Getting Ready for the Heartache to Come or A Body Intercepting Light," "If It's Magic," "Skipping Stones," and "Solstice." In *Starlight & Error.* Doha, Qatar: Diode Editions, 2017.

Didion, Joan. *The Year of Magical Thinking.* New York: Alfred A. Knopf/Doubleday, 2005.

"Eric Garner, Mike Brown and Now, Rumain Brisbon: White Officer in Arizona Shoots and Kills Unarmed Black Man." HNGN: Headlines and Global News, December 4, 2014, https://www.hngn.com/articles /51824/20141204/eric-garner-mike-brown-now-rumain-brisbon-white -office-arizona.htm.

Four Tops. "Standing in the Shadows of Love." Track 8 on *Reach Out.* Motown, 1967, album.

Heinz, Kurt. "The Book of Voices: Patricia Smith." Website. December 31, 1999. http://voices.e-poets.net/SmithP.

Holman, Bob. "Patricia Smith, Journalism & Poetry: Shall We Meditate on Truth?" Modern American Poetry (website), 1998. maps-legacy.org /poets/s_z/p_smith/about.htm.

Oxford English Dictionary. Online ed. Oxford: Oxford University Press, 2019.

Smith, Patricia. *Big Towns, Big Talk.* Cambridge, MA: Zoland, 1992.

———. *Incendiary Art.* Evanston, IL: Triquarterly, 2017.

———. "Introduction." In *What We Ask of Flesh: Poems,* by Remica L. Bingham, Wilkes-Barre, PA: Etruscan Press, 2013, xv–xvi.

———. *Life According to Motown.* Sylmar, CA: Tia Chucha, 1991.

———. "Motown Crown." In *Shoulda Been Jimi Savannah.* Minneapolis: Coffee House Press, 2012.

———. "Pearl, Upward." In *The Best American Essays 2011*, ed. Edwidge Danticat and Robert Atwan. New York: Mariner, 2011.

———. Personal interview. Association of Writers and Writing Programs Conference, Austin, TX, March, 11, 2006.

———. *Teahouse of the Almighty*. Minneapolis: Coffee House Press, 2006.

REVISION AS LABYRINTH

Bingham, Remica L. "Sighting." In *Conversion*. Detroit: Lotus Press, 2007.

Bingham-Risher, Remica. "Fast Animal Nominated for a National Book Award!" *Remica L. Bingham Blog*. October 10, 2012, http://remical bingham.blogspot.com/2012/10.

Harvey, Yona. "Yona Harvey on Sonia Sanchez's 'Summer Words of a Sistuh Addict.'" *Poetry Daily*. https://poems.com/features/what-sparks -poetry/yona-harvey-on-sonia-sanchezs-summer-words-of-a-sistuh -addict.

Phillips, Carl. *The Art of Daring: Risk, Restlessness, Imagination*. Minneapolis: Graywolf Press, 2014.

Rich, Adrienne. "When We Dead Awaken: Writing as Re-Vision." In *Arts of the Possible*. New York: W. W. Norton, 2013.

Rukeyser, Muriel. *The Life of Poetry*. Middletown, CT: Wesleyan University Press, 1996.

Seibles, Tim. *Body Moves*. New York: Corona Publishing Company, 1988.

———. *Buffalo Head Solos*. Cleveland: Cleveland State University Poetry Center, 2004.

———. *Fast Animal*. Wilkes-Barre, PA: Etruscan Press, 2012.

———. Personal interviews. Old Dominion University, Norfolk, VA, May 9, 2004, and via email, December 12, 2013.

———. "Trying for Fire." In *Hurdy-Gurdy*. Cleveland: Cleveland State University Poetry Center, 1992.

Walcott, Derek. "Love After Love." In *Sea Grapes*. New York: Farrar, Straus and Giroux, 1976.

COME THROUGH

Bingham, Remica L. *What We Ask of Flesh*. Wilkes-Barre, PA: Etruscan Press, 2013.

Blain, Keisha N. "Ep. 150 An Invitation to History with Keisha N. Blain," interview by Traci Thomas. *The Stacks*, podcast. February 10, 2021. https://thestackspodcast.com/2021/02/10/ep-150-keisha-n-blain.

Brown, Jericho. "As a Human Being." In *The Tradition*. Port Townsend, WA: Copper Canyon Press, 2019.

Eady, Cornelius. *You Don't Miss Your Water*. New York: Henry Holt and Co., 2005.

Francis, Vievee. *Forest Primeval*. Evanston, IL: Triquarterly, 2015.

Gay, Ross. *Catalog of Unabashed Gratitude*. Pittsburgh: University of Pittsburgh Press, 2015.

———. *The Book of Delights*. Chapel Hill, NC: Algonquin Books, 2019.

Hamer, Forrest. Personal interview. April 24, 2015.

Jess, Tyehimba. *Olio*. Seattle: Wave Books, 2016.

Kearney, Douglas. *Patter*. Pasadena: Red Hen Press, 2014.

Kendi, Ibram X., and Keisha N. Blain, eds. *Four Hundred Souls: A Community History of African America, 1619–2019*. New York: One World, 2021.

Micheaux, Dante. *Circus*. Brooklyn: Indolent Books, 2018.

Rasmussen, Matt. *Black Aperture*. Baton Rouge: Louisiana State University Press, 2013.

Shockley, Evie. *the new black*. Middletown, CT: Wesleyan University Press, 2012.

Spielberg, Steven, dir. *The Color Purple*. 1985; Burbank, CA: Warner Home Video, 1997. DVD.

Walker, Alice. *The Color Purple*. New York: Harcourt Brace Jovanovich, 1982.

CREDITS

INDEX

Note: Page numbers with an added "n" refer to notes at the end of the book.

acceptance, human need for, 107
Achebe, Chinua, 82
Acts 17:28, 199
"Adam's Conversion"
    (Bingham-Risher), 53
addiction, 87–88, 174, 177
Affrilachian Poets, 194
"Africa" (Bingham-Risher), 9–11
African American Literature and Its
    Cultural Traditions class, 65, 126
African American Review, 194
"After All" (Seibles), 182
The Age of Phillis (Jeffers), 32
Ai: *Cruelty*, 146; death, 57; "Elegy,"
    151; exposing the unthinkable,
    145–46; fragment written in honor
    of, 149–50; "The Good Shepherd:
    Atlanta, 1981," 147–48; "Hitch-
    hiker," 146; on human possibility,
    149, 151–52; "Life Story," 146; mul-
    tiethnic heritage, 149; *Vice*, 145–46
"Ain't No Way" (Franklin), 29
Alexander, Elizabeth: appreciation for
    craft, 89; *The Black Interior*, 82;
    grief/grieving, 121–22; intended
    audience, 89; on Rodney King,
    93; as model/mentor, 88–89; on
    revolution, 89–90
All For Love (New Edition), 98
ancestors, elders: "*Honor the el-
    ders' voices. Honor your own*"
    (Bingham-Risher), 89; recognizing/
    honoring, 25–27, 196–98

Anglesey, Zoë, 8
"To Anita" (Sanchez), 81
"—answer to yo/question / of am i
    not yo/woman / even if u went
    on shit again" (Sanchez), 87
Appiah, K. Anthony, 78
Arcade (Hunt), 120
"Arrival" (Hamer), 101
The Art of Daring (Phillips), 181
The Art of Death (Danticat), 152
"As a Human Being" (Brown), 194
assonance, 3, 157, 181
"Assuming the Mask: Persona and
    Identity in Ai's Poetry" (Jackson),
    149
Atlanta, Georgia, child murders, 143,
    147–48
Augusta, Georgia, Bingham home in, 1,
    18, 148
avant garde, Hunt's explorations, 119,
    132–33

BaddDDD Sonia Sanchez (film), 81
Baker, Josephine, 69
Baldwin, James: on the cover of *Time*
    magazine, 8; in the film *I Am Not
    Your Negro*, 191; importance to
    Black American writers, xii; "the
    terror of being destroyed," 143
ballad, 141
Baobab Collective, 194
Baraka, Amiri, 85n
Barthes, Roland, 142n

BART/S (Black Arts Repertory Theatre/ School), 85n
"be," in Black English, 84
Bellocq, E. J., 141
Bellocq's Ophelia (Trethewey), 141–42
"Benediction" (Bingham-Risher), 159
Bennington College: advice from Ochester, 34–35; Bennington Bitch Club, 27; poetry program, 27–28; studies with Jeffers at, 29; studies with Miller at, 3. *See also* Jeffers, Honorée Fanonne; Miller, E. Ethelbert
Betts, Reginald Dwayne, 36
Beyoncé: as a feminist, 107–8; *Lemonade*, 102; as link with Sonsoréa, 100–101; name, 101, 109; self-reinvention, 103
Beyoncé (album), 103
the Bible: Bible study, 71, 81, 126; as a kind word from a good friend, 40; language in, 46, 113; love for, sharing with Jeffers, 39–40; rereading, 123; retellings of, 50, 52; sensuality in, 52. *See also* Jehovah God
Bingham, Doris Knight: explanation of God, 115; family in Norfolk, 1–2, 14, 41; love for reading, 118; move to Phoenix, 5, 12, 119; and Mrs. Myers, 11–12; pride in daughter's poem, 10; as a reader, 117; reading aloud by, 119; reading of Psalms, 1; remarrying Robert, 185; single parenting, 118
Bingham-Risher, Remica: : "Adam's Conversion," 53; "Africa," 9–11; "Benediction," 159; "The Body Speaks," 56, 149; *Conversion*, 3, 149–50, 185–86, 191–92; "Distant Lover," 70–71; "Genesis," 50; "Getting Ready for the Heartache to Come or A Body Intercepting Light," 169–70; "*Honor the elders' voices. Honor your own*," 89; "I am small as nothing but armed," 174; "If It's Magic," 158; "I found yesterday," 163–64; 174;

"I Go Back to September 1975," 186; "The Lost Gospel of Peter," 117; "Love in Stereo," 100–101; "Missing You," 2; "My Aunt says *Now the real work begins*," 180; "Noble & Webster, Shadow Sculptures," 168; "Our child is not yet ten and we are clearing his closet," 93–94, 125; "The Principal Calls and I Understand I Will Be Held Accountable," 128–29; "Regents Prompt: What are the best ways for step-parents to deal with the special problems they face?" 168; "The Ritual of the Season," 19; "Sighting," 185–86; "Skipping Stones," 166; "Solstice," 160–61; "Sonsoréa (\sahn-soar-ray\)," 104–5, 110–11; *Starlight & Error*, 70, 77, 125, 155, 158–59, 166, 184–85; "What We Ask of Flesh," 144; *What We Ask of Flesh*, 148–50, 170, 192; "young, small and growing, often violently," 40–41
Bingham, Robert: addiction, 5, 11, 12; at daughter's wedding, 185–86; gifts from, 180; military career, 1, 147–48; rehabilitation in New Jersey, 179–80; remarrying Doris, 185; shadow memories, 174–75, 177–78
biographical poetry, 32, 75–76, 120–21, 178. *See also* persona
"Biographical Suite" (Hunt), 120
Black Americans: Black English, 25–26; "the Black interior," 88–89; capturing pain and love of, 3; complexity of experience, 16–17, 88–89; importance of family/home, 18, 34–35; importance of remembering history, 194; innate fear, unrest, and longing, 19, 143; loss/grief, 20, 69, 121–22; male/female relationships, 67; pragmatism, 33–34; self-reinvention, 102–3; skin color variations, 56; stereotyping of, 88

Black Aperture (Rasmussen), 192

Black Arts Movement: history of, ix, 85n; Hughes's contributions, 7; Hunt's involvement with, 131; loving one's and others' Blackness, 1; Sanchez's work associated with, 84

Black children/youth: activist role, 85; current freedoms and limitations, 92–93; Sanchez's focus on, 85; worrying about, 6–7, 129, 159. *See also* parenting

black/dark, as negative terms, 50

The Black Interior (Alexander), 82, 88–89

Black Lives Matter movement, 71, 156

Black Nature: Four Centuries of African American Nature Poetry (Dungy), 19

Black Panther (movie), 77

The Black Poets (ed. Randall), 13–16

Black studies field, 86

"The Black Woman Speaks" (Catlett), 90–91

Black women: diversity of, 133; efforts to ignore or destroy, 30; honoring, 141; multiple identities of, 69n, 133–34; power of, 30; stereotyping, 67

Blain, Keisha N., 197

Bland, Sandra, 71

Blessing the Boats (Clifton), 53–54

"blk/rhetoric" (Sanchez), 85

"Blues Aubade (or, Revision of the Lean Post-Modernist Pastorale)" (Jeffers), 9

The Bluest Eye (Morrison), 139–40

the body: celebrating, 50–52, 182–83; demanding respect for, 56; feeding, along with the soul, 189–90; loving, 56; power of, 56

"The Body Speaks" (Bingham-Risher), 56, 149

Boland, Eavan, 141

Book of Judges, rape in, 149

The Book of Life (Clifton), 53

Boston Globe, Smith's resignation from, 167

"The Boy Died in My Alley" (Brooks), 129

Braithwaite, Kamau, 132

Brisbon, Rumain: childhood friendship with, 161–62; last visit with, 162; poem about, 168–69; police killing of, 155–56, 159–60, 165; retrieving honest memories of, 162, 165

Broadside Press, 15, 85n, 87

Broadside Quarter, 85n

Brooks, Gwendolyn, 128, 158–59

"Brother" (Derricotte), 56

Brown, James, 85

Brown, Jericho, 193

Brown, Mike, 156

Brown, Sterling, 3

Browne, Mahogany L., 112

"Building Nicole's Mama" (Smith), 171

Burgess, L. Ralph, 194

Burke, Thelma, 83

Butler, Octavia, 62

Byrd, Otis, 31, 33

Callaloo, 194

Callaloo Creative Writing Workshop, 97, 100, 140–41

Campbell, Christian, 37

"Carver" (Nelson), 75

Catalog of Unabashed Gratitude (Gay), 193

Catlett, Elizabeth, 83, 90–91

Cave Canem retreats, ix–xi, 34–37, 49–50

Césaire, Aimé, 132

Chance the Rapper, 92

"Chapter 2: Back-Home" (Hunt), 119

Charleston, South Carolina, Emanuel AME Church massacre, 62–63, 71

Che, Michael, 71

children: and childlessness, 124–25; fear of harming, 121, 128, 129; murdered/martyred children, 148, 169; and self-understanding, 105; tending students as, 126–27; worrying about, 166; writing for, 133

The Cineaste (Jordan), 64, 75, 76

clarity, as a goal, 32, 50, 179, 194

Clarke, Cheryl, 47
clichés, avoiding, 67, 182
Clifton, Lucille: on being both/and,
 69n; *Blessing the Boats*, 53–54;
 The Book of Life, 53; at Cave
 Canem, 49–50; death, 57; dis-
 covery of, 47; on efforts to erase
 or ignore Black women, 29–30;
 emphasis on transformation,
 50–51; "fat fat water rat," 50; first
 manuscript sale, 48; generosity of
 spirit, 54–55; *Good Woman*, 48;
 grief/grieving, 122; at Howard
 University, 48; integration of spirit
 and body, 49; love for language/
 words, 46–47; minimalism, 47;
 Next, 48; photograph of, 44;
 Quilting, 49, 52, 57–58; respect
 for, 49; scriptural influences, 46,
 51, 52; sensual womanist themes,
 50–52; on speaking the "unsay-
 able," 45–46; "surely i am able to
 write poems," 49; on truth-telling,
 59; "why people be mad at me
 sometimes," 26; womanist themes,
 50–51; "won't you celebrate with
 me," 127; writings and awards, 48
"Clitoris" (Derricotte), 56
Coleman, Monica A., 63
collaging, 123–24
*Collective Brightness: LGBTIQ Poets
 on Faith, Religion & Spirituality*
 (ed. Simmonds), 109
the Collective "I," 88
The Color Purple breakfast, 189–91,
 194, 197
Coltrane, John, 131
"Come In Heaven (Earth Is Calling)"
 (Vega), 177
"Common Betrayal" (Hamer), 103
community: and being the "only" in
 a room, ix; among Black poets,
 xii; *The Color Purple* breakfast,
 189–91, 194–95; family as, 40–41;
 importance of, 195, 198; loving,
 Cave Canem as, 34–35; loving,
 families as, 33–34; poets' need for,

34–35; Sanchez's Collective "I,"
 88. *See also* Cave Canem retreats
Conversion (Bingham-Risher), 3,
 185–86, 191–92
1 Corinthians 10:13, 147
"A Coronary Artist" (Hunt), 120, 124,
 133
cotton bolls, 17–18
Cox, John, 66
Cox, MacNolia, 66, 69
Crisis, 7
"Crossroads" (Hamer), 101
Cruelty (Ai), 146

dancing, 66, 71, 90, 106–7
Danticat, Edwidge, 152
"Dark Night in Bennington" (Miller), 38
Dark Room Collective, 194
Davis, Borbie, 72
deafness, Hamer's, 100
death: and faith, 30–31; and loss, 163;
 and memory, 8; premature, 140;
 violent, 84; zombies, 107
DeBerry, Jarvis, 34
"Delicious" (New Edition), 98
Derricotte, Toi, ix, 49, 54–58, 72
Didion, Joan, 162–63
Discovery Award, National Endowment
 for the Arts, 48
Disneyland trip, 11
"Distant Lover" (Bingham-Risher),
 70–71
the Divine. *See* Jehovah God
Dodge Poetry Festival, Stanhope, New
 Jersey, 54–55
Domestic Work (Trethewey), 141
Do the Right Thing (film), 63–64
Dove, Rita, 75, 195
Doyle, Erica, 37
Drake, 98–99, 101
Du Bois, W. E. B., 7, 86
Dunbar, Paul Laurence, 84
Dungy, Camille, 19

Eady, Cornelius, ix, 54, 72, 192
ecopoetics, 19
"Edge" (Hamer), 105–6

Einstein, Albert, 75
"Elegy" (Ai), 151
end rhyme, 157
enslavement: and facing loss, 140; researching family experience of, 102; uncovering depths of, 84
erotic realm, 183
Espada, Martín, 141
Essence, 34
Ethnic Notions (film), 127
Eve, reimagining of, 52
"even the forgotten and unutterable" (Bingham-Risher), 149–50
The Evidence of Things Not Seen (Baldwin), 143

faith: and being seen, 39; as belief, trust, 30–33; as a collective term, 33; as devotion to the truth, 33; as duty owed ancestors/elders, 25–27; finding spirit, 41; in God, 40; grounding from, 41; heart-mending, 27–30; in revolution, 92; as sincerity of intention, 37–38; and trauma, 168–69. *See also* Jehovah God
family: Doris Bingham's, 1–2, 14, 41; Robert Bingham's, 179–80; as community, 34–35, 40–41; Derricotte's focus on, 56; Jeffers's elegies to, 28, 31; and names, 109; as source of joy, 74; voice of, incorporating into poetry, 40–41, 72–73
Fast Animal (Seibles), 176
"fat water rat" (Clifton), 50
Fathering Words (Miller), 8
fear: and the Black experience, vii, 19; conquering through love, 170; efforts to explain, 143; facing, 143; living beyond, 168, 185; naming and facing, xiii, 57–58, 170; and worry, uselessness of, 186. *See also* Black Americans; parenting; race
feedback: as nurture, 8, 8n; patronizing, 117; the value of kind words, 40
feminism, 50, 51n, 84, 101, 108

Finney, Nikky, 47
"Flounder" (Trethewey), 141
Forest Primeval (Francis), 192
forgetting: fear of, 92, 133; the personal past, 144, 160–61; willful, 144
Foster, Frances Smith, 74
Four Hundred Souls: A Community History of African America, 1619-2019 (Blain et al.), 197
Four Tops, 167
Francis, Vievee, 192
Franklin, Aretha, 29
freedom: of Black children, 92–93; and fearlessness, 185; practicing, as Hunt's goal, 135; self-reinvention as, 184; writing as opportunity for, 182
The Friends (Guy), 46
Fulkes surname, 102
Full Moon of Sonia band, 83
Furious Flower Poetry Center, 57, 194

Gabbin, Joanne, 57
Garner, Eric, 156
Gates, Henry Louis, Jr., 25n
Gay, Ross, 193
Gaye, Marvin, 3
"Genesis" (Bingham-Risher), 50
"Genus Narcissus" (Trethewey), 141
Georgia, enduring love for, 28, 39
"Getting Ready for the Heartache to Come or A Body Intercepting Light" (Bingham-Risher), 169–70
Ghebreyesus, Ficre, 121–22
Giovanni, Nikki, 57, 85n
Girmay, Aracelis, 36
"Giving Thanks for Water" (Jeffers), 31
The Glory Gets (Jeffers), 32
Glück, Louise, 147
God. *See* faith; Jehovah God
With Good Reason, 122
"The Good Shepherd: Atlanta, 1981" (Ai), 147–48
Good Woman (Clifton), 48
"The Gospel of Barbecue" (Jeffers), 31
Gourevitch, Philip, 143, 150
grandmother, truth-telling by, 119–20
"Gratitude" (Eady), 72

Greenfield, Eloise, x
"The Green Shirt" (Olds), 121
"grew me up" term, xii
grief/grieving, 62–63, 121–23, 169
Guillén, Nicolás, 82, 132
Guy, Rosa, 46

Haiti, 107
Hamer, Forrest: "Common Betrayal,"
    103; "Crossroads," 101; deafness,
    100; discovery through language,
    100; early encounters with poetry,
    113; "Edge," 105–6; goals as
    poet, 190; heritage in writings of,
    9, 105–6; *Middle Ear*, 100, 101;
    music references, 101; personality,
    demeanor, 97, 100; photograph of,
    96; reverence/spirituality, 109–110;
    Rift, 103; transformation as subject
    for, 103; on unintended impacts of
    actions, 97
Hamilton, Bobb, 85n
Harlem Renaissance, ix–xi, 7
Harvey, Yona, 181
Hayden, Robert, 48
Hayes, Isaac, 6
Heinz, Kurt, 166–167
Hemings, Sally, 150–151
historical events: in Jeffers's poetry, 31;
    living in the grip of, 137; and mem-
    ory, 118–120, 194; the punctum of
    photographs, 142n; serendipitous
    discoveries about, 163; Trethewey's
    focus on, 141, 143–145. *See also*
    Black Arts Movement; Harlem Re-
    naissance; racism; violence/trauma
"Hitchhiker" (Ai), 146
Holman, Bob, 167
home: author's early loss of, 119; and
    the challenge of Black identity, 2;
    complexity of relationship with,
    19–20; as ideal/memory, 18; and
    loss, 20; place vs., 18; poem about,
    18; revisiting, value for women
    writers, 20–21
Home Coming (Sanchez), 84
Honey, I Love (Greenfield), x

*"Honor the elders' voices. Honor your
    own"* (Bingham-Risher), 89
Howard University: African American
    Resource Center, 3; Clifton's time
    at, 48
Hughes, Langston, ix, 6–7
humans: humanizing, 127; innate flaws
    in, 166; interconnection, 146; nam-
    ing, 109; resilience, 143; wonders
    of, embracing, 4–5, 63
Hunt, Erica: *Arcade*, 120; on becoming
    an adult, 133; at Cave Canem,
    116; "Chapter 2: Back-Home,"
    119; "A Coronary Artist," 120,
    124, 133; critical approach,
    117–118; efforts to expand the
    limitations of language, 131; ex-
    ploration of the avant-garde, 119;
    family background, 132; impacts
    of motherhood/caretaking of others
    on poetry of, 120; on the impor-
    tance of naming, 111; on impro-
    visation, 123; influence of music
    on, 131; interest in the philosophy
    of language, 135; as "language
    poet," 116; *Local History*, 120,
    131; meandering nature of work
    and poetry, 123; on meaning of
    avant-garde, 132–133; opposi-
    tional poetics, 124; photograph,
    114; poems as letters to the future,
    196–197; poets admired by, 132;
    resources collected by, 128; search
    for authentic identity, 130–131;
    "Second Voice," 131; *Time Slips
    Right Before Your Eyes*, 119; use
    of improvisation, 132; on Wright's
    scope, 128
Hurdy-Gurdy (Seibles), 173, 175
Hurston, Zora Neale, 84
Hurston/Wright Foundation, 194
Hutson, Jean, 15, 86–87
hybrid, invented poetic forms, 76, 101,
    190

iambic pentameter, 72
I Am Not Your Negro (film), 191

"I am small as nothing but armed" (Bingham-Risher), 174
identity: authentic, and self-exploration, 130–131; limiting, avoiding, 149; questioning/discovering, vii
"I End in Winter"(Jeffers), 32
"If It's Magic" (Bingham-Risher), 158
"I found yesterday" (Bingham-Risher), 163–64
"I Go Back to May 1937" (Olds), 187
"I Go Back to September 1975" (Bingham-Risher), 186
improvisation, 123, 132, 132n
"Incident at Cross Plains (The Lynching of William Luke, 1870)" (Jeffers), 31
"Indianapolis/summer/1969/poem" (Sanchez), 87
In Search of Color Everywhere (ed. Miller), 7, 16–17
In Search of Our Mothers' Gardens (Walker), 82
intention: Jeffers's clarity of, 32–33; making sure poetry communicates, 182; sincerity of, 37–38
"Invisible Dreams" (Derricotte), 58

Jackson, Major, 26, 149
Jackson, Michael, 67, 106
Jeffers, Honorée Fanonne: *The Age of Phillis*, 32; at Bennington College, 27–28; "Blues Aubade (or, Revision of the Lean Post-Modernist Pastorale)," 9; on changing roles of Black poets, 31–32; on the elders and the politics of race, 26; on faith, 25; friendship with, 39; "Giving Thanks for Water," 31; *The Glory Gets*, 32; "The Gospel of Barbecue," 31; historical research, 32; homages to family and home, 28, 31; "I End in Winter," 32; lessons from, 39; on "letting go," 42; love for jazz/blues, 28; mentorship from, 39; moniker for Bingham-Risher, 38; mourning Clifton, 57; photograph of, 24; on

plain speaking, clarity of intention, 32–33; poems about grief, 31; on race as a complex construct, 182n; *Red Clay Suite*, 39; relationship with father's poetry, 40; "Singing Counter," 32; singing with, 29; "The Subjective Briar Patch: Contemporary American Poetry," 29–30; "What Grief Is," 31; "Where the Song Stops," 31
Jeffers, Lance, 40
Jehovah God: Bingham-Risher's mother's explanation of, 115; gifts from, 175; and the human capacity to endure, 146–47; to seek, 121; inspiration from, 199; Morrison's dissections of, 140; possibilities of the Divine, 173; questioning faith through poetry, 168
Jess, Tyehimba, 192
Jet, 34
Johnson, Georgia Douglas, 7
Johnston, Amanda, 35–36
Jordan, A. Van: biographical storytelling, 75; breadth of cultural references, 75; *The Cineaste*, 64, 75, 76; on envisioning the future by salvaging the past, 76; focus on male vulnerability, 66; identification as an African American poet, 78; learning to write, 64; love for film, 63–64; love poems, 66, 75–76; *M-A-C-N-O-L-I-A*, 69, 75; music for, 65–66; "Notes from a Southpaw," 64; on Oscar Micheaux, 76; photograph of, 60; "Poem about My Rights," 4; *Quantum Lyrics*, 75; on racism and race, 78; response to Eady's "Gratitude," 72; *Rise*, 64, 66; sensitivity to female experience, 66–67, 73; singing one's own stories, 66; stories of historical figures, 69, 75; "Tamara's Dance," 66; "Thought Experiment #1: E=MC²," 75; "What Does It Mean When a Man Dreams of Lingerie?" 66

Jordan, Bessie, 73
Jordan, June, 4
joy: in excellence, 200–201; expressing through poems, 194; finding in family and relationships, 74; Gay's ability to voice, 193; joyful memories, 186, 193; radical love, viii, xii

Kearney, Douglas, 99n, 192
Kendrick, Dolores, 3
A Kind of Freedom (Sexton), 118
King, Martin Luther, Jr., 18
King, Rodney, 93
Knight, Etheridge, 85n
Knight, Mary, xiii
Komunyakaa, Yusef, 195

language: attending to closely, 100; Clifton's, 46–47; compounding in English, 191–92; erotic, 183; improvised, Hunt's, 116, 135; invented, Morrison's, 137; kind words, value of, 40; limitations of, 131; love for, 46–47; and the music of real speech, 190; playful, 132n; in poems, evaluating during revision, 182; the power of words, 3; rhythm, 25; as tool for discovery, 100; using Black vernacular, 84; words as comfort, 46
Language Poets, San Francisco, 130
Lawrence, Jacob, 83
Leaving Saturn (Jackson), 26
Lee, Spike, 63–64
Lemonade (Beyoncé), 102–3
Let the Circle Be Unbroken (Taylor), 46
Life According to Motown (Smith), 159
The Life of Poetry (Rukeyser), 188
"Life Story" (Ai), 146
The Light of the World (Alexander), 121–22
listening: close, and imagining what is missing, 100; hearing the voice of love, 73, 109; importance, for a poet, 98. *See also* language; music
literary politics, 3

Local History (Hunt), 120, 131
Lorde, Audre, 47
Lordi, Emily, 65
loss: Black experience of, 6, 19–20, 119, 140; and death, 163; and revision, 186. *See also* grief/grieving
"The Lost Gospel of Peter" (Bingham-Risher), 117
Lotus Press, 3
love: and being remade, 183; Black women's, reflections of in *Lemonade*, 102; from father, examples, 177–78; celebrating, xiii, 62–63; as the center of revolutionary struggle, 82; childhood experiences of, 155; conquering fear of, 170; Jordan's explorations of, 66, 75–76; and listening to New Edition, 98; old love, reconnecting with, 67–69; writing about, 67, 69–71, 73–74; young love, 61–62
"Love After Love" (Walcott), 127, 180
Love and Marriage in Early African America (ed. Foster), 73–74
"Love in Stereo" (Bingham-Risher), 100–101
"Love Is Jes' a Thing o' Fancy," 74
lynching, 31–32
lyric poetry, Hunt's, 116

M-A-C-N-O-L-I-A (Jordan), 69, 75
Madhubuti, Haki (Don L. Lee), 85n
male vulnerability, Jordan on, 66
Marquez, Gabriel Garcia, 123
Marshall, Paule, 25
Martin, Trayvon, 92
martyr children, 169
McDonald, Laquan, 156
McMillan, Terry, 118
Memorial Drive (Trethewey), 145
memory: collective, 141, 153; of elders/forebears, 197–98; of father's love, 177–78; and grief/grieving, 8, 160; importance to Trethewey, 137; of mother's love, 115; poetry as, 133; re-remembering/re-constructing, 128, 187; and secrets, 119; as

unreliable, imagined, 18–19, 62, 143
"mess," as a term, 85
metaphor: evaluating during revision, 182; explaining, joy of, 126; Morrison's use of, 140
Micheaux, Dante, 191–92
Micheaux, Oscar, 76
Middle Ear (Hamer), 100, 101
Miller, E. Ethelbert: the African American Resource Center at Howard, 4; on the Black Arts Movement, 1; "Dark Night in Bennington," 38; emphasis on the ordinary, the impact of daily livings, 4; home and office, 7–8; *In Search of Color Everywhere*, 7, 16–17; inspiration from, ix–x; as a literary activist/archivist, 3, 7; loving relationship with Jordan, 4; "October 31," 4, 8; on open mics and spoken word movement, 22; photograph of, xiv; role as mentor, 8, 38; *Season of Hunger/Cry of Rain*, 3–4; on successfully living as a poet, 20
"Missing You" (Bingham-Risher), 2
"Missing You" (Ross), 1, 3
Monticello, Charlottesville, Virginia, 150–51
Morning Haiku (Sanchez), 85
Morrison, Toni: capacity to create beauty, 139; death, 137; on human responses to chaos, 137; importance to Black American writers, xii; love as motivation for truth-telling, 138; Nobel Prize, 195; poetic gifts, 138; use of metaphor, 140
motherhood/mothering: author's experience of as a child, 117–18; as caregiving, 129–30; childlessness, 124–25; and dead/martyr children, 169; dilemmas of, 120–21, 124, 131; as fluid practice, 133; Hunt's examination of, 124; and love, 128; mothers as artists, 120–21, 124; and the revolutionary life, 91;

Sanchez's poems involving, 87–88; truth-telling, 119–20; worry about sons, 6–7, 9, 159
"Mother to Son" (Hughes), 6–7, 9
"Motown Crown" (Smith), 157
Mullen, Harryette, 132n
multiracial background, 141, 149
music: in Bingham-Risher's work, 157; in Hunt's work, 131; in Jordan's work, 64; in poetry, 101; as poetry, 157; in poetry, 190; and rhythm, 190; role in Black culture, 65, 106; and the sound of words, 182
"My Aunt says *Now the real work begins*" (Bingham-Risher), 180
Myers, Darlene, 6, 11–12
"My Papa's Waltz" (Roethke), 141
"Myth" (Trethewey), 141

names: Browne's wish about, 112; and describing experience, 111–12; embodying, 104; family, owning and passing on, 109; growing into, 103; importance, 97; and self-reinvention, 101–3; taking oneself seriously, 37–38; as terms of endearment, 38
Naomi Long Madgett Poetry Award, 3
National Poetry Slam, 166
Native Guard (Trethewey), 141
Neal, Larry, 85n
"The Negro Artist and the Racial Mountain" (Hughes), 20
"The Negro Speaks of Rivers" (Hughes), 7
Nelson, Marilyn, 75
Neruda, Pablo, 82
the new black (Shockley), 192
New Edition, 98
New Jersey: Robert Bingham's family in, 179–80; Dodge Poetry Festival, 54–55
Next (Clifton), 48
Ngũgĩ wa Thiong'o, 82
nigger, as a term, 13, 16
"Noble & Webster, Shadow Sculptures" (Bingham-Risher), 168

Norfolk, Virginia.: author's grandparents' home in, 2; family's return to, 14; Seibles in, 175
"Notes from a Southpaw" (Jordan), 64

obsession, meeting head on, 168
Obsidian, 194
Ochester, Ed, 34
"October 31" (Miller), 4
Ogawa, Ai. *See* Ai
Old Dominion University, Norfolk, Virginia, 175
Olds, Sharon, 121, 187
"old souls," 61
Olio (Jess), 192
oppression, revealing/countering, 63, 145–46
the other, giving voice to: in Ai's poetry, 147; as empowerment, 150; impacts on self-understanding, 108; Seibles's perspective, 178–79. *See also* biographical poetry; persona
"Our child is not yet ten and we are clearing his closet" (Bingham-Risher), 93–94, 125

"Papa Don't Take No Mess!" (Brown), 85
Parable of the Talents (Butler), 62
paradise: Butler's definition, 62; and community, 77; finding joy, 74; and hope, 71; and self-understanding, 62; and the wonders of being human, 63, 77
Paradise (Morrison), 118
"Paradise is one's own place,/. . ." (Butler), 62
parenting: and emotional overload, 121; fears of doing harm, 121; learning and experiencing, 108–9, 110; raising a son, 125; and self-reinvention, 186–87; as the work of revision and transformation, 185
Parks, Gordon, 142n
Patter (Kearney), 192
Pecola Breedlove (Morrison character), 139–40

persona: in Ai's poetry, 147, 149; in biographical poetry, 32; challenges of using, 169; in Hughes's poetry, 6; in Smith's poetry, 160. *See also* the other, giving voice to
Phillips, Carl, 181
Phoenix, Arizona: Black population in 1988, 5; departure from, 162; move to, 5, 119; racism and poverty in, 12–13
photographs, Trethewey's interest in, 142n
Pilgrim, David, 140
plain speaking, 32–33
"Poem about My Rights" (Jordan), 4
"poem pieces," 184
Poems in Conversation and a Conversation (Alexander and Van Clief-Stefanon), 90
poetics: Alexander's emphasis on, 89; and art for art's sake, 90; avoiding absolute closure, 181; ballads, 141; as collaging, 123–24; the craft of poetry, 176, 178, 181; end rhyme, 157; Hunt's explorations, 119, 130–31; hybrid, invented forms, , 76, 101, 190; and innovation, 132–33; the limitations of language, 131; lyric poetry, 116; opposition, 124; punctum, 142n; repetition, 101, 157; rhyme, 141, 157; rhythm, 25, 190; Smith's, modeling, 157; sonnets, 157; syllable count, 181; unstructured structures, 85; Volta in, 190. *See also* language; writing poems
poetry: as art form, Jordan's understanding of, 72; being fed by, 190; as caring for others, 54; changing one's perspective, 190; clarity, tenderness, and preservation in, 194; combining allure and clarity, 179; countering societal oppressions, 63; dealing with race in, 9; discovering, x, 100; emotional impacts, 121; envisioning the unseen, 77, 197; facing the unfaceable, 31, 57–58, 145; as

fluid practice, 133; hearing your own voice in, 72–73; illuminating the extraordinary in the ordinary, 146; intimacy provided by, 46–47; love poems, 4–5, 67, 182–83; as a melding of feelings and beliefs, 188; as memory, truth-telling, 133; as mining, 155; Morrison's writing as, 140; and permission to represent subjective experience, 30; political vs. "artsy," 9; popularity of, 22; potential of, x; a providing access to shared experience through, 61; queer writers, 47; as a reflection of actual lives, 195; relief and release provided by, 196; rereading, 181, 192–93; revealing small beauties, 193; as snapshot of universals, 40; as storytelling, 75; synthesizing function, 196; and transformation, 31; value in the real world, 195. *See also* revision; writing poems

poetry slams, 158, 166

poets, Black American: changing roles of, 31–32; and community/collective understanding, xii, 33, 77, 191; duty, 82, 86–87, 89; exposing common humanness, 127; expressions of love and fear, xiii; female intimacy, 46–47; fluidity and diversity of, xi–xii; identifying contemporary needs and possibilities, 91–92; and the importance of context, 16; importance of music, 65; importance of recognizing the elders and their contributions, 196; interviewing, goals and structure, ix; lack of common familiarity with, 72; lack of recognition/recompense, 33; during the last part of the twentieth century, 195; limits and possibilities, 119; living as political, 49; living/identifying as a poet, viii, ix, 20–21, 72, 78, 117, 149, 173–76; and the musicality of language, 95; music as manifestation of thriving, 65; negative criticism, 197;

the poet's Collective, 34; privileges afforded, 106; reflecting of reality by, 195; relationship with historical movements, 127; as revolutionary, 81–82, 90–91; role in transmitting culture, 8–9; transcending and transforming lived experience, 179, 185; use of Black vernacular, 84; using understandable language, 32; as witnesses/truth-tellers, 193; women, and representation, 56–57

the Poets in the Kitchen, 25, 40

Power and Possibility (Alexander), 89

Prince, 103

"The Principal Calls and I Understand I Will Be Held Accountable" (Bingham-Risher), 128–29

Proofs & Theories: Essays on Poetry (Glück), 147

Proverbs 25:11, 40

Pryor, Richard, 66, 69

Psalm 39:6, 169

punctum, 142n

Quantum Lyrics (Jordan), 75

"Quantum Lyrics Montage," 75

Quilting (Clifton), 49, 52, 57–58

race: as a construct, complexity of, 182n; and erasure, 46, 75; as informing everything, 105; race riots, 18; racism vs., 78; Seibles's efforts to reenvision, 182–83; as a term, Jeffers's construct, 26n; writing about, 9, 26n, 32, 67, 92

racism: history of, in Jeffers's poetry, 31; Jordan's portrayals of, 69, 78; in Phoenix, 12–13; as subject in feminist poetry, 84

Radio Raheem (movie character), 63–64

Randall, Dudley, 13–17, 87

Rasmussen, Matt, 192

"Really Breathing" (Seibles), 182

Red Clay Suite (Jeffers), 39

"Regents Prompt: What are the best ways for step-parents to deal with

the special problems they face?"
(Bingham-Risher), 168
repetition, 101, 157
research, role in writing poems, 18, 32,
73, 102, 128, 141, 176
resilience: as human characteristic,
143; hybrid poetry, 190; joy from,
xii; manifesting through song and
dance, 106
reverence: for ancestors, 25; in Hamer's
poetry, 109; Seibles's expressions
of, 173. See also faith
revising: as a metaphor for transforma-
tion, 174; returning to poems that
resist closure, 181
revision: definition, 185; eliminating
"poem killer" modifiers, 181–82;
goal, 176; and letting go, 174,
178–79; and loss, 186; as a meta-
phor for finding new life directions,
174; removing or rewriting poems,
184; and solving life problems,
181, 185; starting again, 180; the
work of parenting as, 185. See also
writing poems
revolution: Alexander's perspective,
88–89; as both noun and verb,
86; and the Collective "I," 88; as
complex and messy, 90–91; regular
work associated with, 86; role of
artists, 81–82; Sanchez's focus on
change, 85; as a term, multiple
meanings, 90
rhyme: and Smith's early experiences
with song lyrics, 157; Trethewey's
use of, 141
rhythm, 25, 190
"Ribbon in the Sky" (Wonder), 183
Rice, Tamir, 156
Rich, Adrienne, 174, 179
Richardson, James William, Jr., 32
Rift (Hamer), 103
Rise (Jordan), 64, 66
Risher, Michael, 16, 67–69, 92, 110,
122–23, 125, 139
Risher, Michael K., 77, 93–95, 99, 121,
125, 139, 165–66

Risher, Sonsoréa (Farmer), 98–100,
102–105, 107, 112, 139
"The Ritual of Season" (Bingham-
Risher), 19
"The River Will Not Testify" (Espada),
141
Rodgers, Carolyn, 57, 84
Roethke, Theodore, 141
Ross, Diana, 1, 3
Rukeyser, Muriel, 188
Rumain. See Brisbon, Rumain
"Run, Nigger, Run!" (folk poem), 13–14
Ruth Lilly Prize, 48–49
Rwanda, genocide in, 143

Sanchez, Sonia: "To Anita," 81; Black
studies as field, 86; "blk/rhetoric,"
85; candidness, 87–88; and the cul-
pable responsibility of revolution,
89; documenting personal and ra-
cial pain, 81; early teaching career,
86–87; gatherings, community, 83,
88; *Home Coming*, 84; "India-
napolis/summer/1969/poem," 87;
intended audience, 89; introduction
to Black literature, 15; on lifting
oneself and others, 83; *Morning
Haiku*, 85; on motherhood, 87–88;
on the musicality of Black lan-
guage, 95; photograph of, 80; on
real vs. superficial change, 85–86;
on revealing Truth, 90; revolution-
ary and shocking language use, 84;
Sister Son/ji, 69n; "summer words
of a sistuh addict," 87–88, 181; on
survival, change and love, 81; on
telling stories of everywoman and
everyman, 82; *We a BaddDDD
People*, 82, 84–85, 87
Schomburg Center for Research in
Black Culture (New York Public
Library), 15
Scotland Neck, North Carolina, 2
Scott-Heron, Gil, 177
Scripture. See the Bible
Season of Hunger/Cry of Rain (Miller),
3–4

"Second Voice" (Hunt), 131
Seibles, Tim: "After All," 182; efforts to re-envision race, 182–83; erotic realm, 182–83; *Fast Animal*, 176; *Hurdy-Gurdy*, 173; on love for writing, 182; photograph of, 172; on poetry as both truth and fiction, 178–79; on poetry as a life's work, 185; on the possibilities of the Divine, 173; "Really Breathing," 182; seeing the spiritual in sexuality, 183; as teacher at Old Dominion, 175–76; "Trying For Fire," 173; vision of a better life, 188; on white space, 182
self-care: and fostering inner strength, 150; making time for oneself, 115–16; writing as, 57, 107
self-criticism, 186–87
self-invention, 103, 112
Sexton, Margaret Wilkerson, 118
sexuality, 50, 183. *See also* love
shadow, as a term, 168
"Shall We Meditate on Truth?" (Holman), 167
Shange, Ntozake, 84
Shockley, Evie, 192
"Sighting" (Bingham-Risher), 185–86
signifying, as a term, 25–26
silence, destructiveness of, 56, 110, 144, 151–52
Simmonds, Kevin, 109
"Singing Counter" (Jeffers), 32
Sister Son/ji (Sanchez), 69n
"Skipping Stones" (Bingham-Risher), 166
small beauties, noticing, 193
Smith, Patricia: Brooks's influence on, 158–59; "Building Nicole's Mama," 171; discovery of poetry, 158–59; on early experience of mother's records, 157; and giving voice to others, 156; on God's presence, 170; impact of father's murder, 160; introduction to *What We Ask of Flesh*, 156; on learning from students, 171; *Life According to Motown*, 159; lifelong obsession with music, 157; "Motown Crown," 157; and performance poetry, 166–67; photograph, 154; on poets' responsibility, 159; references to news stories, 159–60; resignation from the *Boston Globe*, 167; skill with persona, 160; on sudden change, 155; *Teahouse of the Almighty*, 159; "Terrell's Take on Things," 26; unmaking and remaking her life, 167
"Solstice" (Bingham-Risher), 160–61
Song of Solomon (Morrison), 137–38
sonnet, 141, 142, 157
"Sonsoréa (\sahn-soar-ray\)" (Bingham-Risher), 104–105, 110–11
soul culture: Black survival, xiii, 57; as expression of Black thriving, 65; as a phrase, viii
soul music, 156
The Source of Self-Regard (Morrison), 137
the South, as home, 20–21
sparse enjambment, 157
Spillers, Hortense, 105
spoken word movement, 22
"Standing in the Shadow of Love" (Four Tops), 167
Starlight & Error (Bingham-Risher), 70, 77, 125, 155, 158–59, 166, 184–85
storytelling poems, 75–76
"The Subjective Briar Patch: Contemporary American Poetry" (Jeffers), 29–30
"Summer Soft" (Wonder), 98
"summer words of a sistuh addict" (Sanchez), 87–88
"surely i am able to write poems" (Clifton), 49
surrealism, 132
syllable count, 181
symbolism, 182

"Tamara's Dance" (Jordan), 66
Teahouse of the Almighty (Smith), 159
Tender (Derricotte), 55–58

Terkenli, Theano, 18–19
"Terrell's Take on Things" (Smith), 26
"They Want EFX" (Das EFX), 99n
"Things" (Greenfield), x
Thomas and Beulah (Dove), 75
"Thought Experiment #1: E=MC²"
(Jordan), 75
"Thriller" (Jackson), 106
"By the Time I Get to Phoenix"
(Hayes), 6
Time Slips Right Before Your Eyes
(Hunt), 119
touch/intimacy, as a paradox, 105
Touré, Askia, 85n
Toys "R" Us, 118
The Tradition (Brown), 193–94
Transfigurations (Wright), 123
transformation: in children, 105;
Clifton's emphasis on, 50–51; as a
goal, 185; Hamer's emphasis on,
103; and parenting, 185; remaking
oneself as an artist and human be-
ing, 103, 179; revising as metaphor
for, 174. *See also* faith; revision
trauma. *See* violence/trauma
Trethewey, Natasha: *Bellocq's Oph-
elia*, 141–42; at Callaloo Creative
Writing Workshop, 99–100, 141;
Domestic Work, 141; "Flounder,"
141; "Genus Narcissus," 141; on
importance of remembering, 137;
inspiration from, 141; as keeper of
collective memory, 141, 153; *Me-
morial Drive*, 145; mixed-race heri-
tage, 141; mother's murder, 144–45;
"Myth," 141; *Native Guard*, 141;
photograph of, 136; poetics, 141;
use of photographs, 142n; on writ-
ing about past traumas, 144
"Trying For Fire" (Seibles), 173
Turner, Mary and Hayes, 32

"The Unglamorous but Worthwhile
Duties of the Black Revolution-
ary Artist, or of the Black Writer
Who Simply Works and Writes"
(Walker), 82

Unite the Right Rally, Charlottesville,
Virginia, 150
"Urban Renewal—Block Party" (Jack-
son), 26

Van Clief-Stefanon, Lyrae, 30, 90
Vazirani, Reetika, 8
Vega, Táta, 177
Vice (Ai), 145–46
violence/trauma: Ai's approach to re-
vealing, 145–46; complexities of,
166; coping with by forgetting,
144; enduring, 147, 160; facing
and addressing courageously, 82;
forging new beauty from, 180–81;
grappling with, 138–39, 144–45;
and guilt, 144–45; memories
of, ongoing impacts, 93–94;
Sanchez's portrayals of, 87–88;
sudden, impacts of, 160; and
sustaining faith in God, 168–69;
as a theme, 148–49; transcending,
151–52
Volta, 190

Waiting to Exhale (McMillan), 118
#WakandaSoLit, 77
Walcott, Derek, 127, 180, 195
Walker, Alice: and the hard labor of
revolution, 89; *In Search of Our
Mothers' Gardens*, 82; on the mess-
iness of truly revolutionary art, 88;
on revealing the Black Truth, 90;
on true revolution, 86; who she is
speaking to, 89
Walker, Margaret, 67
Washington, Booker T., 33
We a BaddDDD People (Sanchez), 82,
84–85, 87
Weems, Carrie Mae, 142n
*We Wish to Inform You That Tomor-
row We Will Be Killed With Our
Families* (Gourevitch), 143
"What Does It Mean When a Man
Dreams of Lingerie?" (Jordan),
66
"What Grief Is" (Jeffers), 31

"What We Ask of Flesh" (Bingham-Risher), 144

What We Ask of Flesh (Bingham-Risher), 16, 90, 148–50, 170, 192

Wheatley, Phillis, 32

"When My Father Was Beating Me" (Derricotte), 56

"When We Dead Awaken: Writing as Re-Vision" (Rich), 174

"Where the Song Stops" (Jeffers), 31

white space, 182

"Whitey on the Moon" (Scott-Heron), 177

"why people be mad at me sometimes" (Clifton), 26

Wilson, L. Lamar, 71

Wizard of the Crow (Ngũgĩ wa Thiong'o), 83

women: experiences of, 50–52, 124; fear of harming loved ones, 121; heavy lifting by, 90–91; and re-visioning, 174; as revolutionaries, 90; the womanist aesthetic, xiii, 50, 108

Wonder, Stevie, 158, 183

"won't you celebrate with me" (Clifton), 127

words. *See* language; poetics; writing poems

Wright, Jay, 123–24, 128

writing poems: achieving clarity, 179; Bingham-Risher's, 176; embracing absurdity, 33–34; expanding, broadening ideas, 192; finding time for, 81; importance of white space, 182; judging effectiveness, 190–91; multiple drafts, 196n; poetry workshops, 116–17; role of research, 18, 32, 73, 102, 104, 128, 141, 176; as an uneven process, 187; visual elements, 182; as work, 126. *See also* revision

The Year of Magical Thinking (Didion), 162–63

You Don't Miss Your Water (Eady), 192

"young, small and growing, often violently" (Bingham-Risher), 40–41

Zephaniah 2:3, 121

"A Zombie Is a Slave Forever" (*New York Times*), 107

zombies, 106–107

ABOUT THE AUTHOR

Remica Bingham-Risher, a native of Phoenix, Arizona, is a Cave Canem fellow and Affrilachian poet. Her work has been published in the *New York Times*, the *Writer's Chronicle*, *Callaloo*, and *Essence*, among other journals. She is the author of *Conversion* (Lotus, 2006), winner of the Naomi Long Madgett Poetry Award; *What We Ask of Flesh* (Etruscan, 2013), shortlisted for the Hurston/Wright Legacy Award; and *Starlight & Error* (Diode, 2017), winner of the Diode Editions Book Award and a finalist for the Library of Virginia Literary Award for Poetry. She is currently the Director of Quality Enhancement Plan Initiatives at Old Dominion University and resides in Norfolk, Virginia, with her husband and children.